UXBRIDGE
• COLLEGE

THEORISING VIDEO PRACTICE

MIKE WAYNE

LAWRENCE & WISHART LTD
LONDON

Lawrence and Wishart Limited
99A Wallis Road
London
E9 5LN

First published 1997 by Lawrence and Wishart, reprinted 1999

British Library Cataloguing in Publication data.
A catalogue record for this book is available from the British Library.

ISBN 0 85315 827 4

Typeset by Francesca Hamon, London.
Printed and bound in Great Britain by Redwood Books, Trowbridge

CONTENTS

ACKNOWLEDGEMENTS

In writing this book I received help, advice and encouragement from a number of people to whom I would like to express my gratitude. Terry Tiernan helped enormously in clarifying the idea for this book in its initial stages and generously contributed to the formulation of the practical exercises in the book. Many thanks also to Pete Keighron for his time in comprehensively reading and commenting on draft versions of the book and Dave Chapman for his thoughts on video practices. Bob Barker has offered support, encouragement and intellectual comradeship both in relation to this project and my teaching and research over a number of years. My thanks also to Vicky Grut for her careful editing of the manuscript. I would also like to thank Media Services at Brunel University College for their help and patience. Thanks to Columbia University Press for permission to reproduce several passages from Film Sound, Elizabeth Weis and John Belton (eds), © Columbia University Press. Finally, a great debt is owed to the students from Brunel University College and the University of North London. Their audiovisual creativity inspired this book and made the writing of it seem worthwhile.

Introduction

Politics and Culture

Today on the domestic market the camcorder is now as familiar as the still camera. Basic but adequate editing facilities can be accessed through educational institutes, video collectives or, at more expense, commercial facility houses. There is even the possibility of planning editing sequences on the simple portable domestic editing equipment now available on the market. On a scale never seen before, people have the chance to produce their own sounds and images, their own representations. The question is what will we do with this opportunity? There is the possibility for an enormous diversity of uses for video, and a plurality of audiovisual expression could be tapped and generated at the grass roots level where all this video hardware is located. However, there are a number of complex problems to be negotiated in order to bring this potential to some fruition. The central argument in this book is that the problems and potentialities of access to video can only be identified and addressed if we contextualise our practice historically and understand it theoretically. This book offers itself as a contribution to that task.

In my view, the three distinct but interfacing moments of production, text and consumption all form part of a single term, 'video practice', although this book focuses primarily on the negotiation of formal strategies at the point of (video) production. This book, however, will not help you to operate a camera, light a scene, or find your way around a video editing suite. There are plenty of books available with that kind of technical information on offer. What is rather less common are books which encourage a critical relationship with this productive hardware. A critical engagement requires us to think about the contexts in which audiovisual production and consumption takes place, the components of audiovisual language and the relationships between production, consumption and texts. In trying to address these questions, this book falls into two parts. Chapters one, two and three discuss the institutional/industrial structures and historical contexts in which video practices may be located. These opening chapters may seem very distant from the 'practicalities' of practice, and indeed in one sense they are. These chapters seek to interpose themselves between you and the immediacy of the technology in order to give some context to that relationship so that you may reflect critically on it. Subsequent chapters are then devoted to the various levels at which meaning is constructed in the audiovisual text. In the final chapter I take a more extensive look at the documentary, a mode of audiovisual practice which crops up throughout the book. At the end of each of these chapters on signifying strategies, I have suggested some exercises that might help translate some of the theoretical ideas discussed, into practice.

To understand video practice requires that we look at theories developed to explain cultural practices other than video. In the following chapters I draw on a range of theories developed to illuminate specific kinds of cultural artifacts (literature, theatre, painting, photography); I draw on theories of communication (linguistics, sociology of culture); and obviously I also draw on theoretical work developed in relation to film, television and video. However, I am not concerned to develop a 'video aesthetics'. I see video very much as part of a broader audiovisual culture, making its own impact on that culture, certainly, but also largely explicable within the terms and debates which have been developed in relation to that culture. For this reason, the reader will find that film theories constitute the dominant, though by no means exclusive, theoretical reference point in this work.

In terms of textual practices, many of my examples are drawn from the low/no-budget video work produced by students themselves. This is important for several reasons. Although relatively few readers will have actually seen these videos, their inclusion testifies to the argument that 'amateur' cultural production need not be a pejorative term. Part of the debate around video is that the technology widens access to cultural production. But critical discourses must also widen the range of cultural artifacts they are prepared to discuss. I believe that 'amateur', low-budget video production can be as complex and intricate as anything produced by the mainstream or independent sectors of the audiovisual industry and thus that student videos are cultural objects worthy of serious analysis. There is another reason connected with a specific and central argument in this book. One of my main concerns is to explore the pragmatics and politics of low-budget audiovisual production. My discussion of students' videos is intended to show concrete examples of how theory works in practice and how it works particularly well for low-budget practice. My argument is that theory can help you negotiate the resource limitations of low-budget practice, it can broaden the repertoire of textual strategies at your disposal and build your confidence to explore, experiment and develop. The ultimate aim of my interrogation of practice is to stimulate the reader's creativity. If that seems paradoxical, it is only because the division between theory and practice has become so unproductively entrenched. Chapters one, two and three will offer theories and histories that can account for that division. Subsequent chapters will, I hope, show just how false a division it is, by showing the theory 'in action'.

This book does not aim to be narrowly prescriptive, but it would be disingenuous to imply that it is not selective. Aesthetically, and against the grain of recent discussions around postmodernism, I shall argue that modernism remains an important (even if often unrecognised) reference point for cultural workers. There are two reasons for this. Firstly, modernism provides a fertile cultural resource and, I shall argue, many of its strands have not yet exhausted their complex relationship to society. This argument will be elaborated in chapter two. Secondly, I shall argue that the textual characteristics of modernism are very suited to the resource limitations generated by low-budget cultural production. This pragmatic strand will be a running theme throughout the book. I think it is also fair to say that this book is weighted towards narratives, although I am interested in expanding the possibilities of storytelling and I do also consider non-narrative structures and strategies as well as the documentary, a tradition of audiovisual practice which may be related to, but cannot be subsumed within narrative. It is not only aesthetic preferences which exert their influence on this book, but political ones as well. The politics which selects, synthesises and assesses the cultural theory is marxist and feminist in its orientation.

Marxism is hardly flavour of the month in academia at the moment, nor is its stock very high in wider political circles. Many have confidently predicted its death in practical political terms, having equated it (mistakenly in my view) with the former, now defunct regimes of Eastern Europe. Marxism may well be in crisis but in all honesty what political projects, from secular neo-liberalism to Islamism, are not in crisis as they try to come to terms with the dislocations and rampant inequalities of late twentieth century capitalism?[1] For me, marxism remains incomparable as a theory of history and this informs my understanding of the history of the media and related cultural forms. Marxism provides an analysis of some of the major faultlines of social life under capitalism. The two key issues which impinge on our subject are: the contradiction between the potential and actual uses of new technology (in classical marxist terms, the contradiction between the forces and relations of production); and the contradiction between bourgeois economics and bourgeois ideology (or between base and superstructure). We will come back to these issues in subsequent chapters. Since the theme of this book is to link theory and practice (albeit in relation to video) I would just say that the jury of history is still out as far as I am concerned. Confident predictions that marxism will never again inform the political practices of the masses seem to assume that capitalism (particularly its democratic variant) has achieved a profound stability and legitimacy. Yet this is a view which is hardly supported by the historical record, nor is it shared by many liberal commentators who are profoundly anxious that capitalism may be undermining its own democratic institutions.[2]

Feminism also seems to be undergoing something of a crisis if it is judged by its once radical ambitions. Its past, as Susan Faludi has documented, has been subject to relentless attacks and misrepresentation by the mainstream political and cultural currents.[3] At present, the Super-Fems (as one writer dubs such high profile spokeswomen as Naomi Wolf and Camille Paglia), 'propagate a new message of adaption and conformity'.[4] This media-friendly feminism which has accommodated itself with individualism, consumerism and careerism, is very much the end product of a broad ideological assault on the more radical feminism of two decades ago. The rise of 'respectable' feminism is not unconnected with the rise of a 'respectable' alternative to the failing social and economic policies of the New Right. As one commentator puts it:

> Power feminism ... is an ideal focus for the [Labour] party of the future. It's lean, it's clean, it's light-weight. It looks towards the future, averting its eyes from the muck and grime of the present. It functions, in short, as a freeze-dried, vacuum-packed dietary replacement to fill up the hole in Labour thinking that was once taken up with poverty, exploitation and class. Let us not bother thinking about the boring fact that women in general continue to work for lower wages than men do.[5]

By contrast, the political ascendency of feminism in the 1970s single handedly put gender on the agenda in the teeth of opposition and derision. Such political struggles informed the cultural analysis of gender in ways that remain fruitful and on which I draw, although with a distinctly 1990s slant.

Since this book is addressed primarily to students, it makes sense that the videos I discuss in the book have been made by students. One of the themes which emerges in the video work I have selected to look at, is the crisis of identity which men are undergoing. This focus is perhaps not surprising. Suicide rates for young men are on the increase while job prospects are decreasing. Roles within the family are changing with women outperforming men in education and increasingly present in the labour market. Perhaps what is surprising is how often men figure as a subject of exploration in videos, even where women have been the driving force behind a production. Yet the way men and women behind the camera look at men in front of the camera, often appears to be nuanced in quite distinct ways. Women appear to be having a lot more fun reconstructing the male in relation to masculinity and femininity. I am reminded here of another example of 'amateur' cultural production – this time in the print media – which has been discussed by Constance Penley. She explores a particular spin-off of Star Trek fanzines produced and circulated by the Star Trek fans themselves. This is 'slash literature', which takes as its premise an explicitly sexual relationship between Captain James T. Kirk and Spock. Yet the people who produce this literature are almost all women and overwhemingly heterosexual. Trying to account for the fact that these women produce romance/pornography involving two men, Penley argues that, in trying to construct a fantasy of professional and sexual equality in a patriarchal society, it is easier to do this between two men than it is between a man and a woman.

> Every slash story ... tries to show how there could be a sexual relation: it is up to us (meaning feminists studying popular culture) to deal with the fact that the women fans can imagine a sexual relation only if it involves a childless couple made up of two men, who never have to cook or scrub the tub, and who live three hundred years in the future.[6]

I suspect something analogous often goes on when women get behind the camera and use the male body to reconstruct gender (using, for example, cross dressing) for their own purposes. On the one hand, this could indicate, as Penley suggests, the redoubtable qualities of patriarchal ideology, setting the agenda and making certain kinds of relationships difficult to imagine. On the other hand, such reconstructions of the male body indicate some of the fissures and cracks opening up in patriarchal ideology. The tone of this reconstruction appears altogether rather different when men (at least straight men) gaze at the male body. The mood is often more sombre, with an emphasis on the male as an isolated figure prone to destructive and self destructive urges. Gendered ways of looking, then, constitute, along with questions of class, two main themes in the discussions around representation.

One particular component of film theory/practice that will crop up frequently in the following pages, and provides much of the inspiration for the kinds of video practices that attract me, is 'third' cinema. The term refers to a cinema which emerged in the 1960s in some parts of Latin America and Africa, but it is a cinema which is defined primarily not by its geographical location, but, as Tesholm Gabriel argues, by its commitment to political liberation and change.[7] In this capacity 'third' cinema differentiates itself in name and in its practices, from 'first' cinema (dominant, industrially and culturally) and 'second' cinema ('art' cinema, committed to authorial expression).[8] Stated so baldly this is a problematic set of categories, but nevertheless, 'third' cinema is a useful reference point for this book for several reasons: it is often, like video practice, a 'poor' cinema; it implicitly or explicitly interrogates dominant cinema (both in its mass entertainment and art cinema manifestations); it is interested in integrating theory and practice; finally, and refreshingly, these days, it situates the politics of cultural activities within a wider culture of political traditions.

Let us pull the threads together. The politics of culture and the culture of politics do indeed remain linked in complex ways. These links may sometimes be oblique and even negative in the sense that the culture of politics seems very moribund and, as numerous commentators have observed, increasingly distanced from the concerns and values which touch people in their everyday lives.[9] For one commentator, politicians across the political spectrum fail to even speak the same language as the people they are supposed to represent:

> New Labour speaks a different dialect from the Government's, but not a different language ... On the central question now facing the political economies of western Europe, new Labour and the new right are at one. Both accept the same vista of relentless global competition; both believe that there is and should be no shelter from the gales of globalisation; neither acknowledges the Hobbesian wisdom that choice is empty without security.[10]

This consensus on matters of political economy underpins a looser though definite conservative consensus on a range of other issues which intersect directly with political economy, including, as I have already indicated, gender, but also the environment and race, as well as a more general conservativism in terms of sexual and cultural choices. With access to the means of representation spreading, the gap between the culture of the professional politician and everyone else becomes more discernible, more evident in the sounds and images videomakers produce. The politics of culture is today marked by a rejection of the established and institutionalised political cultures. This rejection may be very explicit and articulate in video work, or it may be rather coded, a matter of tone and style. Certainly my impression of the range of work which many students have left behind as they exit academia, suggests noirish anxieties about a world which promises little more than downward mobility.

But it is not just the language of established politics which needs to be re-thought, it is the language of the media as well, a language which, as this book will explore, is political in its own right. The technology is there and so too is one very important resource: time. It is scarce but it can be found. If one thinks of how much time people have put into producing their own music culture, then I think one glimpses the possibilities of an independent video culture. There is a long way to go and perhaps independent video will never become that popular; perhaps the medium will be overtaken by other cultural and communication possibilities: in the meantime theorising video practice seems a useful thing to do.

Notes

1 D. Harvey, *The Condition of Postmodernity*, Basil Blackwell, Oxford 1989, pp. 353-355.
2 The very titles of the following examples indicate the concern: W. Hutton, 'Gambling with the World's Welfare', in the *Guardian*, June 19th, 1995, p.17; M. Woollacott, 'Our World at Risk as Free Trade Goes into Free Fall', June 16th, 1993, p.19; R. Dowden, 'A Troubled World Primed to Explode', in the *Independent*, January 2nd, 1995, p.8.
3 S. Faludi, *Backlash: The Undeclared War Against Women*, Chatto and Windus, 1992
4 M. Benn, the *Guardian*, March 8th, 1994, p.23.
5 J. Turner, the *Guardian*, July 29th, 1995, p.23
6 C. Penley, 'Feminism, Psychoanalysis and the Study of Popular Culture' in *Cultural Studies*, L. Grossberg et al (eds), Routledge, London 1992, p.495.
7 T. Gabriel, *Third Cinema in the Third World*, UMI Research Press, 1982.
8 F. Solanas and O. Getino, 'Towards a Third Cinema' in *Movies and Methods*, vol. 1, B. Nichols (ed), University of California Press, 1975, pp.44-64.
9 M. Kettle's complaint that '[p]olitics has never seemed less related to the condition of everyday life than it does today' is a commonplace one; the *Guardian*, June 5th, 1993, p.27.
10 D. Marquand, the *Guardian*, June 5th, 1995, p.14.

Chapter One

Theory and Practice

What is practice and how does it differ from theory? Conversely, what is theory and how does it differ from practice? Where and how do the two meet? We shall see that trying to reconcile theory and practice is useful but difficult: the difficulties have deep historical roots and are embedded in the structural organisation of society and culture. This chapter endeavours to address the above questions and sketch in some of the problems that hinder the integration of theory and practice.

Defining Practice

For our purposes there are two definitions of practice which are important. One dictionary definition of practice is very familiar: practice means activity which attempts to acquire a particular level of competence in an activity through repeated exercise. Certainly when you first engage with video production it is this sense of practice that you are most likely to be aware of. You have to learn basic technical knowledge about the camera and its ancillary equipment (microphones, tripods, editing suites etc), to become familiar enough with it to operate it comfortably. Perhaps by now you have picked up a video and shot some tape with it. You look at it. But what do you see? Your attention is likely to be drawn to the technical flaws and mistakes. This is understandable and you will want to engage in practice (i.e., acquiring a particular level of skill through repeated exercise) to address these problems within the technical and temporal resources available.

However, there is something much more interesting going on, something much more intangible, more difficult to investigate. I am referring to the complex lines of influence that are at work in quietly shaping your decisions and giving meaning to your practice in quite another sense of the word. For practice also means customary or usual action (as in 'it is the practice to behave in such and such a manner'). So while you need to acquire and hone the technical knowledge which is indispensable for any form of cultural production, it is that cultural knowledge (or custom) you have already acquired, or rather how you mobilise this knowledge, which constitutes our main concern and difficulty. This second definition of practice alerts us to the need to ask some simple but basic self-reflexive questions. For example, what are the implications of setting your camera in such and such a place, at such and such an angle? What conventions are you drawing on to provide links between one shot and the next?

The fact that such questions need not be uppermost in your mind in order to produce images and sounds tells us something interesting about practice. Prior to learning anything technical about video, it is clear that you have internalised a vast store of audio-visual cultural knowledge which you have learnt at the point of consumption. On the plus side this means that you can go out with a video camera for the very first time and already have an instinctive grasp of the grammar, say, of an interview situation. The down side of this situation is twofold. Firstly there may be a very large gap between your ambitions – acquired by consuming professional and well-resourced cultural products – and your own resource and skills base. This gap needs to be acknowledged and addressed or it can become very demoralising. Secondly, practice, of a cultural or any other nature, can be undertaken with very little understanding or questioning of why we do things in particular ways. Practices can function quite happily and autonomously from any self-interrogation. If practice was not to some extent autonomous from rigorous self-consciousness, then simple and relatively uncontentious acts would start to occupy disproportionate amounts of our thinking; no doubt insomnia would ensue. However, the disadvantage here is in losing sight of why we do things in particular ways; we become slaves to a particular kind of practice and rule out alternatives. This feature of practice may become very debilitating.

Defining Theory

What is the role of theory in the interrogation of practice? What features has theory got which makes it useful in understanding what we do? Implicit in the definition of practice as customary action is the idea that it is governed by gradations of habitual thinking. The Italian marxist, Antonio Gramsci, called this kind of habitual thinking 'spontaneous' consciousness. The inverted commas indicate, of course, that what we may feel to be spontaneous is precisely the opposite, a response so ingrained and preconditioned that it bypasses thought in any active and reflective sense. Gramsci posed this question:

> is it preferable to 'think', without having critical awareness, in a disjointed and irregular way, in other words to 'participate' in a conception of the world 'imposed' mechanically by external environment ... or is it preferable to work out one's own conception of the world consciously and critically, and so out of this work of one's own brain, to choose one's own sphere of activity, participate actively in making the history of the world, and not simply accept passively and without care the imprint of one's own personality from outside? [1]

We can transpose these concerns about the role of culture in society generally to the modest context of video production. In order to have critical awareness rather than spontaneous consciousness, in order to 'participate actively in making [cultural] history rather than having our cultural dispositions shaped 'mechanically by external environment', e.g., the dominant media industries, we have to be aware of how cultural history has left us with (following Gramsci) an 'infinity of traces gathered together without the advantage of an inventory'.[2] The aim of this book is in large part to sketch in such an inventory, to explore the possibilities and difficulties of adapting it to your work as a low-budget videomaker, and to suggest some alternative inventories as well. Theory gives us the ability to reconstruct such an inventory. How?

Firstly, theory can make connections. For example it can help you clarify what your work has in common with and how it departs from other cultural artifacts. Most of the time you will be able to locate your work in some kind of connection with a particular tradition of representation. Without theory though, your understanding of how and where your work connects with and departs from particular traditions, will inevitably remain rather impressionistic. You may say to yourself, I want to make a documentary in the Desmond Wilcox mould, and although you will have an idea of what a Desmond Wilcox documentary looks like, translating that into practice without an informed theoretical approach could mean that you end up with a video rather different to the one you thought you were making. For theory can really clarify the most minute components of a particular tradition of representation. And it can clarify how that tradition of representation differentiates itself from others, some of which might be widely different and some of which may run alongside and have meeting points with the tradition of representation you are initially attracted to.

Secondly, theory can clarify the effects in terms of the meanings produced by a set of conventions or strategies. Take for example the 'twist in the tale' plot device, a formula which establishes audience expectations only to then undermine them. Of course this is a common trope of the classical narrative or variants of it. But in appropriating this device what can easily be missed is the fact that the 'surprise' ending is already built into the device: the audience expects it. The surprise, baldly presented, surprises no one because it is already demanded by the audience once they detect the game being played with them. Studying a mainstream film or television production that uses this device shows that everything depends on the build-up and presentation of the twist. Moreover build-up and presentation may take time (viewing time and production time) and other resources which are not available to you. So you need to think carefully about how you can appropriate various strategies. To take another example, you may want to make a short fictional piece that has a 'strong' female character in the lead. Popular culture offers various types of 'strong' women (e.g., femme fatales and career women). In order to understand the definitions of strength being offered and how precisely these are activated by a web of representational strategies, you will again require some theoretically informed thinking.

Finally, theory relativises practice. If practice is customary or usual action then it has been forged and disseminated by collective habit, communication and interaction. Theory provides us with the vocabulary to interrogate the assumptions secreted into those habits, those apparently spontaneous reflexes. Theory allows us to examine the internal workings of a set of conventions and thus understand that they are not universally valid and that there are other ways of doing things. But whatever you produce, whatever its relationship with identifiable conventions and representations, you will want to appreciate it in its proper complexity. It is extraordinary but commonplace that students and others engaged in cultural production can be responsible for producing work that obviously embodies complex ideas, and yet so often they cannot talk or write about what they have made at anything like the same level of complexity. And yet theory, which could unlock that complexity and therefore contribute to the development of their cultural work, is so often viewed with indifference at best, hostility and suspicion at worst.

One of the ironies of human practices is that they often begin life alongside explicitly articulated principles which become, over the course of time, taken for granted and implicit. If practice is only naturalised theory, then explicit theorising need not be seen as something alien and threatening to the cultural worker. Rather than seeing theory and practice as distinct and separate activities, we need to see them as part of a continuum. The terms 'theory' and 'practice' refer to those circumstances and contexts in which either reflection on practice (theory) or the implementation of theory (practice) predominate. Ideally, during any single unit of video making and across numerous units of video making, these two activities should be constantly at play, emphasising now one, now the other.

The above formulation – that theory and practice refer to the emphasis of one in a continuum in which both are always present in some combination – allows the objection to spontaneous practice per se to be relinquished. It would indeed be absurd to urge that all spontaneity be excised from all practice. The ability to improvise, to do the unexpected, the unplanned, to experiment, to try something where the meaning and effect is not immediately clear, is very obviously conducive to genuine creativity. All I have been trying to point out so far is that, less obviously, a practice that is not informed by critical reflection generates what we might call a spontaneity of confirmation, the unquestioned sense that 'this is how things are done', which is a less than authentic spontaneity. Integrating theory into practice allows for the possibility of a genuinely experimental spontaneity. Yet if we can theoretically integrate theory and practice, we must also acknowledge how, in terms of institutionalised practice, they have been separated and held apart in the two dominant models of cultural production which we have available to us.

Two models of cultural practice

In the education system a tripartite division has developed between: a) theoretical courses in film, television and media studies; b) vocational courses which aim to train labour for its insertion into the day to day running of film and television organisations; c) practical arts-based courses which aim to cultivate individual authorial expression. The bifurcation in the practical courses b) and c) has a long historical genesis and is embedded in some of the large scale structural transformations of the last four hundred years. It is worth sketching this history in, for its consequences abut right up onto the present, offering two models for conceptualising cultural practice. I want to suggest that both models have something to offer, but that both have to be in some sense transformed if they are to be useful for the purposes of empowering the videomaker.

The craftworker

Before the Renaissance the concept of authorial expression, as we understand it today, simply did not exist. The cultural worker was conceived in terms similar to those governing the vocational orientated courses today. The artist was seen very much as a craftsperson, someone who learnt the skills of a trade and applied them. There was no sense of artistic production being the province of the gifted few, or that cultural workers were engaged in a magical or mysterious process. They were simply doing a job, much like any other worker. The reason for this conception of course is that in the feudal era, mysterious or transformative powers belonged to God, not ordinary mortals. Despite its basis in feudal ideology this evacuation of mystery from creativity has something to recommend it. It makes creativity earthly, physical. In this conception creativity requires a constant learning process, a sense that the cultural worker is always an apprentice to knowledge. Creativity in this conception requires planning and preparation. It requires such raw materials as equipment, locations and time. In this conception of cultural practice, creativity is embedded in the material, everyday world. It is not something so precious and rare that only a few can hope they have been born with it.

The down side of the medieval conception of the craftworker was the requirement that they be totally subordinate to their patrons (the church, the aristocracy). Similarly today, craftworkers in television (technicians, writers, directors) deliver a product under instruction and close supervision of the organisation. The difficulty with uncritically celebrating cultural production as ordinary work is that in advanced capitalist society, work is generally a rather degraded, disenfranchised sphere of activity . Stuart Hood, a one time BBC controller, has written eloquently about the craftworkers' alienation from the products of their own labour. It is worth quoting from him at length:

> Film crews, for instance, will find themselves scheduled to shoot material for a programme about which they know little and about which they have not been consulted. The result is that they often have scant interest in what they produce. They will turn up on the right day at the right time and carry out their work 'professionally' – which means that they will bring to bear on the task in hand a number of known and tried skills that will produce predictable results. The exposure time will be correct and the picture sharp; the subject will be shot in such a way that the pictures can be edited together into a coherent narrative; the sound will be clear and capable of being easily synchronised with the pictures. They may then move on, on the same day, to another assignment for a different programme about which they are also ill-informed but which they will shoot with the same professional skill. Apart from checking on the technical quality of their work, the team will show little interest in how their pictures are used and have no say in that use ... it would, in management terms, be uneconomical for a film crew to be involved in the discussion of programme ideas of how the programme should be shot. Time spent in this way would, from management's point of view, be wasted time – time in which the crew might have been producing more material, shooting more film, and so justifying the cost of their wages.[3]

What Hood captures here is the practical consequences and human cost of what the sociologist Max Weber called rationalisation. For Weber, a central feature of modern capitalism was the development of predictable and routine patterns of work and administration in which the relations between people are governed by impersonal laws. The space for labour to consider the peculiarity and specificity of particular situations, to experiment and to make mistakes, shrinks massively in favour of systems geared towards the calculation, costing and predictable co-ordination of work. A strict division of labour characterises such systems, operating not only between mental and manual labour, between those who conceptualise and those who execute the work, but amongst the 'executors' themselves. Thus there is little in the way of rotating specific jobs. A camera person is always the camera person, other facets of the work process are divided off from them. The reason for this is simple. If jobs are rotated and/or decisions shared, then everyone has a broader input fostering the kind of discussions which, as Hood points out, capital regards as wasted time. Yet if you are working in a group outside the industry, and if the members of the group are 'volunteers' rather than 'wage slaves', the industry's hierarchical working practices may not be the best way of motivating and involving people. Some flexibility of roles (for example, sharing and/or rotating roles) and/or group decision making (balanced by the need to get things done) can bind people together through job satisfaction as effectively as the coercion of rationalised systems.

Rationalisation impacts not only on practice, but on consciousness of practice.[4] For the craftworker's labour becomes so streamlined in the name of efficiency that they become wedded to a very narrow range of conventions of representation. Obviously a more diverse and exploratory attitude to representation would run counter to the organisation's needs to produce material economically. Thus rationalisation performs an essential service for capitalism. Both are compulsively homogenising forces, assimilating the different and the particular qualities of things to the quantative drive to accumulate more capital. Television's news and current affairs programmes are a particularly striking case where a select number of templates of representation are fitted onto the most diverse issues, events and situations. This means that little consideration is given to how issues, events and situations may require a rethinking of previous assumptions about representation.

This triumph of quantity over 'quality' would seem to be contradicted by the emphasis which organisations and institutions of all kinds, place on 'quality controls'. Aside from the fact that the parameters which determine 'quality' are firmly subordinated to the rationalising imperatives of capitalism, notions of quality often function to depoliticise the craftworker's relationship to their own work. The social and political questions generated in the process of work, get transformed into less highly charged notions of what is and is not 'professional' practice. The film *Acceptable Levels* (John Davies, G.B., 1983) offers an illustration and critique of the way this works. The film is a fictional account of a BBC production team that go to Northern Ireland to film a documentary showing how children live with 'the Troubles'. The film's title refers to the levels of violence in Northern Ireland that have become normalised. The news media's formulaic approach to the conflicts in Northern Ireland can be seen as a key contribution to this process of normalisation. In *Acceptable Levels*, while the film crew are interviewing a child on an estate, another child is shot and killed by British troops using plastic bullets. The team rush out and film the aftermath. Initially outraged by the incident, the director gradually whittles it down to a brief mention in the programme's final cut. This is justified by the 'poor' quality of lighting in the footage, and by the shift in form and tone from carefully researched documentary to cinema-verite images of confusion, grief and a 'hysterical women waving a plastic bullet' as the director puts it. The director can only consider it 'unprofessional' to combine different documentary forms (when in fact such a formal dislocation within his documentary might have brought home just how unacceptable the levels of violence are in the region). Thus the highly charged material can be excised without any sense that this is a political, rather than a purely professional, decision.

While the craftworker has, in the main, little choice but to adopt the working practices of the organisation which employs them, the independent videomaker may have considerable latitude regarding working practices and means of representation. To make use of that, though, requires an interrogative attitude to your own cultural practice, one that eschews fetishising particular methods and making them sacrosanct by equating them with 'quality' or 'professionalism'. It should be clear why integrating theory into this model of cultural practice has been problematic. If the craftworker, the product of vocational training and apprenticeship, draws on theory, then that might bring them into conflict with the spontaneous practice required by the culture industries. They need labour to be routinised and regimented in order to produce culture in enough quantity and with enough degree of similarity to compete in the market place. Thus the only 'theory' which can be tolerated is the uncritical codification of what the cultural worker is or should be doing. Here 'theory' is reduced to normative prescriptions. Far from relativising practice, this kind of 'theory' only passively reinforces it (we shall explore this in more detail in chapter two).

The author

Unless you come from a background in the industry or have gone through vocational training, the model of cultural practice you are likely to lean towards is that of authorship. This is because authorship has such a high status in western culture. It is seen as a mark of value in cultural artifacts if an author can be clearly discerned. It is the central categrory by which evaluative judgements are drawn between high culture and popular culture and between the best and the mediocre of popular culture. Its appeal is also likely to lie not only in the implicit value it gives to your work, but the associations it has with autonomy and independence.

These associations are once more embedded in history. The concept of authorship has its origins in the emergence of capitalism. Great philosophical and cultural shifts accompanied the decline of feudal society in the face of the more dynamic forms of wealth creation associated with trade, merchants and competition for markets. One of the great contributions which capitalism made to consciousness was to begin to place, theoretically at least, the individual at the centre of society. This was congruent of course with the entrepreneurial activities of the merchant class, but it also helped provide a greater legitimacy to the artist as someone having rights and interests independent of (separate from) the patron.

Yet capitalism's philosophy of individual autonomy, while remaining crucial to legitimise private property, comes, by the twentieth century, to be in contradiction with capitalism in its monopoly phase. Here capitalism's rationalising logic intensifies, driving out individual 'units' of capital in favour of fewer but larger corporations and industrial combinations. Rationalisation of working practices inside organisations therefore also intensifies, penetrating industry, state and culture. In this context, the notion of the intuitive artist becomes even more appealing (if ever more illusory) in an attempt to preserve some realm of activity beyond the reach of ruthlessly systematising forces. The idea of the author expressing their own personal preoccupations comes into conflict with the commercial pressures and demands of the capitalist market, certainly, but it also leads to a rejection/suspicion of all theorising, as yet another attempt to harness the cultural worker to a system apparently every bit as abstract and formalised as a Ford factory production line.

The contradictions between bourgeois ideology (with its notion of individual creativity) and bourgeois economics (with its emphasis on profitability) requires cultural production to be split into two sectors. One is geared to the mass market and is the domain of the craftworker. As we have seen, the craftworker is someone who has command over certain technical knowledge but whose skills are employed for a task set by someone other than themselves so that they deliver their skills without putting anything of 'themselves' into the work. The author on the other hand is given license to produce distinct and individual work. The author/artist comes to be seen as someone fundamentally different from others, an outsider, often 'exempt from all normal rules of social intercourse'.[5]

We can see this division very clearly in television. Soaps and series employ a roster of writers who make little discernible difference to any particular episode of our favourite soaps. This is because the skills they are being employed for are to write within the already constructed formula for the series. On the other hand, authors like Dennis Potter, Fay Weldon, Troy Kennedy Martin, etc. produce work that has certain thematic and compositional qualities which are associated with and are marketed as being particular to that author. We have seen that one of the pluses of the craftworker model of cultural practice is the stress on the material, everyday nature of cultural production. Its weakness lies in its unthinking internalisation of the values and assumptions that are part of that everyday spontaneous practice. Conversely, what is valuable about the authorship model of cultural practice is the stress it places on the individual's role in shaping the end results of cultural production. Yet, though this independence is eminently preferable to the craftworker's subordination, the great weakness of the category of authorship as it has been largely understood, is the way that it prises the individual out of any consideration of their context or influence by social, political and cultural forces. For the mainstream cultural critics who feed into and off this kind of cultural practice, it is considered the height of praise to explicitly celebrate the author's apparent transcendence of social particularity, claiming universal status for their work. This can instantly defuse and transform the most powerful of social critiques. Writing of the critical reception to the feature film *Distant Voices, Still Lives* (Terence Davies, 1989), Peter Keighron observes how 'a film that shouts of class society, poverty and history'[6] is transformed into a metaphor for the 'human condition', something which exists, to the relief of the privileged, quite independently of 'class society, poverty and history'.

The role of this conception of authorship in denying the social, has implications when it comes to adopting this as a model for cultural practice. Here we have a different kind of spontaneous practice, one that is legitimised not by notions of 'professionalism' as with the craftworker, but by a notion of creativity as something issuing forth from the individual author with very little mediation by society. The Bolivian filmmaker and theorist Jorge Sanjines has written scathingly of how this model for the cultural worker encourages 'the overblown expression of an individual talent'. He goes on to identify the ideological coordinates of this apparently subversive cultural production:

> [if the artist] continues to believe in his or her own right to create without reference to anyone else, and to think that what counts is the release of his/her own 'private demons', with no concern for intelligibility, then s/he is locating her/himself clearly within the key ideological postulates of bourgeois art.[7]

If we return to Gramsci's call for the critical maturing of consciousness, we may think that all Gramsci is asking is that every individual should think for themselves. But Gramsci explicitly rejects an image of society being made up only of discrete individuals. In Gramsci's words, every individual is always a 'conformist to some conformity'.[8] As we have seen, theory has a special role to play in making you aware of how, as cultural producers, your work connects up with different levels and types of 'conformity'.

We must also recognise that, just as practice without theory can be detrimental to practice, theory divorced from practice can also quickly lose its benefits. A striking example of how the division of labour between practice and theory can be detrimental to the latter can be found in Roland Barthes' readiness to declare the 'death' of the author and proclaim a republic of readers. Writing as a post-structuralist, Barthes promulgated the notion of intertextuality. This concept suggested that the cultural text did not 'belong' to the author and could not be understood as a product of their personality. Instead the text was to be seen as composed of fragments of other texts – cultural, social, political and so on. The text is a 'tissue of quotations drawn from the innumerable centres of culture'.[9] Nothing is original in the sense that all texts depend on pre-existing ones and beg, borrow and steal from them in order to construct themselves. To a large extent this is incontestable. I cheerfully admit that nothing in this book is 'original' in the sense that the ideas have not been expressed in some form by others. But in attacking high bourgeois notions of originality and individual ownership of meaning, Barthes bends the stick too far the other way. If in some ways Barthes' notion of a 'tissue of quotations' has some affinities with Gramsci's notion that we are composed of an 'infinity of [cultural] traces', Gramsci, as a marxist, also holds on to the other horn of the dilemma. For if we are all in some sense the product of our contexts, then we are also, in minute ways individually and in rather larger terms collectively, producers of our contexts. It is this duality of human experience which we need to hang on to.

To contemplate your 'death' as an author of culture at the very moment you get your hands on the means of cultural production, would seem, then, unnecessarily demoralising. As a 'scriptor' (as

Barthes chooses to rename the author), I am very much aware that this work is composed of thousands of fragments from other texts. What distinguishes this text from those other texts is the particular synthesis of writings, interpretations and emphases that I choose. Similarly, you will make decisions, selections and choices at the point of production that crucially determine the meanings of your video work. Moreover, video has so miniaturised and simplified the technology and processes of production, that it is quite possible to produce work outside of the collaborative conditions which characterise most film work. The whole point of this book is to help foster a spirit of cultural work that seeks to be conscious of how and why you make particular decisions, selections and choices and therefore meanings. Undoubtedly those meanings can be traced back to a variety of different cultural sources and are therefore not 'original' in the sense that they will have no derivation. This 'levelling down' of culture may shock the bourgeoisie, but it is hardly very radical for all that. Nor should you despair if your visions of expressing your 'inner self' are crumbling before you! While the concept of intertextuality rightly absorbs the author and the text back into the cultural and social matrix from whence they came, the specific synthesis of 'texts' and meanings are not so predetermined that decisions, choices, selections and the weighing up of combinations on your part, become redundant. What should become interesting to you as you struggle to understand your cultural work, is the how and why of a particular textual synthesis, and an appreciation of its significance should be related not only to your own creative development, but to the historical context of its production and reception. If the term 'history' seems too grand to apply to your own cultural practice, then that is only because the dominant notions of who makes history and how, have been thoroughly undemocratic ones.

Theory and political correctness

We have seen thus far that many of the difficulties involved in integrating theory and practice and many of the reasons why cultural workers may be sceptical about theory arise out of the specialisms and divisions of labour characteristic of capitalist class society. Nevertheless it has to be immediately acknowledged that there have been abuses of theory which can only reinforce widespread prejudices and misconceptions concerning theory. Such abuses turn the liberatory potential of theory into something rather more debilitating. I am thinking of what has come to be called Political Correctness (PC). Producing video work for widespread distribution and exhibition could well mean falling foul of some very draconian censorship laws on the medium. Videos drawing on religious iconography can be banned under blasphemy clauses for example.[10] The politics of Political Correctness, however, are not as in this example associated with the right (although clearly the right has its own canon of what is Politically Correct), but rather with the left; and the censorship which PC may exert for you as a videomaker is more likely to be a form of self-censorship and/or peer group pressure. For PC is a rather disparate and diffuse phenomenon:

> Despite the capital letters it is not an organisation, a campaign or even a movement. There are no recognised PC leaders, no official or even unofficial PC programme or manifesto. Nor is it even possible to identify key theoretical texts which exemplify the PC outlook. At most, perhaps, it could be described as a trend, a cultural phenomenon, a series of attitudes and practices which are an effect or residue of certain aspects of the movements for black, female and gay liberation.[11]

For the right, the term Politically Correct is a new expression of a very old objection to progressive social policies. Such policies are underpinned by theories which seek change by identifying patterns of human relationships and then insisting that these relationships are neither natural nor inevitable, but rather they are the product of human history. Before PC, conservatives used the term ' ideology' to describe ideas about the world and human relationships that went against what the right perceives as commonsense and 'natural'.[12]

Clearly, critiques of the unequal distribution of power and status along lines of gender, race and sexuality, depend on theory to identify how and why sexism, racism and homophobia operate. In the United States, where the PC debate has been most fierce, these questions of power have tended to revolve around the teaching curriculum. In recent years, real and unambiguous advances have been made within areas like literature, which are heavily fortified by tradition. Thus women's writing, post-colonial writing, working-class literature, have all been admitted to the curriculum. These genuine advances though have been occasionally marred (the furore has been massively over-amplified by the media) by PC tendencies which become embarrassed about or hostile to all cultural expression not deemed to be unequivocally 'pro' oppressed groups.

Such a stance is another way of asking for 'positive images', which in itself is not a bad thing as long as it is understood that what constitutes positive representation is contestable, open to debate and open to change and development. In the UK the struggle against homophobia and racism takes different forms and is associated with different organisations with different and even conflicting ideas about the images that are 'positive' in the fight against discrimination and hostility. The attempt to codify and list positive images is typically a bureaucrat's solution to what is a political debate. To try and impose what constitutes positive images is to freeze and arrest the complexity and development of culture's relationship to the world outside culture. The favoured work, the work that conforms to the 'rules' becomes increasingly sterile (just as socialist realism was to once it was codified and imposed on Soviet artists by Stalin in the 1930s).

If one impulse behind the PC approach to culture is to sever its connection with social change, another contradictory impulse is to collapse social inequality and cultural representations together and treat them as if they were the same thing. But they are clearly not. Cultural artifacts will be consumed in different ways by different people at different times. It was widely reported that David Mamet's play *Oleanna* – which takes PC as its subject matter, and looks at the shifting power dynamic between a (female) student and her (male) lecturer – was quite often read very differently by women and men. But one cannot 'consume' pay differentials between women and men or between black and white people as anything other than being sexist or racist. In the UK, the head teacher who blocked a school trip to see *Romeo and Juliet* on the grounds that it was 'heterosexist' was making a similar error, merging a cultural artifact with discriminatory practices. Again the difference between the two is that while gay and lesbian spectators can find their own spaces, interpretations and meanings in a cultural artifact, the same cannot be said in the case of actual discrimination. (It is instructive to note that the disproportionate response of the education authorities who called for the headteacher to be sacked, indicates that PC has little institutional purchase in the UK education system).

Of course, irrespective of how particular audiences consume a text it might be argued that cultural artifacts encourage or lean towards particular interpretations and that they are underpinned by, for example, sexist or racist assumptions. In what sense is the fictional text different in this regard to, say, the tradition of racist literature which claims that there is scientific evidence (IQ tests and the like) which 'proves' that black people are less intelligent than white people? I think we can draw a distinction which broadly holds true, between, for example, racist political or academic material and a Hollywood movie (or a high art painting) exhibiting racist assumptions. Political and 'scientific racism' as it is sometimes called, are orientated towards advocacy and influencing public/policy action and initiatives. Seeking political or academic influence, they are systematic attempts at 'theorising' society, genetics, or whatever. The cultural text is generally different for contextual and textual reasons. It is not that the cultural text transcends the social world, but that it generally operates in a different register of social activity. Advocacy for specific political or scientific outcomes tends to be downplayed and a rather looser, more ambiguous mode of address is deployed in the name of entertainment and pleasure. Internally, while the cultural text may embody 'theories' – often implicit and naturalised ones – they are rarely as coherent or systematic as 'scientific' or 'factual' or political tracts. Indeed, cultural products often reveal the contradictions within a perspective such as racism or sexism as well as registering the presence or impact of oppositional voices. Such contradictions and conflicts demand our attention because they tell us about the structure of ideas which we all inhabit in one form or another. A cultural text may illuminate the appeal of, but also the weaknesses in, such structures of thought and the difficulty they have in maintaining their hold over us. They hint at and illuminate what kinds of transformations in thinking and practice would amount to genuine advances and what might be more superficial. To regard these questions as self-evident and not in need of exploration is to close debate and to fossilise into assertions of self-destructive certainty. There is, then, a secular and political case for thinking that culture is different from other forms of social and intellectual activities and that this 'difference' has important implications for the way we respond to and discuss culture and its relationship to society.

I have been arguing for a political approach to cultural labour and the finished cultural text(s). I have argued that theory is an essential component of any understanding of the relationship between culture and politics. In this sense, a critical theory rebuts the claims of conservatives that discrimination and inequality is somehow part of human nature, somehow inevitable, and somehow harmless. Taking on board the critique of various forms of discrimination is not an attack on 'free speech', and the unthinking reproduction of such values is hardly an enormous gain for the cultural worker. This is as true for the black cultural worker producing representations of gay sexuality as it is of the white cultural worker involved in producing representations of black culture.

At the same time, a truly critical theory will also rebut the censorious attitude and the atmosphere of self-censorship which PC can generate. The realm of culture is a realm of exploration, of testing different possibilities, of registering ambivalences and of shocking and challenging expectations. While theory calls practice into question and provides the analytical tools for dissecting its political implications and elaborate constructedness, practice is always capable of surprising theory, of qualifying it, of being more diverse than theory imagined and illuminating new avenues through concrete examples which theory, with its (necessary and advantageous) propensity for generalisation and schematisation, might have missed.

Conclusion

I want to conclude this chapter with a reference to the Cuban filmmaker and writer, Julio Garcia Espinosa. Writing in the late 1960s, Espinosa produced a very influential and prescient article, and one that was anticipatory in the sense that it dreams of a future glimpsed in the early years of the Cuban revolution.[13] In particular he yearned for the abolition of the division between art and the people, the abolition of the very category of the artist into everyday life. He locates the position of the artist within class society, as someone doubly separated, both from their audience and from wider society. The artist is part of 'a minority which has had the time and the circumstances needed to develop within itself, an artistic culture.'[14] Espinosa asks: what happens if for social reasons such as 'the universalisation of college level instruction' and technological developments (such as video), these divisions between the artist and their audience, between the artist and society in general, are challenged? Espinosa invokes Marx's own utopian vision, that: '"in the future there will no longer be painters, but rather men [sic] who, among other things, dedicate themselves to painting"'.[15] This radical vision seeks to abolish specialisms, professionalisms, divisions of labour and offer culture as something that all can participate in. Dissolving the artist and artistic work as an exclusive group and activity would not only reintegrate art with life but overcome divisions between art and those discourses concerned to explore the body and material life, that is to say, the sciences. Wider access to the means of cultural production will bring with it an invigorating influx of scientific understanding: sociology, anthropology, psychology, economics (and we may add, media theory), which can aid art's understanding of itself and the world. In this chapter I have been discussing how cultural work is divided off from theory as a critical instrument of change (self development and wider change), or in Gramsci's words, as a contributor to a 'historical process of becoming'.[16] We have seen how this theory/practice division is a product of the models of cultural work which capitalism has institutionalised. In the following chapter we shall explore the impact some of these dichotomies have had on the cultural artifacts themselves.

Notes

1 A. Gramsci, 'The Study of Philosophy and of Historical Materialism' in *The Modern Prince and Other Essays*, Lawrence and Wishart, London 1967, p.58.
2 Gramsci, *ibid*, p.59.
3 S. Hood, *On Television*, Pluto, London 1987, p.35.
4 G. Lukacs, *History and Class Consciousness*, Merlin Press, London 1971, pp.88-90.
5 J. Wolff, *The Social Production of Art*, Macmillan, London 1981, p.12.
6 P. Keighron, 'Condition Critical', in *Screen*, vol.32, no.2 1991.
7 J. Sanjines 'Problems of form and content in revolutionary cinema', in *Twenty Five Years of New Latin American Cinema*, BFI/C4, 1983, p.34.
8 A. Gramsci, *op.cit.*, p.59.
9 R. Barthes, 'The Death of The Author', in *Image, Music, Text*, Fontana, London 1977, p. 146.
10 M. Barker, *The Video Nasties*, Pluto, London 1984.
11 J. Molyneux, 'The politically correct controversy', in *International Socialism* no.61, Winter 1993, p. 43.
12 R. Williams, *Keywords*, Fontana, London 1988, p. 154.
13 See V. Geohegan's *Marxism and Utopianism*, Methuen, London 1987, for a comprehensive discussion of 'future dreaming'.
14 J.G. Espinosa, 'For an Imperfect Cinema',in *Twenty Five Years of New Latin American Cinema*, BFI/Channel Four, 1983, p.28.
15 Espinosa, *op. cit.*, p.29.
16 Gramsci, *op. cit.*, p.67.

Chapter Two

Between Art and Industry

In this chapter I want to look at the main areas where video practices are located and the implications these dominant spaces have for the video practices (yours for example) operating outside them. There are two main spheres to be considered in this chapter: the institutions of the art world and the culture industries of the mass media (a third, 'community' video, will be discussed in the following chapter). The conflicting definitions which the world of art and the mass media bring to video are, I shall argue, problematic for the kind of video practice I am advocating. At the same time, some of the actual manifestations of video as art and video within the culture industries, hint at a negation of some of the principles which structure those institutions and industries. Thus there is a dominant logic to these worlds, but also niches for and glimpses of video practices which to varying degrees are in opposition to those logics. In exploring the terms which these institutions each set for video's entry into them, we shall see that the question of form – and more broadly modernist aesthetics – looms large. To anticipate my argument, we shall see that for the institutions of art, questions of artistic form become a major repository of value. What is valorised is art in and for itself. The history of modernist aesthetics has a contradictory relation to this dominant logic, often affirming it, sometimes resisting such aestheticism. Conversely, in the industries of the mass media, questions of form are subordinate to reference points outside the cultural artifact, such as the audience that must be 'entertained' and/or the world, which must be 'convincingly' (an awful lot rests on that word) replicated. These are the antinomies which need to be negotiated if the assumptions which each sphere has vis-à-vis video, are to be interrogated.

Video art

Video's relationship to the art world began to be established in the 1960s, initally by performance artists, especially in New York. Quickly, however, the medium began to be defined not so much as an appendage to other art forms, but as an art form in its own right. It became a bona fide medium of authorial expression, finding – although often tenuously – a place in existing galleries and exhibitions, or establishing its own exhibition networks in venues specifically devoted to video. The question of the medium's formal qualities and characteristics was crucial to video's entry into the world of art. We can begin thinking about the role and function of 'form' in the art world, by asking what might constitute an example of video practice that would not qualify as video art.

The Institute of Contemporary Arts once had an audiovisual library (now just another victim of the arts' retrenchment and contraction in the wake of Thatcherism). Because it was a library rather than an exhibition, you could find works side by side which one would not ordinarily find in the art world. Works on film were listed together with video works – and within the latter category, the library held an unusually eclectic range. For example, one could ask to see work by video artists such as Nina Danino, Nam June Paik, Sandra Goldbacher/Kim Flitcroft, and so on, as well as something like the *Miners Campaign Tapes*, which, amongst other things, explored the role of the miners' wives during the 1984-85 strike, the role of the media and the role of the police. As the plural of 'tapes' in the title suggests, this was an example of video practice and one that depended on the fact that video greatly facilitates the cheap production and distribution of such audiovisual material. As I have suggested, in order to enter the art world, video would have to demonstrate an exploration of its 'specificity' as a medium, which is to say, a self-conscious use of the qualities and characteristics that make video, video. Yet although I have suggested that the *Miners Campaign Tapes* do indeed demonstrate some of the qualities and characteristics of video, the art world would rather define it as 'community' based work.

For the art world, the specificity of the art object resides in the medium itself and the forms it can generate. The example of specificity I have given in relation to the *Miners Campaign Tapes* is far too involved in social practices, far too conditional on video's engagement with practices other than video, to qualify.[1]

To examine further the principles on which cultural artifacts are included or excluded from the world of art, we will need to have recourse to Pierre Bourdieu's sociology of culture. Bourdieu's work stands as a critique of the relationship between cultural forms and social classes. In *Distinction,* Bourdieu explores the relationship between cultural consumption and class. Playing on the double meaning of the word distinction, Bourdieu argues that social subjects (and the dominant classes in particular) draw boundaries (distinctions)between themselves and others and in so doing claim 'distinctiveness' in the evaluative sense, for their tastes.[2] The boundaries are drawn both in terms of what they consume and, importantly, how they consume symbolic goods. All acts of consumption require competences, that is the cultural knowledge that will allow the artifact(s) to be decoded. Without the competences which artifacts demand from the consumer, the latter will feel 'lost in a chaos of sounds and rhythms, colours and lines, without rhyme or reason'.[3]

For Bourdieu the differential distribution of competences are not 'gifts of nature' but the result of informal training (the family background) and formal training (education). His work targets what he refers to ironically as the 'inspired encounters' of high culture, precisely because this cultural field sees itself as gloriously autonomous from anything so 'vulgar' as class.[4] For Bourdieu quite the reverse is true. High culture is nothing more than a valued prize (for some) within the class struggle. Bourdieu calls this field of cultural consumption 'legitimate' taste. It functions to make cultural knowledge, 'come to serve the ancient purposes of ideology in justifying social inequality and domination'[5] by making 'taste' appear to be nothing more than the accomplishment of the individual. Ranked below legitimate taste, comes middle-brow taste. This is characterised by reconciling 'immediate accessibility and the outward signs of cultural legitimacy'. Bourdieu lists some examples of this as:

> accessible versions of avant-garde experiments or accessible works which pass for avant-garde experiments, film 'adaptions' of classic drama and literature, 'popular arrangements' of classical music or 'orchestral versions' of popular tunes...[6]

Below middle-brow taste lies popular taste. Bourdieu reminds us of its lowly status within the hierarchy of taste by sometimes referring to it as 'barbarous' taste. A market logic of supply and demand operates in the construction of this three tiered hierarchy. The more difficult it is to acquire the competences which make the consumption of particular artifacts possible and pleasurable (that is the more supply, through family background and education, is restricted), the fewer people have those competences and therefore the more valuable those competences are for an elitist culture. Bourdieu borrows the terminology of the economist to drive the point home when he refers to such competences/knowledge as a form of cultural capital. Yet of course this market logic which governs the universe of legitimate taste is disavowed by it. For legitimate taste differentiates itself from middle-brow and popular taste precisely on the grounds that they are debased by their proximity to the market, i.e. large (mass) markets where capital hopes to secure rapid returns on investments. Legitimate taste rarely bothers to make an extensive analysis of what exactly it is that the symbolic goods of popular taste are supposed to 'lack'. The judgement is given in advance and is regulated by the fact that such symbolic goods, because they depend upon widely distributed competences, must have a lower value according to the market logic within which legitimate taste operates.

Given this differentiation between legitimate and popular taste, video art must have a highly insecure tenure in the world of art. Video repeats the dichotomy of photography which, Bourdieu has argued, is torn beween legitimate and popular taste and so can never aspire to being anything more than a middle-brow art.[7] Like photography, video's very presence and institutionalisation in the popular world as recorder of family history (holidays, birthdays, marriages, etc.) throws its place in the world of art into dispute (and disrepute). For the key characteristic of legitimate taste is its aesthetic disposition which attempts to cut art off from everyday life (not least because of its contamination by commerce and the masses). This is evident in its contexts of reception, 'the icy solemnity of the great museums, the grandiose luxury of the opera houses and major theatres, the decor and decorum of concert halls'.[8] The formality of the architecture attempts to give art a 'sacred character' as opposed to one that is more profane, from the Latin word meaning outside the temple. (Perhaps the noted tendency of video art to draw on religious themes and icons may be understood in part as an attempt to wrest the technology and its uses from the popular world in order to make it a suitable cultural investment for legitimate taste).[9]

Formality of architecture and conduct is only one facet of the aesthetic disposition's tendency to assert 'the *absolute primacy of form over function*', in the work of art itself, which is to assert the primacy of art over life.[10]

In his discussion of how art has functioned as a motif in bourgeois philosophy over the last three hundred years, Terry Eagleton offers a marxist explanation for this tendency to privilege art over life. The bourgeoisie, Eagleton argues, can find nothing of value, nothing that would help legitimise the social order as meaningful, in its own material practices, doomed as they are to endlessly repeat the grubby cycle of profit accumulation, exploitation and competition. Capital, installed at the heart of the way society produces itself, is fundamentally amoral. Thus morality and ethics must be located in other spheres (art and religion in particular) which are then paradoxically both marginal to the real dynamics of society (profit accumulation, exploitation, competition) and yet, in the legitimising role they have to play, rather important.[11] Just as we saw in relation to authorship and the apparent autonomy of the artist, the ideology of the autonomy of art is the bourgeoisie's way of reconciling its conflicting cultural and economic needs.

We can track this contradiction in the critical reception of the aesthetic experience. It is one of the strengths of Bourdieu's work that he collects such empirical evidence to support his theoretical work. Confronted with a photograph of an old woman's gnarled hands, respondents with the cultural competences to mobilise the aesthetic disposition make references to 'the universe of works of art and its history'.[12] For the junior executive, the photo is reminiscent of Van Gogh's early work, while the engineer is reminded of Flaubert's 'old servant woman'.[13] The picture is further framed within the world of art and removed from the world of the everyday by readings which veer towards the universal, where 'hands, labour and old age function ... as allegories or symbols which serve as pretexts for general reflections on general problems'.[14] What Bourdieu has captured very clearly here is that the move from the particular to the universal and the general catapults the work into a sphere where moral and ethical questions can at least be articulated (as they cannot in the everyday world), but at a price. In other words, the work is placed at such a distance from the material everyday world, as to render any debate on issues like justice or equality quite impotent in practical terms.

Popular taste, by contrast, exhibits what Bourdieu terms as a functional aesthetic, characterised by a 'bracketing of form in favour of "human" content'.[15] Thus, looking at the same photo of the old woman's hands this popular taste does not operate through allusions and references within the world of art, nor does it embark on general and abstract speculations. Rather it moves directly to comment on the immediately human content, that is what those hands mean for the specific individual: 'Oh, she's got terribly deformed hands!...'[16] At its most defensive this functional aesthetic will simply reject what it perceives to be a needless aestheticisation of life, as in the manual worker's dismissal of a photo of pebbles which seems to stress more abstract qualities like shape and texture.[17] More usefully, popular taste can demonstrate a multi-functional aesthetic which acknowledges the relativity of its own judgments and the different uses for art in different contexts and for various audiences. This is an aesthetic which is 'necessarily pluralistic and conditional': ... "As a news photo, it's not bad", "All right, if it's for showing to kids" ... "A photo of a pregnant woman is all right for me, not for other people."[18]

This display of multi-functional sensibilities is in direct contrast to the aesthetic disposition's tendency to locate great art as being universally great, irrespective of time, place, and whoever else might (if they are 'civilised' enough) consume the work. Popular taste's capacity for multi-functional aesthetics gives it an intimacy with the everyday and the ordinary, while conversely, legitimate taste's aestheticising tendencies flow from a disposition that prides itself on being distanced from what it sees as the banal, mundane world of the everyday. Thus the multi-functional aesthetic of popular taste articulates the embryonic and un-theorised principles that could lay the basis for a democratic and progressive theory and practice of cultural consumption and production. Unembarrassed by its relationship to everyday life, willingly admitting its judgments to be relative and contingent, the multi-functional aesthetic fits well with the democratic potential implicit in widespread access to audiovisual production.

As the camcorder finds its way into more and more hands, the attempt to find a niche for video in the temple of art, strikes me as a rather problematic project. Video as art tends to entrench the division between the artist and the amateur, between legitimate and profane culture. At the same time, the latter, whether as pop video, campaigning documentary or as part of a youth project on a housing estate, constantly haunts video art as its disreputable alter-ego. This is not to say that all video art accommodates itself to the spaces for art practices unproblematically. Indeed those spaces may manifest a tension between the prestigious exclusivity of the art world and questions of access which video raises, as the changed name of one video facility and distribution organisation – London Video Arts, to London Video Access, suggests.[19] Within such spaces, those examples of video art informed by socialist and feminist critiques of the social order are particularly problematic for the logic of the art world to absorb, precisely because they challenge the traditional separation between art and politics.

A brief history of Modernism

If Bourdieu's work rescues popular taste from disdain, illuminating its multi-functional aesthetic, there are implications in his arguments around form which are problematic for the videomaker. I want to offer some criticism of Bourdieu on this score via a detour through modernism. Modernism has had an extraordinarily fertile interaction with the major social, political and cultural forces of the twentieth century. It is, I believe (although others would disagree), both clearly definable and still an important reference point for any cultural producer today. The drift of Bourdieu's argument, of course, is fairly hostile to modernism. His position, at least in *Distinction*, is that all formal exploration is necessarily caught up in the socially grounded desire for prestige and status. Thus *Distinction* has particularly pessimistic conclusions for any socialist, feminist or other political approach that aims to reconcile an aesthetic that is 'functional' while exploring the processes of meaning production, perception and interpretation. Peter Burger's work suggests that such a reconciliation is possible when he argues that the radicalism of the avant-garde movements (1890 – 1930 approximately) such as early Surrealism, Dada and post-1917 Russian Constructivism, lay in their attempts to integrate art into daily life. Allied to a politics of social change, formal experimentation functioned to call into question the idea that everyday life need necessarily be lived in this or that particular way.[20] This project, to 'lead art back into social praxis,' required the avant-garde to attack the established institutions of art from within.[21] These institutions insisted on regarding art as an activity quite separate from life. As we have seen, Eagleton suggests that this separation of art from life provides the grounds on which art can function to legitimise the status quo (although such autonomy may occasionally provide the political and economic spaces for genuinely oppositional artistic practices). Bourdieu's sociology discovers how the apparent construction of a discrete world of art helps to reproduce the social order on a more mundane everyday level. The terrain of art becomes the site where individuals can accumulate fortunes of a kind, in the form of cultural capital. For the dominated fraction of the dominant class (intellectuals in the broad sense, meaning those who produce knowledge and information) cultural capital works not only to establish distinctions between themselves and those 'below' them, it also offers some compensatory status in relation to the dominant fraction of the dominant class (owners of capital) by establishing a realm of value outside but not necessarily in conflict with the province of economic capital.

An early although only partial manifestation of the avant-garde's attack on the institutionalised separation of art and life can be found in the Cubist innovation of collage. Here fragments of the everyday are incorporated into the picture surface.[22] Picasso, the most radical of Cubist painters, used collage to show both the continuity between art and life and the fluid, changeable nature of both by transforming a piece of flowered wall paper into a table cloth or a piece of newspaper into a violin. As Picasso said:

> If a piece of newspaper can become a bottle, that gives us something to think about in connection with both newspapers and bottles, too. This displaced object has entered a universe for which it was not made and where it retains, in a measure, its strangeness. And this strangeness was what we wanted to make people think about because we were quite aware that our world was becoming very strange and not exactly reassuring[23]

The world has hardly become less strange or more reassuring since Picasso's time and so the question of whether modernist techniques and strategies remain relevant in providing new connections in a changing world, raises itself for us today. Burger in fact makes a distinction between the avant-garde (which he associates with the project of dismembering art's special confinement), and modernism, which he associates with many of the features which postmodernism has come to criticise: i.e., elitism and its insistence on art as autonomous entity, divorced from social practice. Perry Anderson, however, offers a historical account of modernism which covers both its radical period – Burger's moment of the avant-garde – and its subsequent decline and institutionalisation into an older bourgeois idea of art's separation from life. In this scheme, the rather homogenous interpretation of modernism encouraged by its apparent successor is replaced by a view of it as a much more contradictory phenomenon, located in history.

Anderson argues that modernism flourished in those times and places where the present seemed to break most forcefully with the past, while the future had yet to crystallise into any definite political shape. Key centres of modernism – Germany, Russia, Italy, France – were undergoing rapid urbanisation and industrialisation. The effect of these momentous transformations was to snap the cultural and economic links with a past dominated by an older agrarian capitalism and even, in Germany and Russia, a residual aristocracy. There was then a peculiarly heightened and acute sense of change in relation to the past. But even as monopoly capitalism developed the transport and communication links which so fascinated the modernist movement, it also seemed to be fuelling the forces of its own destruction. Mass labour movements emerged to combat exploitation within the factories, at national and international levels, and capitalism did indeed appear to be producing, as Marx argued in *The Communist Manifesto,* its own 'grave-diggers'. This historical conjuncture produced 'an openness of horizon, where the shapes of the future could alternatively assume the shifting forms of either a new type of capitalism or the eruption of socialism.'[24] Modernism, then, is the aesthetic in which important features of the early twentieth century – changing relationships with what has been, uncertainty in the realm of what might be – are most keenly felt.

Eugene Lunne has very usefully identified four major features of modernism which all relate to this conjuncture.[25] Firstly, modernist art emphasises montage: the juxtaposition of different textual materials. This puts an emphasis on the work of art as an assembled product, constructed from disparate materials, and this clearly chimes in with an era of mass industrial production. But it is not only the external world which is being vastly reconstructed under the awesome powers of change generated by capitalism. It is the human subject and the very nature of personality itself which threatens or promises to undergo transformation. This is the second theme of modernist art, the sense in which a unified, monadic, integrated subject is undergoing transformation. In some strands of modernist art, the reconstruction of the subject is welcomed and celebrated, while in others the loss of individuality is feared and mourned. This ambivalence on the question of the individual subject is a facet of a general ambiguity, a general indeterminacy of meaning or (not quite the same thing) a clash between different meanings. This, the third feature of modernism, can be related to the experience of capitalist modernity itself. As Marshall Berman puts it:

> To be modern is to find ourselves in an environment that promises us adventure, power, joy, growth, transformation of ourselves and the world — and , at the same time, that threatens to destroy everything we have, everything we know, everything we are[26]

Franco Moretti has suggested that modernism's celebration of semantic plurality, indeterminacy, ambiguity and irony, although 'an extraordinary cultural achievement'[27] does have its darker side. For the space it opens (for both the text and the audience) for complexity and richness of meaning, can become so elastic, so pluralistic, so 'open', that neither the text nor the audience need ever make any decisions and choices in relation to the historical forces whose effects Berman so eloquently describes above. Modernism, as Moretti puts it, can cast a spell of indecision. As I have said, a clash of meanings and values is not quite the same as indeterminacy, since a clash suggests conflict between forces in relation to which the spectator (and the text?) have to make choices. Of course conflict is the stuff of drama, of narrative, and this is precisely why, Moretti suggests, modernism so often suspends both in order to give free play to the plurality of meaning. But most cultural artifacts can be located somewhere between the most 'closed' drama and the most semantically indeterminate text. What you as a videomaker have to decide is where and when your work will benefit from ambiguity, from diffuse layering of meanings, from celebrating its gaps and fissures, and where it needs some marking out of the boundaries of meaning potential, some delimitation of what x or y 'means', some prearranged symmetry and patterning to the work.

Finally, modernist art is characterised by a heightened self-consciousness of its status as art, exhibiting an exaggerated capacity for self reflexiveness. This may manifest itself as quoting and alluding to the history of art (at the very point where relations with the past are becoming frayed), or perhaps conversely, the allusions may reveal unexpected correspondences between the past and the present; or in explicit acknowledgement of the work's consumption by an audience (thereby perhaps trying to renegotiate or challenge the terms of that consumption, or simply acknowledge that the work does not exist in glorious isolation but depends on audiences to 'complete' its production of meaning). These four characteristics of modernism: montage/juxtaposition; demise of the autonomous integrated subject; ambiguity; and self-consciousness, are recurring themes in the texts, and indeed the theories, which I discuss throughout this book.

Modernism and Bourdieu's baker

The collapse of the avant-garde or 'radical' modernism before the second world war lay principally in the rise of fascism across much of western Europe and Stalinism in the Soviet Union. Both were intensely hostile to what was perceived as the decadence of modernist sensibilities. Nor was this a momentary interruption of modernism's great flowering. The post-war period was characterised precisely by a closure of horizons, not only politically with the onset of the Cold War, but socially and economically. Post-1945, capitalism was triumphant: its centres of production and consumption were entrenched in powerful oligopolies, its bureaucratic logic was expanding everywhere while the labour force was largely compliant, acquiescent and incorporated. In this context, Anderson argues, modernism severed its links with its own turbulent past, when it threw itself into the contradictory dynamics of life, and instead withdrew into the established institutions of the art world, opting for the solace of artistic autonomy in the face of an 'interminably recurrent present'.[28]

Anderson suggests that the conjuncture which produced modernism, at least in the advanced industrial countries, has now passed. There is no space here to discuss whether the social, economic and political differences between the present and the past outweigh the continuities to the extent that we could say we are living in a new era. I would agree with Callinicos that they do not.[29] As far as looking at the cultural evidence, it appears that modernism's death has been greatly exaggerated. Indeed video art emerges during the 1960s when some of the worst excesses of modernism's 'splendid isolation' from social praxis were being challenged. Video art for example took an interest in that most mundane and profane of things, television: arguably this is the one major innovation in the post-war period which has affected the daily life of people on a par with the transport and communciations revolution in the hundred years after 1850.[30] But this interest in television is nothing new or 'post modern', since it merely repeats an older modernism's interest in the functional uses of technology, industry and science (for example in movements like Futurism, Constructivism, Bauhaus, etc).

At the level of the texts themselves, a glance through a London Video Arts catalogue published in the late 1980s bears out the continuing importance of modernist strategies. For example, Colin Scott's *Italo Svevo* (UK, 1987,) is reviewed in these terms: 'Video technology, texts, signs and meanings scrambled in a melee of sophisticated effects, disparate images and possible relationships. Meaning is elusive here — instead, a network of mysterious connections arise in a sophisticated mesh of moving images'.[31] This sounds suspiciously like modernist juxtaposition and indeterminacy of meanings. Another example, Bill Viola's *Anthem* (1983, USA) has this blurb: 'A single scream by a young girl becomes a vocal accompaniment to a lamentation on the existence of humankind in a fragmented, post-industrial and technological world. Viola carefully links images of commerce, leisure, nature and industry to intimate man's removal from the environment and the resulting separation of body and spirit'.[32] Here the review emphasises the modernist strategy of juxtaposition and, in humanity's alienation from its environment, the demise of the integrated subject. Indeed the tape seems to hint self-reflexively at a precursor: Edvard Munch's mourning for the individual subject in *The Scream*. At any rate many other tapes exhibit even more explicitly the modernist concern for self-reflexivity, such as Stephen Littman's *In The Name Of The Gun* (1987, UK): 'A nightmarish piece in which a gunman fires repeatedly straight at the viewer. Littman makes deft use of video effects to multiply this single image into a whole army of crazed assassins. The tape sets out to produce a critique of male behaviour by turning male aggression back on itself; the result is chillingly hypnotic'.[33] This review identifies self-reflexivity both in the way the tape manipulates a single popular culture icon of masculinity, and in the way it directly addresses the viewer and their relationship to this fantasy of power and aggression.

This is not to say however that the term postmodernism does not describe some new features in contemporary culture. The vigour with which mass culture in its restless search for novelty, has reached into the temple of high art and disinterred many of the modernist strategies and techniques, is perhaps a new development. The question is whether to identify this new development in terms of a fundamental break with what has gone before and thus recast the modernist textual features to be found in popular culture, as 'postmodernist'. The term I believe tends to inflate certain developments in popular culture into major cultural transfomations. In this regard, the prefix 'post' is, I would argue, unhelpful. Television has been particularly keen to appropriate such modernist strategies as self-reflexivity (as any episode of *Red Dwarf* will show) and the suspension of narrative (see, for example, *Baywatch*). Bourdieu's own research makes this clear, although his discussion of the reception of these strategies by the working class is problematic:

> ... when formal experimentation insinuates itself into their familiar entertainments (e.g. TV variety shows with sophisticated technical effects...) working-class viewers protest, not only because they do not feel the need for these fancy games, but because they sometimes understand that they derive their necessity from the logic of a field of production which excludes them precisely by these games: 'I don't like those cut-up things at all, where you see a head, then a nose, then a leg ... First you see a singer all drawn out, three metres tall, then the next minute he's got arms two metres long ... I don't see the point of distorting things' (a baker, Grenoble).[34]

Crucially, though, the empirical research which underpins Bourdieu's arguments in *Distinction*, derives from interviews conducted in the early and late 1960s. The post-1960s spread of videotape editing on television has made sophisticated special effects common, which makes some of Bourdieu's respondents sound extremely old-fashioned. The restructuring of perception, 'distortion' as Bourdieu's baker puts it, is, as we have seen, a central feature of modernism. The historical impasse which led to the failure of the avant-garde project to break down the divisions between art and everyday life, are replayed here as farce, or postmodernist parody. The appropriation, say, of surrealist techniques for advertising, integrates avant-garde art into our daily experience, but on capitalism's own terms (to sell cigarettes for example). Yet since mass culture and the mass audience have been permeated by sophisticated techniques, the question arises whether these strategies can be reappropriated and then reconnected with human needs beyond the commodity. Perhaps today there are far more audiences equipped with the cultural competences to read complex and challenging work than the early modernists could have hoped to reach. Of course such a possibility is not only a question of cultural education, it is also an infrastructural question of distribution and exhibition, which would in turn have to encourage cultural competences (the theoretical possibility of consuming particular goods) into cultural dispositions (the actualising of those competences into systematic consumption habits). We will return to the question of accessing audiences in chapter three, but certainly widening access to the means of audiovisual production renews the question of formal exploration and the legacy of the artistic past. As I shall argue below, as far as cultural production is concerned, the bracketing of form is not an option for the videomaker. For pragmatic reasons alone, the low budget context of most video work outside the dominant audiovisual institutions, demands that the videomaker engages with the questions and problems of form.

Video and the culture industries

As a component of established media structures, video as tape has a carrier function for pre-recorded material which, for example, has helped to extend Hollywood's hegemony in film markets around the world. When I was in Cancun, Mexico recently, I visited a cultural centre where I came across a weighty three-volume history of Mexican cinema's first 30 years of production. Squatting nearby was a large Blockbuster video store (Hollywood's main distribution chain, owned by Viacom/Paramount), displaying the same American films to be found in my local North London Blockbuster store. There was no evidence of the impressive history of a national Mexican cinema in Blockbusters, Cancun, let alone any concessions to local/regional audiovisual culture.

As this facet of video's identity demonstrates, the meaning of video practice is very much tied in with questions around the ownership and control of media industries, questions which shape who is showing what to whom. Yet because videotape is a cheap, easily transported means of distributing electronic signals which can be converted into sounds and images on domestic VCRs and television monitors, the medium has another set of possibilities: it offers the chance for people to communicate with one another outside the dominant audiovisual industries. (Cancun for example is located in a region close to the state of Chiapas, where peasants exploited by Mexico's powerful landowners have instigated an armed uprising and seized control of a number of small towns. One can imagine a situation where videotapes detailing the insurgents' grievances and aims could be circulated in the area). While the actual and potential spread and reach of alternative distribution is certainly dwarfed by the use of videotape to carry the pre-recorded symbolic goods of Hollywood, and other corporate structures, the fact remains that the uses of this technology are a site of contestation and struggle.

Within dominant cinema and what we might call the 'independent' sector operating within the orbit of dominant cinema, the instant replay facility of video has been incorporated into film both as subject matter (*Sex, Lies and Videotape*, 1989, USA) and as a device for structuring the narrative. In *Thelma and Louise* (R. Scott, 1991, USA), Thelma's robbery of a grocery store is seen by the viewer (and the police in the film) after the event has taken place in the story. In *Henry, Portrait of a Serial Killer* (J.McNaughton, 1990, USA) we watch two serial killers watching, after the event, their recording of the murder of an entire family. In both cases our relationships to the events in the film have been significantly, if subtly, altered by the introduction of material taped when we the spectator were 'absent' from the narrative and then later played back to us within the world of the fiction. In *Thelma and Louise* the professionalism which the surveillance camera gives to Thelma's heist contrasts comically with our knowledge that she is imitating the words and actions of a thief she has only just met. This comic contrast is doubled by the fact that the viewer watches the replay of the robbery in the company of the police/FBI. The dislocation between the action and the viewing of it helps distance the viewer enough to underline Thelma's transformation from oppressed housewife to independent woman. At another level, because we see the replay of the robbery from the point of view of the police/FBI and her husband, the video surveillance camera functions as a metaphor of patriarchal surveillance, a patriarchy which Thelma has transgressed against.

In *Henry, Portrait of a Serial Killer*, the material becomes doubly agonising for the viewer since we know as we watch the tape with the killers, that these people must already be dead, and that there can be no expectation that the family, or any member of the family will escape. Thus the video replay brutally refuses some of the psychological drives and investments (what will happen? will they be rescued?) which we associate with mainstream cinema. At the same time the sequence foregrounds our fascination and voyeurism around such images and narratives of 'otherness' which the serial killer represents, through a grisly parody of the family video. What is revealed in these examples is the possibility of incorporating the video/television viewing situation into the text as a way of exploring the relationship between identity and media forms. A student video called *Trevor and Leonard*,[35] for example, uses the scenario of two men watching *Thelma and Louise* as a trigger for a fantasy in which they cross dress and 'live' the film's narrative of escape and empowerment: this against the backdrop of the bored, unsatisfied lives they both lead. Certainly the iconography (defined as recurrent visual patterns) of watching video/television is an interesting one to explore further.

We are in little doubt, however, when watching *Thelma and Louise* and *Henry, Portrait of a Serial Killer*, that we are watching films (even if we are not sitting in a cinema theatre). The former has the stars and the high production values associated with dominant cinema, the latter defines itself as a low budget film by its adult and shocking subject matter and approach. Indeed, in both these examples the identity of film itself remains unchallenged, while video is defined and contained as a minor novelty. However, a Mexican 'text' called *Homework* (Jamie Humberto Hermosillo, 1990) is much more difficult to pin down. Is it film, television or video, and what do we mean when we make these distinctions? *Homework* is the length of a feature film and contains explicit sexual material, which television tends to see itself as denied licence to produce although it may broadcast such material once it is defined as 'film' — a definition which clearly requires more than shooting with celluloid. But *Homework* has the low production values of television, featuring only two actors and shooting all the action in one room (significantly it is a domestic location, the social geography so central to television's soaps and situation comedies). Yet most of the action of *Homework* is mediated through a video camera that is in itself part of the story.

Homework begins with a woman, Virginia, setting up a camcorder under a table in her flat. At first our viewpoint alternates between the video camera and the unseen, unacknowledged omniscient camera familiar from conventional cinema. After Virginia has checked that microphones around the flat are working, the doorbell rings and our viewpoint returns to the camcorder where it will be located for the rest of the film. We can see a room, a section of a hallway, and then another room across the hallway. Off-camera to the right is the front door through which the two main characters enter and leave. When Marcelo first arrives it becomes clear that these two people are ex-lovers who have not seen each other for a number of years. Marcelo, however, does not know that he is being recorded (video as surveillance). The characters wander in and out of shot. When they are close to the camera we see only their legs (video as 'amateur' home movie). At one point Marcelo puts his jacket over the chair under which the camcorder is placed, thus blocking our view, until Virginia removes it.

Marcelo attempts to seduce Virginia but she is worried about Aids. Later she attempts to seduce Marcelo, but he spots the camcorder and, realising that he is being taped, leaves in outrage. Virginia then addresses the camera, suggesting that the intended video of herself and Marcello having sex was part of a college project (video as educational tool), but she then goes onto to talk about her sense of identity, what she perceives to be her shortcomings, and so on (video as diary). Marcelo then comes back to collect his tie and is persuaded to complete the vaguely outlined college project. A long sex scene in a hammock follows. When Marcelo has gone, Virginia puts away the hammock, has a shower offscreen and returns to the room. Then Marcelo reappears, but not as her recently reunited ex-lover, but as her husband with their two children in tow. It transpires that the couple have staged an elaborate sexual fantasy (video as home made pornography). After shooing the children into another part of the flat, they briefly argue about the mistakes each made in the script, before the 'text' finishes with them deciding to go into shooting pornography as a profession. The appearance of the children is a nice touch since one of the most contentious issues surrounding video is that it might introduce into the domestic family context adult images outside the policing and control of the authorities responsible for broadcast television.

Homework then dramatises a gamut of uses and applications of video which, while indicating that it is a highly fragmented field of activity, also suggests that one aspect of its relationship to film and television may be its potential to undermine their identity and challenge their definitions and practices. What is film? What is television? Video implicitly asks these questions by its very difference and its very lack of definition. Video practices may occupy spaces outside the reach and/or concerns of the established media. By virtue of its accessibility, video also has the potential to undermine the divisions between the professional and the 'amateur'.

What differences there may be, however, between film and television (and video) are not due to some intrinsic technological property of each medium. The differing licences which film and television have, for example with their respective censorship apparatuses, derive from complex and contradictory social relationships around the family and leisure time. For example, television's domestic and private mode of reception significantly determines its relationship to censorship and the form and content of its programmes. Yet its mode of reception is not an intrinsic property of the technology. The application of broadcasting in terms of central transmitters and domestic receivers emerges out of a contradictory project around the family. Raymond Williams has situated the emergence of this technology in its determining social and historical context:

> The new homes might appear private and 'self sufficient' but could be maintained only by regular funding and supply from external sources, and these, over a range from employment and prices to depressions and wars, had a decisive and often a disrupting influence on what was nevertheless seen as a separable 'family' project. This relationship created both the need and the form of a new kind of 'communication': news from 'outside', from otherwise inaccessible sources. Already in the drama of the 1880s and 1890s (Ibsen, Chekhov) this structure had appeared: the centre of interest was now for the first time the family home, but men and women stared from its windows, or waited anxiously for messages, to learn about forces, 'out there', which would determine the conditions of their lives.[36]

Similarly, a theme of many of the videos discussed in this book is precisely an interest in exploring the private/personal/domestic/fantasy world and its relationship with the public world of wider society. Like television, and often through television, video is embedded into our daily social relationships and it has become a mediator of those relationships in a disparate number of ways. On television, video is incorporated as part of the flow of images, from the use of replays in sports coverage to video editing in pop programming and commercials, to computer generated manipulation of material recorded on video.[37] We have already seen in the discussion of Bourdieu and modernism, that this diffusion of video effects within the mainstream of television has some interesting implications in terms of cultural consumption. Simultaneously, video is more and more widely used to broaden access to programme making, particularly in the documentary genre (see chapter three). Thus within television, video has two quite conflicting manifestations broadly correlating to its location within two paradigms for television. Video is both a component of television's (increasingly?) corporate identity under the model of broadcasting as advertising, with its implicit address to the viewer as consumer; and a component of television's (dwindling?) identity as public service broadcasting with its implicit address to the viewer as citizen.[38] I am not trying to load the debates about public service broadcasting and the market onto these examples of video practice and then identify what is the 'good' object and what is the 'bad' object. The main question, having acknowledged that this is the wider context for video practice, is this: how is the videomaker to interpret these quite conflicting manifestations? How, if at all, can they be used? This is a question to which I will return to in chapter three.

Monopoly, normative models and video

A historical perspective on video immediately invites us to be cautious about some of the claims that can be made concerning its radical social possibilities. Stuart Marshall points out that one strand of the origins of video technology lies in commercial and military investment for the purposes of commercial information storage and surveillance.[39] Thus, as Nicholas Garnham argues, the redefinition of the technology's social purposes in terms of:

> community action, public education and 'every citizen his own TV producer' all made good advertising slogans to assist the unloading of portable video equipment on the civilian market.[40]

Garnham is rightly concerned that we do not mistake the domestic video market for real empowerment. The history of the development of the mass media in the twentieth century is a story of how large corporations have emerged and grown larger by increasing their control over the means of media production (technology, labour, finance). In chapter three we will look in more detail at the way various groups have struggled to claw back some of this monopolised power of representation. Yet they have only been able to engage in this struggle because, while on the one hand centralising the means of production, the capitalist development of the mass media has, on the other hand, attempted to sell back to people what they, the corporations, have monopolised (i.e. access) in the form of offering small scale production equipment such as the 16mm camera and the video camcorder. Perhaps exasperated by those who see video technology in itself as an answer to what are in fact social and political questions concerning media access, accountability and openness, Garnham largely discounts the possibility that this dual aspect of capitalist mass media development (the centralisation of the means of production and the expansion of the domestic media market) is a contradiction to be worked on. For example, one of the claims which could be made for video is that by offering access to the means of production it may contribute to demystifying the media. As Garnham rightly points out, however, non-professionals working with low-grade video equipment

> will be constantly comparing their results against the professional models and when they fail to match the model, they exhibit reinforced alienation ... Far from demystifying the media, nothing so rapidly teaches respect for professional media skills and output as the average person's contact with portable video.[41]

Yet this is precisely why the professional model needs to be theorised and critiqued if practice is to be liberating rather than alienating. Garnham is in danger of implying that because low-budget video does not allow one to produce audiovisual material of the 'standard' or 'quality' equal to that produced by the dominant corporations in the film and television industry, then engaging in video is largely a battle already lost. However, these standards were not developed in a vacuum; they emerged from very different contexts to the ones in which the low-budget videomaker works. Production costs in the American film industry, for example, were deliberately escalated as part of a strategy by larger firms to drive out competitors by ensuring that audiences equated 'quality' filmmaking with big budgets and the visibility of high production values.[42] Thus it is clearly problematic for the impoverished videomaker to unthinkingly draw on cultural traditions that were forged in the struggle for market supremacy. Not only will the finished product be demoralising for the videomaker, it is likely to make 'painful viewing and listening' for the audience.[43] There is then a straightforward pragmatic reason why historical and theoretical perspectives can help you negotiate the difficulties and possibilities of audiovisual production. There is also a political issue at stake. The success of the large corporations in centralising control of the means of film production ensured the disenfranchisement of the majority from cultural production. Cheap, lightweight and easy to use video equipment may contribute modestly to making inroads into that disenfranchisement. If, however, the videomakers' cultural frames of reference remain locked uncritically into dominant cultural traditions, then widespread access to video will simply extend the power of those dominant traditions in defining the horizons of our thinking. This has indeed largely happened to photography which has been, in its private and domestic usage, defined by 'Kodak culture' as the preserver of 'happy families.'[44]

The dominant traditions of cinema and television permeate the instruction manuals in film, television and videomaking. These manuals (to say nothing of the weekly and monthly magazines), are as we shall see, extraordinarily prescriptive and dogmatic when it comes to discussing how video (or film and television) may be used. Lacking theoretical and historical perspectives, they cannot reflect critically on where their ideas come from. Not only do they act as a conduit for the dominant practices of the mainstream industry, but they disseminate and reinforce a highly selective and reified account of those practices.

Reading instruction manuals critically

Instruction manuals are useful in so far as they inform the reader about how the equipment works, how to operate it, what different effects various features of the equipment will achieve. A good instruction book will offer sound advice about planning and preparation and will certainly have plenty of useful tips about approaching subjects and resolving problems. However, at the same time all this technical information is inextricably bound up with evaluative assumptions about what constitutes good or 'quality' practice. Some of the better ones, such as Brian Winston and Julia Keydel's *Working With Video* will at least acknowledge the existence of a variety of traditions of representations even if these only creep into the margins of their main discussion. Focal Press offer a gamut of media manuals with such titles as *Basic Film Technique* (Ken Daley), *Effective T.V. Production* (Gerald Millerson), *Motion Picture Camera Techniques* (David W. Samuelson), and *Video Camera Techniques* (Gerald Millerson). The frequency of the word 'technique' in the titles is significant. As a word, 'technique' implies learning both about how a particular technology works and the most 'skilled' application of that technology. The two can all too easily be collapsed indissolubly, instead of recognising that the latter area, the area of evaluation, is, or should be, open to debate and discussion. The manual on television production is even more blunt, simply using the word 'effective' to close down any sense of relativity in the ideas propounded or that there may be alternative possibilities.

Single Camera Video Production by Robert B. Musburger (Focal Press, 1993) is typical of these manuals in many ways. We are offered an introduction to the technology although, as with most manuals, there is little in the way of historical explanation of how the technology was developed, who by, for what purposes and how that agenda shaped the characteristics of the technology. The vocabulary used to explain how video converts sound and image into electronic signals, how such features as the aperture work, etc., is understandably scientific. But when we pass from how the technology works to its application, the scientific, objective tone does not change. The book passes quietly onto discussing strategies of representation with the same sense of certainty, the same confidence in articulating inviolable rules that it displays when discussing physics or electronics. This is scientism, the uncritical application of scientific principles to inappropriate areas, and it runs rife throughout such manuals.

One of the main aesthetic assumptions which this scientism lends support to is the notion that good video making looks 'naturally' made. There is then a usually unacknowledged passage from this assumption to the stipulation that 'natural' means disguising the effects of the choices that have gone into the construction of the piece. Why we should find these assumptions compelling, both as distinct and linked propositions, is rarely discussed. It is just taken as unquestionable commonsense. Yet a clue as to the line of logic being followed here is given in the opening sections of Musburger's book. It begins with various comparisons between the sound/image recording capacities of the human senses and video technology. 'The human eye can focus from the end of the nose to infinity instantaneously,' declares Musburger on page four, while of course the video camera cannot. As a discrete observation this is true, but the comparison should set alarm bells ringing since nothing strait-jackets discussion of audiovisual aesthetics more effectively than the assumption that it should be measured against ordinary, everyday seeing and hearing. It is a poor basis on which to construct an aesthetic simply because there are so many dimensions of the audiovisual text which are not strictly comparable with ordinary seeing. For example, the mobility in time and space which editing gives the videomaker is quite unlike the fixed viewpoint of the human eye. Indeed it was precisely because of this *dissimilarity* that the Russian filmmaker and champion of editing, Dziga Vertov, insisted that film liberate itself from trying to mimic the human eye.

Yet if deriving aesthetic preferences from some arbitrary comparisons between the human and technological senses is problematic, so is the whole definition of naturalness and how it manifests itself. Discussing composition in *Video Camera Techniques*, Millerson suggests that the arrangement of figures and objects in front of the camera should look:

> ... so convincing that it all seems to have happened naturally. If a shot is badly composed it will look muddled, allowing the viewer's attention to wander, failing to hold their interest. Where shots are too obviously 'organised', they are likely to look contrived, stylised or mechanical.[45]

The contradictions in this passage are revealing. While it is recognised that organisation is necessary if the shot is not to 'look muddled', composition must not appear to have been subject to human intervention. If it does then the image will be open to a string of pejorative terms ('contrived', 'stylised' 'mechanical') which by implication define the natural as that which is 'untouched', 'spontaneous', the opposite of 'organised'. Yet since the organisation is inevitable and important, naturalness – which is also important for this aesthetic – turns out to be little more than an appearance of things (one might even say a deception of things).

Why then, is so much invested in this appearance of naturalness? This question is not explicitly posed let alone answered in these manuals, and so one has to dig more deeply into the assumptions underpinning the text to come up with an answer. Implicitly invoked in the above passage is the human eye of the viewer receiving the image after it has been subject to the videomaker's organisation. It is once more the human eye which is being offered as a norm against which the image is to be judged. It as though the image, while it may only muster the appearance of 'untouchedness', by doing so approaches albeit imperfectly (because it is only appearance), the 'ideal' of the human eye which may be said to truly observe without organising that which it observes. Yet if this is the unstated argument, then it is problematic insofar as it relies on some of the more questionable grounding that Western science and philosophy has been laying since the Renaissance.

The notion that the human senses are natural – insofar as they are untouched by *a priori* conceptions, schemas and assumptions derived from class, gender, culture and history – belongs to the empiricist tradition of thought in which the senses are conceived of as neutral receivers of information, not organisers of it. The empiricist's stress that human knowledge can only be founded on those experiences open to detection by the human senses was in its day (the seventeenth and eighteenth century) a powerful attack on religious superstition and metaphysics. Today the empiricist approach tends to be conservative and unquestioning of the status quo. This approach is alive and well in the pages of instruction manuals whose aesthetics suggest that video can at least aspire to (although never achieve) the 'natural purity' of the human eye.

The reference point for such aesthetic practices (again usually unacknowledged by the manuals) is the 'classical' cinema of the studio era. Discussing the most successful and powerful example of this cinema, Hollywood, David Bordwell writes that: 'the classical [film]...encourages us to see it as presenting an apparently solid fictional world which has simply been filmed for our benefit.'[46] In other words, as if the fictional world somehow predates the act of narration. While the Hollywood studio manuals would describe their techniques as invisible, Pierre Sorlin observes that the classical film: 'does not conceal its operations but it offers them as a transposition of a preexistent reality.'[47] Again all evidence of the organisation of that reality has been minimised. This rules out any modernist independent expressiveness on the part of the medium and any possibility for the manner of the presentation to comment upon the content. One of the recurrent themes of this book is that such possibilities are an important resource for the low-budget videomaker to draw on.

It is worth noting that the manuals under discussion have an extremely impoverished concept of audiences. When the question of audiences is raised at all, it is generally amid warnings that if they do not stick to the rules of classical construction, they risk losing the attention of an audience unable to follow what's happening, or simply unwilling because a text offers them something that does not appear to be 'natural'. The idea of 'the audience' functions in the discourse as little more than a surveillance force, policing the reader's cultural practice. This conception of the audience is symptomatic of one of the major ironies of these manuals: they appear to be stuck in something of a time warp. Lacking any historical knowledge they cannot register the changes and diversity of aesthetic principles that have taken place even within dominant cinema (and therefore the cultural competences of the mass audience) since the decline of the studio system in the 1950s. Sorlin goes on to to discuss the challenge within European films to Hollywood and Europe's classical cinematic model as films came to increasingly acknowledge that the subject did not exist independently of the means and techniques by which they are presented. Pasolini, a contemporary of these aesthetic shifts, remarked, 'the maxim of wise filmmakers in force up till the 1960s – "Never let the camera's presence be felt" – has been replaced by its opposite.'[48] This stylistic, narrative and generic self-reflexiveness also marks one of the shifts within at least some of the output of Hollywood from the late 1960s and is the basis on which Thomas

Schatz makes a distinction between the Hollywood of the old studio system and 'new' Hollywood.[49]

Similarly, the image of television conjured up by such manuals over-homogenises the actual diversity of aesthetic strategies at play across the medium. For example, there is rarely any acknowledgement that television is composed of multiple genres. Rather the assumption appears to be that television is a window on the world, a transparent medium. Clearly a discussion of genres would start to complicate that. If different genres are recognised by these manuals, their aesthetic strategies are kept strictly separate despite the evidence that television's generic boundaries are fragile and permeable. In *The Videomaker's Handbook* Roland Lewis discusses pop videos and, in stark contrast to much of the rest of the book, places emphasis on 'creative possibilities', and the opportunity to try out 'striking electronic effects by imaginative manipulation of your video'. The reader is encouraged to 'let rip' and '[b]reak the rules' but is also reminded that the pop video offers an opportunity to 'experiment with effects that would be inappropriate in most other video subjects'.[50] Here the pop video genre is constructed as a site of hedonistic experimentation, which ignores the extent to which the genre has its own conventions and formulas. At the same time it is carefully policed. The stress which the pop video lays on constructing a performance for the camera cuts against the aesthetic principles reigning, for Lewis at least, across 'most other video subjects'. Thus, earlier on Lewis drops in the suggestion – again without any reference to the source of these values – that: '[t]o get a natural feel to your videos, avoid shooting people looking directly at the camera lens. This looks rehearsed and artificial'.[51] I am not making radical claims for pop videos just because they disrupt classical forms, a trap which Simon Frith has rightly cautioned others to avoid.[52] I am just pointing out that television articulates a variety of aesthetic strategies which can, as we shall see in subsequent chapters, be worked on and transformed. It is this diversity and this potential which is not recognised by the instruction manuals.

The scientistic vocabulary of these manuals, the sense that they are initiating the reader into a finite and fixed set of techniques, will periodically provoke an anguished gesture towards 'creativity' and 'innovation'. Here we see the tensions between the two models of cultural production discussed in chapter one – the skilled but obedient craftworker and the apparently autonomous author – flaring up openly. Thus Musburger breaks off to remind us that:

> In the midst of all these 'rules' one cannot forget that there are no absolutes in any aesthetic field. All of the suggestions made...are intended to be used only as guidelines. Each individual production situation will determine to what extent those suggestions are followed or ignored.[53]

The reader, however, could be forgiven for exactly forgetting that there are 'no absolutes in any aesthetic field' since the whole thrust of the book has been to argue that there are. The reader is given no resources with which to relativise the classical rules. There has been no explanation of where the 'rules' come from, no discussion of their relevance or irrelevance to the low-budget videomaker, no discussion of alternative traditions, and no concrete examples of where it might make sense to break the 'rules'. It would not, for example, take too much imagination for the author of *Effective T.V. Production* to qualify this remark on panning: 'It's wise to avoid panning over a wide arc, e.g. between people some distance apart. It's far better to cut between them.'[54] Yet if one wanted to show distance between people, perhaps of a political, social or emotional kind, the author appears to have ruled out an interesting option just because it does not fit with the 'wise' rules.

Conclusion

We can recap and conclude the main argument of this chapter by returning to Julio Garcia Espinosa's work and in particular his concept of 'imperfect cinema'. This deliberately iconoclastic term is easily misinterpreted. Espinosa is not calling for a cinema that prides itself on rejecting notions of 'quality' simply for the sake of it. Rather he is calling for the rejection of the notion that there is such a thing as timeless, universally valid definitions of 'good' technique and artistic 'quality' which predetermine what the cultural artifact should look like. We have seen that there are two, rather different kinds of rationale for such universalisation. We have seen, through a discussion of Bourdieu's sociology, that one draws its power from its cultural prestige and the legitimisation of 'quality' in terms of 'art'. We have seen in the discussion of instruction manuals that the other rationale for a universal model of cultural practice draws its legitimacy from its brute presence, pervasiveness and economic power in the market place. By contrast to these universal models, I suggested that video practices constitute a diverse field of activities which to some extent escape the definitions of video operating within the institutions of the art world and the culture industries.

But these worlds also provide – as I have tried to suggest in my discussion of modernist aesthetics and the various manifestations of video in the culture industries – the reference points which make any video practice meaningful.

Writing a decade after the 1959 Cuban revolution and with the wider revolutionary struggles in Latin America very much in mind, Espinosa was arguing for a cinema whose practices and aesthetics are flexible and adaptive to its conditions of production and overall objectives. 'Imperfect Cinema...can be created equally well with a Mitchell or with an 8 mm camera, in a studio, or in a guerrilla camp in the middle of the jungle.'[55] While the image of a guerrilla camp in the middle of the jungle may seem a trifle exotic for western readers, the preceding pages have in effect been arguing for a kind of imperfect videomaking. This is one that has a strong functional aesthetic (an estimation of what you can and cannot do in particular circumstances, and a view that cultural 'quality' may be generated in a variety of production and consumption circumstances) tied to an innovative and critically engaged attitude to questions of form. For Espinosa the concept of imperfect cinema means more than simply adapting your formal strategies to your budget. It also carries with it a political commitment to the subject matter and the audiences for that subject matter. 'Art has always been a universal necessity,' argues Espinosa, 'what it has not been is an option for all under equal conditions.'[56] In the present, video practice is neither available to all nor conducted under equal conditions, but it is a small seed from which bigger things may grow if people contest their domination. In the next chapter it is precisely the struggles around access to the means of cultural production, both past and present, which we turn to.

Notes

1 Another example of the 'art' of video as agitation and propaganda was demonstrated by Greenpeace in their conflict with Shell over the dumping of the Brent Spar. Having landed activists on the Brent Spar oil platform, Greenpeace used video to shoot their own footage and then download it , via a Mac computer and satellite link up, to a media base in Frankfurt. From there the sounds and images of the conflict were relayed to television screens across the world. *Guardian*, June 22nd 1995, pp.4-5.
2 P. Bourdieu, *Distinction: A Social Critique of the Judgement of Taste*, (Trans.) R. Nice, Routledge, London 1984, p. 6.
3 Bourdieu, *ibid*, p.2.
4 Bourdieu, *ibid*, p.29.
5 B. Fowler, 'The Hegemonic Work of Art in The Age of Electronic Reproduction: An Assessment of Pierre Bourdieu', in *Theory, Culture and Society*' vol. 11, no. 1 Feb 1994, p.129.

6 Bourdieu, *op. cit.*, p.323.
7 P. Bourdieu, *Photography: A Middlebrow Art* , Stanford University Press, Stanford, 1990.
8 Bourdieu, *Distinction*, op. cit., p.34.
9 See S. Cubitt's *Videography*, Macmillan, London 1993, pp.114-115, for a different view.
10 Bourdieu, *Distinction*, p.30.
11 T. Eagleton, *The Ideology of the Aesthetic*, Basil Blackwell, Oxford 1990.
12 Bourdieu, *Distinction*, op. cit., p.44.
13 Bourdieu, *ibid*, p.45.
14 Bourdieu, *ibid*, p.44.
15 Bourdieu, *ibid*, p.44.
16 Bourdieu, *ibid*.
17 Bourdieu, *ibid*, p.41.
18 Bourdieu, *ibid*, p.42.
19 Indeed the LVA has now become London Electronic Access, an indication that video's interfacing with computer technology is in some contradiction with the art world's traditional focus on exploring the specificity of each discrete medium.
20 P. Burger, *Theory of The Avant-Garde*, Manchester University Press; 1984, p.72.
21 Burger, *ibid*, p. viv.
22 Burger, *ibid*, p.78.
23 Quoted in N. Stangos (ed), *Concepts of Modern Art*, Thames and Hudson Ltd., London 1994, p.63.
24 P. Anderson, 'Modernity and Revolution' in *Marxism and the Interpretation of Culture*, Houndmills, 1988, p.329.
25 E. Lunn, *Marxism and Modernism*, Verso, London 1985, pp. 34-37.
26 M. Berman, *All That is Solid Melts Into Air*, 1983, p.15.
27 F. Moretti, 'The Spell of Indecision' in *Signs Taken For Wonders*, Verso, London 1988, p. 248.
28 P. Anderson, *op. cit.*, p.329.
29 A. Callinicos, *Against Postmodernism: A Marxist Critique*, Polity Press, Cambridge 1992.
30 Callinicos, *ibid*, p.152.
31 London Video Arts, *Video Tape Catalogue*, 1987, p.19.
32 London Video Arts, *ibid*, p.23.
33 London Video Arts, *ibid*, p.15.
34 Bourdieu, *Distinction*, *op.cit.*, p.33.
35 Made by Terry McSweeney, Piers Freeman, Rachel Robinson, Lorraine Gooday, Garret Scally, Senta Siewert, Sam, University of North London, 1994.
36 R. Williams, *Television: Technology and Cultural Form*, 1990, p.27.
37 R. Armes, *On Video*, Routledge, London 1988, p.85.
38 N. Garnham, 'Public Service Versus The Market' in *Screen*, vol. 24, no.1. 1983.
39 S. Marshall, 'Video: from Art to Independence' in *Screen*, no.26, 1985, p.66.
40 N. Garnham, 'The Myths of Video: A Disciplinary Reminder' in *Capitalism and Communication*, Sage, London 1990, p.68.
41 N. Garnham, *ibid*, p.66.
42 G. Mitchel, 'The Consolidation of the American Film Industry 1915-1920', in *Cine-Tracts* no. 6, 1979, pp.5-6.
43 N. Garnham, 'The Myths of Video', *op. cit.*, p.66.
44 J. Williamson, *Consuming Passions: The Dynamics of Popular Culture*, Marion Boyars, London 1986, pp119-124.
45 G. Millerson, *Video Camera Techniques*, Focal Press, 1994, p.88.
46 D. Bordwell, et al, *The Classical Hollywood Film*, Routledge, London 1988, p.24.

47 P. Sorlin, *European Cinemas/European Societies: 1939-1990*, Routledge, London 1991, p.139.
48 P. Pasolini, 'The Cinema of Poetry' in *Movies and Methods*, vol 1, University of California Press, London 1990, p.556.
49 T. Schatz, *New Hollywood/Old Hollywood*, UMI Research Press, 1983.
50 R. Lewis, *The Videomaker's Handbook*, Pan/Marshall, 1987, pp. 140, 142.
51 R. Lewis, *ibid*, p.42.
52 S. Frith, *Music For Pleasure*, Polity Press 1988, pp.205-223.
53 R. B. Musburger, *Single Camera Video Production*, Focal Press, London 1993, p. 138.
54 G. Millerson, *Effective Television Production*, Focal Press, London 1993, p. 52.
55 J.G. Espinosa, 'For an Imperfect Cinema' in *TwentyFive Years of the New Latin American Cinema*, BFI/C4 1983, p. 33.
56 Espinosa, *ibid*, p.30.

Chapter Three

Representation

Having access to the means of audiovisual production raises some general and quite intricate debates around the issue of representation. An understanding of both the liberatory potential and the limitations involved in having access to video production, requires some understanding of the contexts in which that access is achieved. I have touched on this a number of times already, but I now want to consider this area more fully.

The issue of representation is raised at three important levels. Firstly, there are the sounds and images themselves, the texts which construct and articulate representations. Questions raised here are: who is included in such representations? From what perspective? Who and what is left out? Secondly, there are the audiences who consume those representations. Who are the audiences and how do they engage with the questions just asked about the texts? As numerous contemporary audience studies suggest, there is often a complex transaction between the meanings which texts offer and the actual meanings which audiences make of the texts. And thirdly, representation takes place within the industrial contexts of the media industries. These are characterised by particular patterns of ownership which in turn govern access to equipment, human resources, capital and, perhaps most importantly, audiences. These are all brought together and operate according to the industry's working practices (division of labour) and assumptions about what constitutes the 'quality' of the desired product. It is the intractable and consolidated power of this third context – patterns of ownership and control – which accounts for the fundamental limitations of the twentieth century media 'revolution'. But at the same time, understanding the links between this context and questions around power and representation should not induce demoralisation, but rather give a sense of purpose to cultural practice.

The politics of representation

Looking at representation in the sphere of politics illuminates something of the politics of media representation. In the political sphere, the term representation refers to the claim by individuals and organisations to 'stand in for' and articulate the interests of a wider body of people who cannot be physically present or active in the established institutions of political life, except in the most primitive and small scale societies. The importance of political representation increases as the human population grows and disperses geographically, while at the same time, under capitalism, becoming more interdependent, socially and economically. This process of representation in political institutions is not neutral, however, but massively skewed in favour of certain groups within the categories of class, gender, ethnicity and sexuality. Political representation in the UK is proportionally dominated by the middle class (and the aristocracy), by men, by whites, and, at least publicly, by heterosexuality.

The importance of and technical capacity for media representation has developed in tandem with the increasing complexity with which an expanding society's various components interact and effect each other. Hence the media's role in offering to geographically dispersed but socially, economically and politically interconnected human beings, representations which lie outside their direct experience. The individual and collective identities which such representations help to form can be understood as analogous to 'constituencies' in the political sense. Media representations are political in the sense that they signal the power, weight and legitimacy of particular groups, identities and ideas in society. Yet an abundance of theoretical work has unpicked skews of power in the realm of media images similar to those which are so evident in the political sphere. For example, the Glasgow Media Group have produced numerous studies of the systematic anti-working-class nature of television news.[1] Even more theoretical attention has been devoted to analysing how across a whole range of image making the Straight

White Male constitutes the 'norm' which silences, marginalises or judges other socio-cultural constituencies.

While the political realm is itself more of a symptom than a cause of such differentials in the distribution of social power, the political sphere does have a direct impact on media representations in the form of legislation. Typically, new media technologies (like video) attract the interest of the state, keen to regulate the new possibilities of communication, including, almost inevitably, the application of some form of censorship. But the use of any 'new' media technology is also shaped by the already established media corporations, and the economic logic of capitalism (the tendency towards oligopoly control, rising costs of entry into the market, elimination of price competition, etc.). Both the presence of the state and the inescapable economic relations of our epoch determine how and to what extent media representations construct and interpret the networks of social interdependence, shared and unshared experiences and unequal distributions of power that make up the world today. Raymond Williams has described how community and communication are linked components in a dynamic process:

> Human community grows by the discovery of common meanings and common means of communication ... Thus our des-criptions of our experience come to compose a network of relationships, and all our communication systems, including the arts, are literally parts of our social organisation. The selection and interpretation involved in our descriptions embody our attitudes, needs and interests, which we seek to validate by making them clear to others. At the same time the descriptions we receive from others embody their attitudes, needs and interests, and the long process of comparison and interaction is our vital associative life. Since our way of seeing things is literally our ways of living, the process of communication is in fact the process of community: the sharing of common meanings, and thence common activities and purposes; the offering, reception and comparison of new meanings, leading to the tensions and achievement of growth and change. [2]

Here Williams is arguing for a democratic conception of culture, as something which draws on and is integrated with everyday life. And clearly this is an appropriate way of conceiving the cultural contribution of a medium as widely accessible as video. However, in this and other passages from his early work Williams has a conception of society as something rather like an 'organic community',[3] one whose slow evolutionary growth is bound up with the gradual discovery of commonality amongst society's members. There is little sense here that there may be some quite fundamental conflicting interests within 'the community'. Williams' later shifts towards marxism led him to install class differences as a central dislocating tension within social relationships. While retaining his focus on the importance of communication for community, or identity, Williams was able to make questions of power much more central to his writings. Some communities within 'the community' are clearly much more equal than others within bourgeois democracy. Thus we need to look at meanings and representations as a site of contestation and struggle, and to see the amplification or marginalisation of particular 'attitudes, needs and interests' as central to the links between communication and identity. In order to understand the nature of the struggles to define the uses of video today, it is worth sketching in some of the history of such struggles in relation to film.

The struggle over representation: film

The twin pressures of the state and the concentration of property in fewer hands figure prominently in the emergence of the film industry as a form of mass communication. Nevertheless, the late 1920s saw attempts to establish alternative sites of exhibition for films ignored by the mainstream industry and/or blocked by the censors. Representations of class, gender and sexuality had to operate within a very narrow band of acceptability, a band that became even less elastic after the establishment of the 1934 Production Code in America. Mass audiences were denied the chance to evaluate a whole range of material: not just the revolutionary films coming out of Russia but also religious iconoclasm along the lines of filmmakers like Bunuel, as well as overt representations of sexuality such as Hedi Lamarr's *Ecstasy* (1933). Throughout Europe attempts were made to circumvent state barriers to exhibiting radical films made outside the dominant industry. In France a left Film Society was established in 1928. The famous 'Red Belt' in the capital gave the Paris section of the society a membership of around 8,000. However, in the following year the state intervened, banning the exhibition of films without censorship visas, even for private shows.[4]

In the UK, the Federation of Workers' Film Societies (FWFS) was established in 1929. Its aim was to encourage the formation of local workers' film societies, to distribute films and equipment and advise on how to negotiate permission for film screenings with the local authorities.[5] The latter proved to be a continually frustrating experience, since decision makers in the local authorities were largely conservative, both culturally and politically. This particular difficulty over exhibition was eased as 16mm film and equipment became more readily available during the 1930s. In the UK the projection of Kodak's non-inflammable 16mm film did not require legal permission from either the British Board of Film Censors or local authorities. However, although state restrictions might be circumvented, this could only help to construct sites of exhibition on the margins of the film industry. Then, as today, the dominant commercial interests exercised a monopoly on access to mass audiences. Thus the FWFS collapsed financially in 1932, unable to support the distribution of the industry standard 35mm film. Today, the problem of exhibition for film and video makers operating outside the mainstream industry remains central to the issue of power and representation.

The arrival of 16mm film made distribution a more viable proposition, but it also increased access to the means of cultural production since it was easy to handle, light and most importantly, comparatively cheap. Organisations like Kino and the Workers' Film and Photo League (WFPL) were formed working largely in the field of documentary. Both groups were intimately connected with various sections of the labour movement. The WFPL which existed between 1934–38 was extraordinarily prolific, making at least 24 silent films.[6] But how did such groups find their audiences? They tapped the network of informal education such as film societies and summer schools. They also tapped into trade schools and used civic forums such as town halls to set up screenings. The impressive membership of the Left Book Club gave both Kino and the WFPL potential access to a national audience. Kino even had a cinema van with which they toured seaside towns and holiday camps.[7]

Kino and the WFPL could not break into commercial exhibition irrespective of the type or quality of film they produced and/or distributed simply because of the demarcations the industry made between 16mm and 35mm film. The latter was the only one acceptable to the commercial industry. This has parallells with the careful and continuous upgrading of the 'professional' format for video by the television industry today. Such demarcations are not neutral, objective decisions, nor are they inevitable but rather a question of what social and economic priorities are dominant. In this case it is simply another way of raising barriers of entry into the market by raising costs. Again we can recall Julio Garcia Espinosa's critique of 'perfect cinema'. For him what was important was to develop a cinema that was intimate with and relevant to the needs of its audiences. What blocked and frustrated the development of such a cinema was precisely the dominant model, which had developed an insular sense of where and how 'quality' cinema is made, and even what equipment and technology 'quality' cinema is made with. There are areas of television programming today where the industry's own definitions of quality have been undermined by the explosion of channels and the subsequent requirements to fill airtime. However, channel proliferation does nothing to change the terms of the industry's relationship to its audiences. Judging by the launch of Live T.V. on cable, the programming just becomes cheaper but not substantially different, and is recycled to pad out twenty-four hours. One can only feel a profound sense of a wasted opportunity.

In trying to connect with the needs of their audiences, groups like Kino and the WFPL worked largely within the genre of documentary. There are a number of reasons for this. Models for low-budget fiction film production were few and far between. It took the extraordinary circumstances of a war-torn Italy to throw up the first important model for low-budget filmmaking: Italian Neo-Realism. Today, when we have so many cultural traditions and resources to draw on, it is difficult to appreciate how important this moment in Italian film production was in providing a documentary-inspired model for dramatic fiction. The Indian filmmaker Satyajit Ray has commented on the impact that the neo-realist classic, *Bicycle Thieves* (De Sica, Italy, 1948) had on him.

> [I was] pleasantly surprised to discover that one could work exclusively in exterior settings, with non-professional actors, and I thought that what one could do in Italy, one could do in Bengal as well. [8]

However, it was not only the absence of such models in the 1930s which inflected the majority of left cultural practitioners towards documentary filmmaking. Pessimism about the role of mass culture – which was seen as pacifying and numbing the critical faculties of the masses – was widespread on the left. There was a perceived urgency to 'show things as they really are' and where fiction was associated with 'fantasy', documentary could be constructed as an appropriate vehicle for social information and criticism.

Left cultural workers produced newsreels that aimed to record the realities of life marginalised or excluded altogether by the dominant commercial companies, and to offer substantially different explanations of issues such as widespread poverty, the rise of fascism and the Spanish civil war. Most of these documentaries 'were confined to the immediately observable and upheld the importance of visual accessibility ... only a small number of films ... used agitational techniques.'[9] Such aesthetic inclinations derived not only from the deep rooted empiricism of British culture but also because the flowering of modernist cinematic forms in the Soviet Union had been cut off by 1933.

Yet that commitment to the 'immediately observable' was a very important part of the struggle over representation when even the immediately observable can be ignored by the mainstream media. For example in 1934 the commissioner of the London Metropolitan Police asked newsreel companies not to record that year's Hunger March against unemployment. The companies acquiesced. Kino's record of the march demonstrates how access to the means of media representation thwarted the state-corporate nexus which attempted to make oppositional forces invisible.[10]

The struggle over representation: television and video

It is clear that in the 1930s and for some decades after it, oppositional forces were grouped very largely around the various organisations of the manual, usually male, working class. Today, oppositional groups may be organised around numerous other and intersecting sites of interest: gender, sexuality, ethnicity, ecology as well as with a changed and changing working class (the influx of women into wage labour for example).

Such a proliferation of forces does represent an enormously exciting politicisation of issues which have often been marginalised or ignored. Around these issues, organisations have developed and grown, which offer the low-budget videomaker both a potential audience base and perhaps even a source of modest funding for projects. But more than anything, these organisations represent multiple entry points from which to explore the web of social relationships that constitute our experiences of late capitalism. While the world and consciousness of the world has in many ways changed since the 1930s, there are also striking continuities. Not least of these are the polarities between ownership and non-ownership of the means of production, of which the means of audiovisual production are but a component.

The wide availability of video has provided the means of communication to circumvent the dominant media and offer alternative accounts of 'immediately observable' events. For example, in Timisoara, in the heat of the 1989 Romanian revolution, video activists recorded the dying convulsions of the old order until the censored, state run television was liberated. In Czechoslovakia in the same year, students recorded the revolution on video and set up television sets on street corners to play the tapes. In South Korea students were also instrumental in participating in and recording the intense social conflicts between the working class and the capitalist order, with the latter's ever faithful servant, the state, making its customary brutal interventions. Video played a similar role in Taiwan in 1990, and in Bangkok, Thailand, in the same year, video material presented audiovisual representation of the pro-democracy struggle, and was beamed back into the country via satellite. In Brazil in 1984, 'emergency' measures severely restricted radio and television coverage of voting for a constitutional amendment for direct presidential elections. Coverage was, however, carried out by independent video groups: 'This coverage includes sounds and images showing the rallies from the point of view of participants, rather than from specially built platforms that only give general overviews of the action.'[11] Such overviews reduce participants to silent and homogeneous masses.

In the United States, Deep Dish and Not Channel Zero collected video material from independent and 'amateur' sources during the Gulf War and the LA uprising. The latter, of course, was triggered by the video recording of police beating up Rodney King. As with the example from Brazil, the recording of events from different perspectives, as participants and/ or residents, gives a more multifaceted view of situations than provided by the official newsgathering and dissemination organisations. The political rallies in LA during the uprising or the movement against the Gulf War achieved little or no representation on America's big corporate news networks.[12] As in the case of the Thai video activists, however, Deep Dish and Not Channel Zero were able to buy satellite time to broadcast the material they had collected from others. And finally, an example from the Mother of all Democracies: a year after the UK newspaper and television media laid the blame for the 1990 Poll Tax riot squarely at the feet of the demonstrators, Channel Four broadcast *The Battle of Trafalgar* (Despite TV, 1991), a documentary which used video material shot by demonstrators to call into question the role of the police.

The point of these examples is that despite the popular notion that we live in a media saturated world, there remains an important, indeed central role in documenting the experiences and identities which the media marginalise or repress. This is not restricted to moments of large scale social conflict but includes facets of life culled from the mundane and everyday. This documentary impulse – which as we shall see in the next section can be discerned in non-documentary work as well – is built into the audiovisual 'enfranchisement' of wide layers of non-professionals pointing cameras at subjects and/or from perspectives not accessible to, or routinely ignored by, the dominant media.

One significant difference from the situation of the 1930s is that the dominant organisations of television have shown a greater degree of interest in amateur videomakers than the film industry ever showed in those working on its fringes with 16mm. Television is closer to the print media in so far as discourses of access have a greater weight than they do in dominant cinema. So for example in the US major news corporations like CNN have solicited documentary footage of 'news' from anyone who happens to be at the scene of an accident, natural disaster or crime with a camcorder. Far from opening television up to the non-professional, CNN and co are merely extending their definition of what constitutes news and how news should be constructed (the so called 'human interest' angle is set in stone) into a network of cheap, part-time audiovisual workers. The parameters and assumptions of 'news' remain untouched. In the UK, domestic misfortune captured on video is recycled more explicitly as sado-entertainment in the ITV television programme *You've Been Framed.*

More interestingly, and significantly coming out of the ethos of public service broadcasting, the Community Programmes Unit at the BBC has been at the cutting edge of using video as the vehicle for opening television up to non-professional programme makers. The longest running and most critically acclaimed strand to their work is of course the *Video Diaries* series and its specialised offspring, *Teenage Video Diaries*. These personal reflections on the lives of their authors have brought new people, perspectives and subject matter to the television screen. Most impressive is the editorial control which the diarist retains through out the production process. Whereas earlier forms of access programming such as the Open Door series meant that the non-professional had to rely on a professional crew, including the director, producer and researchers, the simplicity of video allows the single person to combine all these roles. While the technology facilitates the editorial centrality of the diarist, it is guaranteed not by technology, but by democratic practices (i.e. the willingness of the professionals at the CPU to have an advisory rather than controlling role.[13] Video has been used in other access series as well, such as *Private Investigations*, where non-professionals try to make various organisations and institutions accountable to the public, while *Video Nation* is a literal interpretation of the notion of representation as 'a slice of life'.

It is intriguing that the perceived 'authenticity' of the video diarist or private investigator is grounded in assumptions which are precisely the reverse of those governing the dominant documentary form on television. Objectivity is the byword for the most prestigious and familiar slots in the television schedule: the daily news broadcasts and weekly 'flagship' documentaries such as *Panorama*. This institutional documentary tradition functions in the economy of documentary as the norm against which all other traditions are evaluated (see chapter eight). Programmes like *Private Investigations* set themselves outside this tradition when they allow the 'ordinary' person licence to reflect and comment on how their interview went with a representative of a company or organisation they are investigating. This moment of reflection is a key trope of authorship and subjectivity, and it would be quite out of bounds in the dominant paradigm since it would indicate partiality and opinion far too explicitly. While the 'authenticity' which governs this tradition is that of institutional 'objectivity', the 'authenticity' of the video access programme is rooted in a notion of the sincerity, the genuineness of the individual author. As Jeremy Gibson at the Community Programmes Unit says of their relationship with the video diarist:

> Your ego, and your attitude and approach can come across from the rushes in a very off-putting way that an outsider wouldn't like. It's our job to identify that and try and turn the diarist to take a less egocentric approach to something and less pushing of aspects of their personality which are difficult or confrontational. The other thing is that they may be very much in love with a very contrived material, terribly in love with some parts that we know are a total contrivance.[14]

Despite the different starting points of the 'professional'/objective and 'amateur'/subjective documentary, both are committed to aesthetic principles similar to those which Ryan finds among the 1930s documentary filmmakers, and which he describes as: 'confined to the immediately observable [upholding] the importance of visual accessibility...[largely rejecting] agitational techniques.'[15] The formal experimentation of 'agitational techniques' undercuts any claim to objectivity since it foregrounds the constructed nature of commentary and interpretation. It would clearly also fall into the category of 'total contrivance' cited by Gibson, since the subjective 'authenticity' he clearly values is precisely the transparent ordinariness, the evident unprofessionalism of the author.

I have stressed the importance of providing documents of the 'immediately observable' in a variety of times and places. This applies no less to television, and so for example the space which *Teenage Video Diaries* offered in allowing working-class youths to become visible is very important. But no less important is the form this takes. At present access television operates within certain aesthetic constraints. In order to trace more oblique connections between things, to be able to work in the register of suggestion as well as statement, to shock and confront as well as show, videomakers require the possibility of formal constructions that would conflict with the claim of objectivity which underpins the mainstream television documentary, as well as the potentially limiting notion of the lay author that currently underpins access documentary television.

None of this is to denigrate an exciting and successful development, one which, because it has attuned television to a less glossy, 'professional' look, has struck an important blow for access television. But it is important to be aware how certain assumptions about what the non-professional video should look like, about what it can and cannot do, are in operation and therefore channelling further advances of access television into certain directions and ruling out other paths. Indeed, if the question of content explains why for the CPU, like Kino and the WFPL before them, documentary was the 'natural' vehicle through which important, 'immediately observable' but largely ignored facets of life could be articulated, the issue of form helps to explain why access television has been contained largely within the documentary genre. For low-budget documentary can be made and still look familiar when compared to the procedures of documentary exposition dominant on television. There are differences as we have seen, but these only mark out access documentary's own peculiar version of 'authenticity'. However, a fictional piece made on a fraction of an average drama budget would simply look cheap because it would have no compensatory ideology of 'authenticity' to legitimise it. The only way out of this bind would be to explore new forms of presentation: the cheaper the budget the more radically innovative the drama would have to be in order to compensate.

Yellow

I want to discuss a student video called *Yellow*,[16] both to anticipate some of the formal strategies discussed in subsequent chapters and to draw together questions of representation touched on in this chapter, with issues around theory and practice which cropped up in chapters one and two. In particular, I want to stress that *Yellow* exceeds both the reified account of dominant practices found in the instruction manuals discussed in chapter two and the actual diversity of practices presently found in the dominant audiovisual industries. In demonstrating this I will focus on the video's subject matter, its mode of address and its subversive contact with and mingling of a variety of audiovisual genres. *Yellow* is primarily a fictional piece, operating in that creative space that has been largely shut off from public service access television. Significantly though, it hardly falls into any of the categories of drama as currently defined by television.

Yellow follows two gay men as they wash and dress and prepare to meet each other for a date, making use of a location which David Hockney has described as having an obvious interest for the painter: 'the whole body is always in view and in movement, usually gracefully, as the bather is caressing his own body.'[17] *Yellow* is constructed primarily through jump cuts (see chapter five) within locations and juxtapositions between the locations of the bathrooms and bedrooms of the two men. *Yellow* offers different and overlapping positions of reading for at least three kinds of audiences: gay men, heterosexual women and heterosexual men. The first two 'constituencies' are offered the erotic spectacle of the two classically attractive male leads, known only in the end credits as the blond and the brunette. Initially, the blond is seen in the bath and the brunette in the shower. In mainstream cinema, eroticism of the male body is common enough in the genre of the musical and the male as erotic spectacle is even more prevalent in the promotional and marketing material of the music industry. With its minimal narrative construction of romance, *Yellow* looks a bit like a pop video, while opening up a space for gay sexuality that the pop video could not countenance, at least not quite as openly. By contrast, gay sexuality has an acknowledged presence in the classical narratives of television and film but only because a range of containment, marginalisation and punishment strategies can be deployed by the classical narrative against gay sexuality. Such strategies are less available to the pop perform in their separate spaces stresses the relationship between the solitary performer and the camera rather than relationships between performers. Thus *Yellow* confronts the audience with its own desires and prejudices rather than locating them amongst fictional surrogates and then manipulating those desires/prejudices through the mechanisms of narrative absorption.

Yellow also draws on and reworks notions of narcissism in interesting ways. Narcissism is a psychoanalytic term derived from the Greek myth of Narcissus who fell in love with his own image. It refers to the processes of identification whereby the sense of self, of the 'I', can be shored up by making an imaginary equivalence between the self and another (or images of others). The 'I' 'falls in love' with itself as it perceives itself in the image of the other, that image being cleansed of all the frustrations and fractures which the self suffers in their everyday lives.

This is nicely illustrated in a student video called *Desperate Minutes,* which uses the iconography of the television viewing situation to comically dissect masculinity as two football fans sit down to watch the 1979 FA cup final. The identification which each has to the teams (Manchester United and Arsenal) is a straightforward example where by the self perceives apparently heroic and admired collective bodies as a suitable site for narcissistic investment. As in *Trevor and Leonard,* the characters' rather frustrated lives (here filmed in black and white) contrast with the glamour of Wembley and the whole event (which remains in colour). However, in *Desperate Minutes,* this mode of narcissistic identification seems both to be dependent on competition, tests of prowess and skills (all important components of masculinity) but also potentially undermined by this because there must be a loser as well as a winner in any contest. Thus each fan tries to undermine the other's narcissistic identification: for example, the Arsenal fan declares that his friend has 'always been a loser' when Arsenal are winning 2-0. There is then something of a sadistic structure to narcissistic identification. But there is also a masochistic element, insofar as the idealised site of identification must logically lose sometimes, therefore placing the (football) spectator in the same position of 'loser' (i.e impaired and inadequate masculinity), which they once attributed to others.

These contradictions of gender also interlock with tensions around sexuality, which narcissistic identification may also bring into play. The themes of aggression, of domination and subordination associated with narcissism are in fact routinely

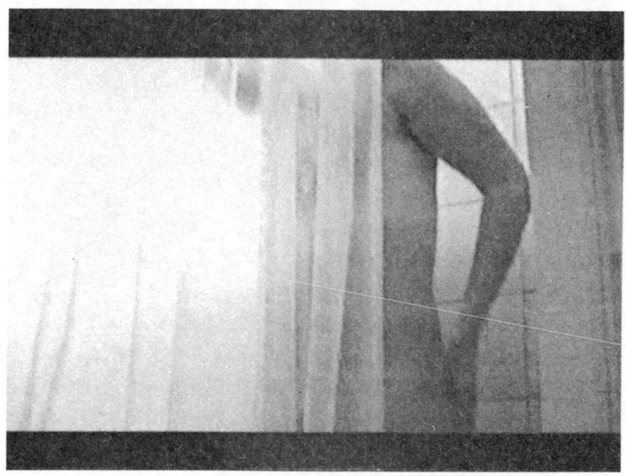

Fig. 3.1

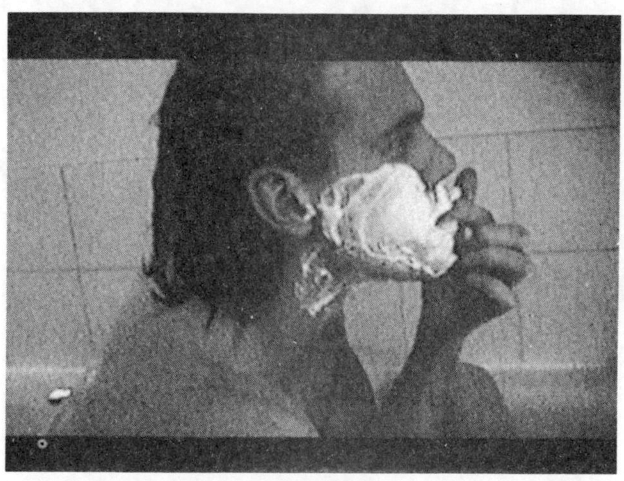

Fig. 3.2

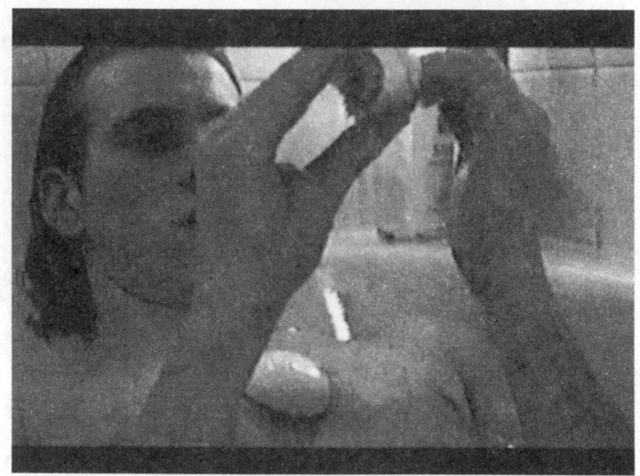

Fig. 3.3

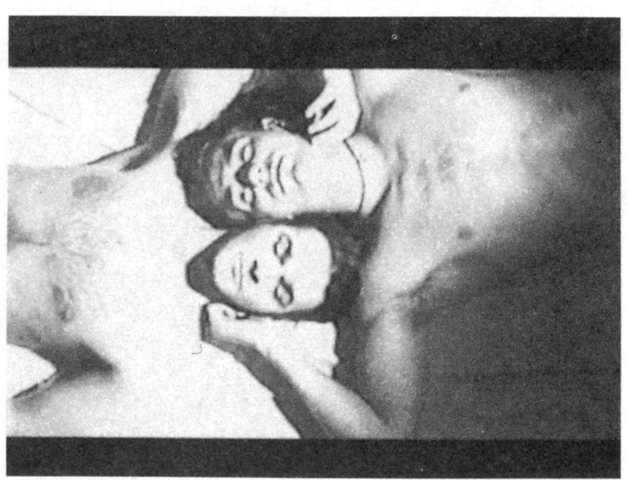

Fig. 3.4

played out across representations of masculinity in action and adventure genres, both on film and television. Drawing on the work of a number of psychoanalytic critics, Steve Neale concludes that such aggression is symptomatic of profound anxieties around looking at the male body. For narcissistic admiration of the idealised (in this case male) body can quickly shift into the register of the erotic, and looking can become or articulate a libidinal desire. But in a patriarchal and homophobic society, this component or dimension of the look must be repressed.[19] The favourite strategy of the action and adventure film is to resort to an excessive machismo,[20] as if neurotically warding off any hint of characteristics that should not belong to a 'real' man (i.e. the feminine), although the gay appropriation of the 'butch man' image has made that particular heterosexual 'retreat' vulnerable. Conversely, the male may be feminised, a strategy particularly favoured by texts (including pop videos) informed by music/performance genres. Yet this feminisation still operates within a patriarchal and homophobic ideology, for it is still in fee to 'those conventions which dictate that only women can function as the objects of an explicitly erotic gaze.'[21] The gaze, as Laura Mulvey argued in her seminal article, remains male.[22]

Adverts adopt and adapt both of these strategies. An example of the former strategy is found in the advert of the male photographer in a politically unstable Latin American country who keeps perspiration at bay with Lynx body spray. An example of the latter strategy can be seen in an advert for a body spray addressed to both men and women, where the man is feminised by his proximity and contact with nature and women (the two are often conflated by patriarchal thought) as he runs naked through a forest, blending with the trees to escape from pursuit by wolves. The spectacle of male bodies in *Yellow* also suggests the visual iconography of advertisments for body cleanliness, appearance and clothes (see Fig. 3.1). However, *Yellow* is bolder and more deconstructive of the rules governing gender and erotic spectacle. Avoiding the polarised options of machismo and feminisation, the video jump cuts between the blond shaving and then scrubbing his nails (see Fig. 3.2 and 3.3). And of course the connotations of confidence and well-being are not linked to the acquisition of commodities[23] but to a celebration of gay sexuality. Thus narcissism, a term which usually has pejorative implications, manifests itself in this video as empowering in the context of a homophobic society.

In drawing on representational strategies associated with the documentary, *Yellow* also rejects the generic separatism encouraged by the instruction manuals. The video displays a keen observational interest with the details of apparently mundane activities. We see the men shaving, washing their hair, ears, armpits, nails, clipping their toenails, brushing their teeth, applying styling mousse on their hair, aftershave and so on, as well as the details of dressing. Again, outside the commodity orientated narcissisism of adverts, these are representations which men rarely see of themselves. Combined with this attention to detail is another classic feature of documentary. Temporal continuity is maintained and duration compressed, not by the classical rules of continuity editing which govern fiction, but by the idea that we are following a process (washing and dressing) in some kind of chronological order.[24] In both of these features there is something of that documentary impulse to give representation to marginalised facets of life. As a political and textual strategy this also clearly works to support the celebration of gay sexuality by integrating it into the everyday.

The shifts between the locations of the two men are each marked by a still frame overhead shot displaying the two men together on a bed in various positions of relaxation and intimacy. This 'flash forward' (see Fig. 3.4) – once the formally daring preserve of art cinema – anticipates the sexual consummation of their meeting and goes against the grain of dominant representations. In the institutions of film and television, visibility for gay men is usually granted only at the price of virtually de-sexualising them. In America advertisers withdraw their money from slots around television programmes at the slightest hint that gay men or women might actually have sex. Recently two British soaps have featured gay women kissing. This seems to have provoked less uproar than when the gay character Colin from *Eastenders* kissed his boyfriend. It seems that in a male-dominated homophobic society the display of gay male sexuality is more threatening than female gay sexuality, which has a long tradition of being integrated into male heterosexual fantasies and has recently become chic in an extraordinarily mainstream way.

The celebration of gay sexuality on the image track is juxtaposed with the recollections of guilt by a voice-over:

> Everyone goes through that torment of: 'I don't want it to be. Oh please don't let it, Just please pass over me'. I went through terrible torment.

Intriguingly, the voice-over is not linked to either the blond or the brunette. It functions outside the fictional mode for the voice-over because it does not offer insights into character psychology nor does it have cause-and-effect implications in the skeletal narrative. The voice-over appears to address the audience directly, but rather than recounting a classical story with a beginning middle and end, it articulates some experiences and memories in a fragmentary way. All this gives the voice-over a documentary status, functioning to contextualise the fictional narrative of same-sex romance within a deeply homophobic society: 'If a gay came on tv my dad would say: "the dirty bastards". It's like, "oh God, it's not normal. Everyone knows its wrong."' As the video progresses the voice-over also becomes more affirmative: 'First love, oh yeah – I went "oh fucking hell", like that. I was just struck.' The voice-over continually provides explicit points of recognition for gay men and challenges heterosexual men and women to confront their own and society's prejudices.

> As a gay couple you're not allowed to adopt and I think I've got as much right as anyone else. I think I've got as much to offer. So I know it's going to sound disgusting — but if I have to I'm going to buy one.

Here the video strikes at what is arguably the institutional and ideological root of discrimination against gays as well as lesbians: the mono-paradigm of the family which, according to the classic marxist case, relieved capital of much of the burden of the reproduction and socialisation of future wage labour. The exclusiveness of the mono-paradigm functions to construct the division of labour and gender identities within the family as natural and inevitable. The oppression of individuals defined as being within society's norms depends in turn on the construction of a whole variety of other kinds of sexual and familial relationships as deviant and therefore subject to official and unofficial discrimination.

Conclusion

I have already referred to Italian Neo-Realism and the strategies it deployed to construct representations on low-budgets. *Yellow* illuminates other possibilities. For example, it is hard to talk of the blond and the brunette as characters since the video uses little in the way of acting as conventionally understood. This represents one solution to the possibility of not having trained or confident actors as a resource. In addition, whereas Neo-Realism suggested the possibilities of doing without studio sets and utilising exterior locations, *Yellow* is completely constructed around the private, domestic space (and the easily accessible props associated with that space). Clearly, such a space attracts the low-budget videomaker precisely because it is easy to access and cheap to construct representations around. Here videomakers should recall the old feminist adage about the personal being political. I hope my discussion of *Yellow* demonstrates that there is no area of private experience which is not charged with the politics of representation.

While *Yellow* is not a documentary, it does have some documentary components/strategies which link back to the project, found in both film and television, of extending representation to that which has been ignored, marginalised or repressed. These documentary components play a crucual role in linking the personal to the public/political domain, thus demonstrating the continuing importance of this genre for low-budget video work. At the same time *Yellow* draws on some of the most commodified aspects of mass culture – principally adverts and pop videos – extracting their utopian energies in the service of progressive representation. Here, then, is one very positive answer to the question of how videomakers might respond to the different manifestations of video practice coming out of the public service and commerce-led paradigms operating across television.

Notes

1 Glasgow University Media Group, *More Bad News*, GUMG/Routledge Kegan Paul, London 1980.
2 R. Williams, *The Long Revolution*, 1961, p.10.
3 T. Eagleton, *Criticism and Ideology*, Verso, 1976, pp.11-43.
4 B. Hogenkamp, *Deadly Parallels: Film and the Left in Britain 1929–1939*, Lawrence and Wishart, London 1986, p.31.
5 Hogenkamp, *ibid*, p.36.
6 T. Ryan, 'The New Road to Progress', in *British Cinema History*, Barnes and Noble Books, 1983, p.117.
7 Ryan, *ibid*.
8 R. Armes, *Third World Filmmaking and the West*, University of California Press, 1987, p.82.
9 Ryan, *op. cit.*, p.127.
10 Hogenkamp, *op. cit.*, p.111.
11 M. Alvarado (ed), *Video Worldwide*, UNESCO, 1988, p.275.
12 M. Lucas and M. Wallner, 'Resistance by Satellite' in *Channels of Resistance*, BFI/C4, 1993, pp.176-194.
13 P. Keighron, 'Video Diaries: What's Up Doc?' in *Sight and Sound* 1993, p.24.
14 Keighron, *ibid*, p.25.
15 Ryan, *op. cit.*, p.127.
16 Made by Vanessa Hodge.

17 'David Hockney: A Drawing Retrospective', Royal Academy of Arts, *Exhibition Gallery Guide*, 1995/1996
18 Made by Helen Austwick, Vicky Duggan, Lee McKillop, Mush Mohammed, Philip Williams (Brunel University College, 1995).
19 S. Neale, 'Masculinity as Spectacle', in *Screening the Male*, Routledge, 1993, pp.9-20.
20 S. Neale, *ibid*, p.14.
21 S. Neale, *ibid*, p.18.
22 L. Mulvey, 'Visual Pleasure and Narrative Cinema' in *Screen*, vol. 16, no. 3, 1975.
23 W. F. Haug, *Critique of Commodity Aesthetics*, Polity Press, Cambridge 1986.
24 B. Nichols, *Representing Reality*, Indiana University Press, Indianapolis 1991, p.20.
25 D. Bordwell, 'The Art Cinema as a Mode of Practice' in *Film Criticism*, vol. 4, no. 1, 1979.

Chapter Four

The Image

In this chapter we begin to focus on the various levels at which an audiovisual text produces meaning(s). Here we begin with the most basic unit of meaning: the image. In the course of addressing the image we will need to look at a number of things. Firstly we will need to distinguish between seeing and interpreting the ordinary and everyday world around us, and the processes involved in constructing and interpreting the image. Then we will need to understand some of the variables involved in constructing the image. Finally, I will suggest some analogous relationships with regard to the image between early cinema and contemporary video making.

Images and the real

Irrespective of the differences between the way celluloid and video tape store and reproduce the image for viewing, and irrespective of the different visual qualities deriving from the technologies, any discussion of the reception and production of the video image must take account of antecedent and ongoing debates about the relationship between the image and the real. To try and have some kind of fit between these two phenomena, to try and see things, via the image, 'as they really are', constitutes the project of realism in art. The very phrase 'seeing things as they really are' implies that some kind of transformation in our perception is required, and that at present, our perception of a subject, or across whole areas, is limited in some way.

But what kind of transformation has the realist project offered? Principally, I would suggest there have been two objectives realist art has concerned itself with: (a) a quantitative adjustment extending representation to subjects formerly excluded from or marginalised by the various media; and (b) a qualitative transformation in how we see.[1] A lot of controversy within realist art turns on conflict between different traditions that lay a greater stress on one or the other of these objectives. There is also considerable room for argument about the degrees to which each has been achieved in any particular example of realist art. For instance, in shifting the focus of the image to the working classes the documentary filmmakers of the 1930s were undoubtedly advancing realist cinema and extending the range of cinematic subject matter. At the same time, extension always leaves something out and that something may signify significant limits to a particular realist tradition. Thus *Coalface* (Grierson/Cavalcanti, GB, 1935) extends the focus of representation to the miners, but in discussing the workings of the industry and the dangers of the job, this short film is symptomatically quiet about the leading role the miners had in the 1926 General Strike. There is also clearly room for disagreements around what actually constitutes a qualitative transformation from one kind of seeing to another. For example, how different is a naturalist audiovisual text produced by say, Ken Loach (a champion of realism insofar as subject matter is concerned), from a film produced in the tradition of big-budget dominant cinema? (I offer this as a genuinely open question).

Such debates around realism may be said to have been something of a burden for the image. It is understandable that the question of realism has been seen to be so central to the production of the image because that is the site where a recognisable world may be most tangibly and concretely materialised. Yet an important facet of realism demands making connections between things [2] and this logically requires debates about realism to be thought at other levels of audiovisual language, such as sound–image relationships, editing, and the larger macro-structures of narrative or non-narrative modes of organisation.[3] Nevertheless, we cannot avoid the issue of realism vis-à-vis the image precisely because many of the arguments touched on here are not merely esoteric and academic, but have filtered into popular, commonsense judgements. The aphorism that 'the camera never lies' today has a counterclaim in the increasingly popular postmodernist position – rooted in various strands of philosophical and cultural relativism – which denies access to the real and the possibility of making truth claims, altogether. This chapter attempts to navigate between these two fallacious positions. The realist position will be represented by the French film theorist Andre Bazin, while the anti-realist position will be discussed in relation to structuralism. The aim of this chapter, however, is not to offer a comprehensive overview of debates around realism. Rather, the main aim is to relate the concept to three specific issues relevant to you even before you place the camcorder viewfinder to your eye. These are: a) your role in the construction of the image; b) how the meanings of the image are generated, and c) the relationship between the image and that which the image is a representation of.

One popular and widely circulated argument is premised on the camera's abilities to accurately record the scene in front of it, thus supposedly giving the medium privileged access to the real world. Andre Bazin's argument was that since the fifteenth century, when painters started to develop the rules of perspective in order to imitate how we see the world, painting has been torn between pursuing a realist path, showing things as they appear to be, and a symbolic path, i.e. exploring the aesthetic capabilities of the medium. However, although painting developed the rules of perspective by which the painter could attempt to reproduce a likeness of something, the painter's work, according to Bazin, 'was always in fee to an inescapable subjectivity'.[4] Thus when we look at a realist painting, our knowledge that this has been produced by the artist using learned and acquired skills, gets between the viewer and the painting. Bazin argued that there is a psychological barrier between the audience and what is represented. The camera, however, frees painting from this realist task, an unsatisfactory preoccupation because of the nature of the medium. For Bazin the camera is more perfectly suited to reproducing the real because the process of reproduction is simply the objective, impassive process of recording light and registering that record on light sensitive film. Thus the viewer is compelled to appreciate the essential veracity of the photographic image.

My account of Bazin's ideas is necessarily schematic, missing out the many points of tension and contradiction in his work. For example, does the 'realism' of cinema reside in the technology's supposed mechanical objectivity or the spectator's ability to convince themselves of the photographic image's essential veracity? This latter explanation for cinematic realism need not necessarily be 'true', it is just something the spectator willingly believes in. Bazin oscillated between the two explanations, trying to make the former buttress the latter. The latter, more sophisticated position, acknowledges that the appearence of 'life likeness' in the image is a carefully crafted illusion with which the viewer is complicit. For Bazin this illusion was to be encouraged because it approximated the viewer's everyday interpretation of the world. Yet even the more subtle position ultimately rests for its persuasiveness on the cruder and ultimately untenable argument that the ontology of the photographic image is its capacity to get direct access to the real without being in fee to human subjectivity. We have seen something of this tension already when I discussed the instruction manual's commitment to this tradition of 'realism'. We saw that there too, the writer was caught between recognising the necessity of human intervention in organising the image, and an aesthetic preference, blown up into a universal 'must', that that intervention should be concealed. Bazin then is only one of the more eloquent advocates of widespread assumptions. Let us start again, at first base, with the technology, and we will find that the camera is as much in fee to human subjectivity – or better, to the outcome of human decision making – as is the painter's brush.

The camera itself has been constructed as a result of human decision making which has given it particular qualities and not others. Firstly, it organises the act of looking within a frame, thus our usually unbounded vision now has a finite space in which to work.[5] The space you select, what you include and exclude from the frame is a basic choice the photographer, the filmmaker and the videomaker alike, must make. Nor should the frame be thought of as some kind of restriction, as an imperfection compared to the ordinary act of seeing. Arnheim, an early film theorist, points out how the vertical and horizontal lines within the shot are supported by the vertical and horizontal lines of the frame while '[s]lanting lines appear slanting because the margins of the picture are straight'.[6] As a simple demonstration of the effect of having a frame, look around the room you are in, then make a square out of your fingers, placing the 'frame' over one eye and 'pan' across the same space. Suddenly the boundaries to your vision bring new definition to the relations between objects and their relation to the edge you have imposed. So the frame is a 'set up', quite literally, in a way that unbounded vision is not. We may also note that the very selection of a frame governed by four 90° angled corners was not inevitable. Given another set of historical and cultural forces, the circle, the square, the triangle or even the hexagon might have been chosen to shape our vision. It should also be noted just how easily the recorded image can be cropped to different sizes and shapes once in the video editing suite.

Secondly, unlike our normal vision which has clarity of focus throughout, the filmed or recorded image is subject to manipulation. Choices are made to focus on foreground or background objects. Even where there is clarity throughout a limited depth of field, such as the deep focus photography which Bazin advocated, this merely relocates choices and decisions into areas such as the placing and movement of the subject in the image. Thirdly, our perspective is subject to alteration depending on the kind of lenses employed (e.g. various degrees of wide angle and telephoto lenses) as against the unvarying perspective of normal sight. [7]

Finally, the ability of a two-dimensional image to produce the effect of three-dimensionality on a flat surface relies on the audience's understanding of the conventions of perspective. These conventions, developed in the early Renaissance, were a great advance in their ability to depict a contemporary, secular world, as opposed to the world of religion, symbolism and mythology which had dominated the art of the feudal era. Yet, as Berger argues, these developments in pictorial seeing were neither inevitable or innocent and value free. There is an ideological congruence between perspectival painting's address, its summoning up of its ideal spectator as a single individual and the emergence of the individual as a central philosophical category of capitalism. Perspectival painting flatters the spectator that they occupy 'the unique centre of the world'. [8] Everything appears to be arranged so that the viewer can cast a masterful, controlling gaze over the scene depicted from a single point in time and space. In doing so, perspectival painting lost the ease with which the older, religious, mythological painting dealt with time and space as a continually unfolding process. The new conventions of seeing froze time and space and, in effect, removed the spectator from history. Yet while the camera's optics inherited some perspectival conventions, they also challenged others. The still camera, Berger argues, 'isolated momentary appearances and in so doing destroyed the idea that images were timeless.' [9] This new stress on the image being snatched from the flow and continuum of life in turn impacted upon painting. The Impressionist movement was precisely about capturing transitory moments, snap shots of life.[10] Later, a still nascent 'moving pictures' industry influenced Cubists to rearticulate the pictorial construction of space. The Cubist painting did not address the spectator as if they occupied a still point in space, but, just as the cinema was beginning to do, it offered the spectator multiple perspectives on the same subject. Thus, while Bazin saw cinema as inheriting and perfecting painting's advances in perspective, I would agree with Berger, that cinema could also be used to challenge some of the older assumptions underpinning perspectival conventions.

Arguments about the camera's faithfulness to that which it records are unhelpful because they block a systematic understanding of how images are constructed. This is a useful term since it stresses the extent to which a text is made, and embarrasses the belief (which Bazin shared) that the image emerges from, is coaxed out of, or reflects the world in any simple one-to-one correspondence. Cultural practitioners who have some investment in the belief of the image as a window on the world are typically self-effacing about their own role in the process of meaning production. For if the camera does have the capacity to record the world without apparently shaping that record of it, then logically what is placed before the camera should aspire to look untouched by artistry and preparation. This artistic practice is a defining feature of naturalism and has been criticised by, among others, the playwright Trevor Griffiths:

> They [the cultural workers] actually believe, I think, that reality is an unproblematical concept, that somehow your job as an artist is to set up a window on the real world, and allow the audience to see the real world through that window that you've introduced into their lives. Now, I suppose that nobody actually practices naturalism quite that way. I mean, they'd be crazy if they did. But that passes for theory quite often, when you push people. [11]

Against the Bazinian type of argument we need to stress that the image and the real, the record and the thing recorded, are two distinct phenomena. This is not to say that there is no relationship between representation (in images, in language or whatever medium) and the real, just that the relationship is a complex and indirect one. Bazin's theory of the relationship between representation and the real belongs to the mimetic tradition. From this position representation works by reflecting or copying a world which exists beyond the medium and which remains 'untouched' by the medium in which it makes an appearance. Yet while the image shares some of the physical and spatial characteristics of everyday, ordinary seeing, this merely classes it as an iconic sign: i.e. one that resembles the thing that it depicts. The emphasis must remain, however, that it is still a sign and like all signs it is the product of human decisions and choices that have gone into the making of it. It is this human labour which mediates the relationship between the image and the real and which makes that relationship complex and indirect. We should also note just how easily the naturalistic qualities of the image can be ruptured at the push of a button when one is working with video.

The construction of meaning(s)

One way of understanding the implications of those decisions and choices in a systematic way is to draw on two concepts developed in linguistics. Meanings, whether in language or the image, are produced by two fundamental processes: selection and combination. You select what goes into the image from a storehouse of possible choices. Linguists call that storehouse a paradigm. Units of meanings selected from one paradigm are then combined with units of meaning from other paradigms. A group of units combined together is called a syntagm. The syntagm represents the actualised image made up of components selected from various paradigms.[12] Fig. 4.1 as actualised could be described thus:

A white/ elderly/ woman/ in profile/ against bullfighting/ posters

And with some of the other possible choices from the various paradigms, our syntagm might look like this:

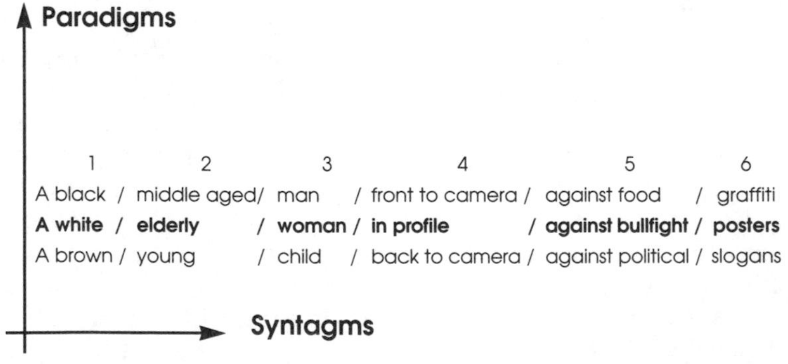

Awareness of the paradigmatic and syntagmatic relations underpinning the visual text alerts us to the way decisions shape the meaning of the image, rather than (as Bazin would have it), the meaning emerging out of a faithfulness to the real built into the apparatus and enhanced by a self-effacing aesthetic. Altering the syntagm by swapping units of meaning from one or more of the different paradigms will inflect or radically reconstruct the possible meanings of the image. Common sense tells us this, but it does not tell us why this is the case. We need to have recourse to the work of the Swiss linguist, Ferdinand de Saussure, if we are to understand why.

If it is clear that the meaning(s) or potential meanings of Fig. 4.1. would alter if other categories were selected from within the paradigms, then we have observed how the production of meaning involves drawing boundaries between and within the various paradigms. Drawing boundaries is another way of establishing difference, which Saussure suggested was so important to the production of meaning. According to Saussure's theory, a sign produces meaning because of its structural relations of difference with other signs in a total system of signs. This difference operates at two levels. A sign, Saussure points out, is

Fig. 4.1

made up of two components: a signifier, which is the vehicle for meaning (inscription, sound) and a signified, which is the concept attached to or associated with the signifier. Firstly, there is differentiation between signifiers. 'Cat' for example is able to produce a concept different to 'mat' because of a phonetic difference (c and m) between the two signifiers. If it is the differences between signifiers which helps produce a sign, then there is no 'natural' intrinsic bond between a signifier and the concept it signifies. The relationship is one agreed by the community that uses the language. This is unproblematic and clearly indisputable. It is proved by the fact that other languages have other words (signifiers) for the concepts of 'catness' and 'matness'.

These arguments were applied to the visual and moving image by semioticians in the 1970s. Here the signifiers of the photographic image were conceived as

> blotches of light, dark, and colour ... articulated via position and opposition to form fragments of recognisable ... [shapes] ... which are themselves articulated into iconic forms such as arms, legs, and trees.[13]

This modernist inspired theory in turn provided the underpinning for experimental film practice, which foregrounded the signifiers of the cinematic sign (specifically, celluloid, grain, focus, lens, contrast, etc.) thus calling into question the 'attached' signified as a natural and unproblematic given. According to Gidal, radical experimental cinema did not seek to obliterate representation altogether in favour of 'pure' light and other cinematic materials. Rather it sought to entice the viewer into meanings and expectations while simultaneously producing them as constructions which undermine the spectator's certainties about meaning. A tension between signifier and signified is set up to explore the contradictions between 'the seen and the meanings inculcated, or the seen in relation to what the viewer thinks he/she "knows" as to the referential meanings.'[14]

We can see this process at work in Fig. 4.2. which is a photograph developed with a high contrast filter. Part of the image, particularly the blank white surroundings and the blurring of the object into that whiteness on the bottom left and top right of the picture, is nothing more than the materials, the signifiers, of the photographic process in an undifferentiated state. Generally, though, the signifiers have been articulated into a set of structural relationships which allow us to differentiate a particular shape to the object overall. And in the centre of the picture we can differentiate not only shapes and angles but definite iconic forms. We can discern girders perhaps made of iron, and in the background some sort of casing or walls which the girders are supporting. We can make out a piece of wood to the left of centre (we can just see the grain), and above that what could be a pipe. Looking at this image we are keenly aware that the meaning(s), the signified(s) to which it may refer is rather less stable and solid than is usually the case.

In reading this or any other image, we bring with us two kinds of 'inculcated' conceptual schemas: those schemas we use daily to differentiate between things (is this a building? a gutted church?), and those schemas specific to cultural artifacts.There are two of this latter kind at work in Fig 4.2. which are important to our reading of the image. Firstly, the area in the image which is most transparently iconic is just to the right of centre. This is one major concession to our expectations since it is a very classical compositional strategy to draw our attention primarily towards the spaces just off centre and in the middle portions of the image. The other convention which invites us to read the image in a particular way is that we imagine the top and bottom of the subject will correspond with the top and bottom of the photograph. This, however, is only a convention and could be

Fig. 4.2

misleading. If the image is turned to the right onto its longest side, one may just be able to disern what could be some water in what is now the picture's bottom right. Developed with less contrast, the surrounding context of sea and sand would become apparent and the building(?) would transform itself into a wrecked boat. As the materiality of the process of construction fades we would make the passage from signifier to signified with more assurance. The element of risk, of hazard and therefore the possibility of questioning our relationship to the image and to the culture of the image, arguably diminishes. Of course, this is an extreme example in which the materiality of the signifier is so foregrounded as to obliterate the object signified. As we have seen from Gidal, experimental cinema theorists often situate their practice as setting up a tension between a foregrounded signifier and a still recognisable but now problematised signified. Similarly, David Hall has argued that video art in the 1970s 'was intended as a "liberation" from the shackles of the object'[15] that is, from a Bazinian 'humility' (evident in the effacement of the medium's formal properties) toward the integrity of the subject matter. At the same time, Hall contends that video art's interest in form was not – at its best – formalistic; rather, it sought to interrogate the socio-political meanings attached to the construction of the signified.

We have seen how signifiers construct signifieds, but what is the relationship between these signifieds and what they refer to? What is the relationship between a picture of a boat and a real boat? Does the latter in any way have an effect on the image, in terms of making it meaningful? This is a huge question and here there is only space to give it a most cursory attention. Let us return to Saussure to see what his theory suggests. In fact Saussure argued that the concepts or signifieds attached to the signifiers are, like the signifiers, only able to produce meanings because of the relations of difference which they establish at a semantic level. Put another way, language produces meanings by its own processes of establishing boundaries between, for example, the concept of 'catness' and other signs which abut onto it. If we are thinking in terms of the larger category of 'pets' , then 'catness' is part of a system which divides up the world of pets and which includes 'dog', 'goldfish', 'hamster' and so on. Advocating this argument, Sturrock argues that, 'we can only delimit the meaning of the signifier "rock" by differentiating it from other signs which abut onto it semantically, such as "stone", "boulder", "cliff"'.[16] I have a problem though with this formulation.

It would seem to suggest that consciousness is produced by language alone, organised into a system of differences quite unaffected and indeed radically cut off from any relationship with the real world or our interaction with the real world. Yet how else can we explain why, in Sturrock's example, 'stone', 'boulder' and 'cliff' abut semantically onto 'rock' rather than such things as 'dog' and 'goldfish' if not because they share certain physical properties quite independent of language? For example, the former is a product of geological forces while the latter group are the product of biological forces.

The tradition of thought Sturrock is advocating is sometimes called conventionalism. From this perspective, meaning(s) are entirely the product of social conventions which have constructed an elaborate field of differences between signs (their signifiers and signifieds). This suggests a separation between representation and the real as problematic as the mimetic tradition's collapsing of the two together. I would argue that the real world independent of language does have certain qualities which exert a strong pull on how we conceptualise or differentiate between phenomena.[17] To return to my own example of pets, no matter what we do with language, a hamster in a tank full of water would not acquire fishlike qualities simply because a community of language users decide that 'hamster' now has a closer semantic relationship to 'fish' than 'gerbil'. Thus while signs construct meaning, their complex relations with the world independent of language cannot be grasped by the notion that one set of differences between signs are *as valid* as any other. Nor is it just that isolated objects or particular living things have certain qualities which set limits on how we can conceptualise them. Social practice (or what Marx called social being) has a very profound and complex interaction with consciousness. As human beings we appropriate and transform nature (turning some animals into pets for example) and thus we transform ourselves (the practice of keeping pets produces such values as care and compassion for animals, which in earlier epochs would have been quite bizarre for most people for whom animals were kept to produce food or become food).

To return to the picture of the woman in front of the bullfighting posters (Fig. 4.1) we can explore this relationship between practice and consciousness in relation to the image. We can see that the act of constructing and interpreting the image involves identifying differences within and between such socially significant categories as ethnicity, age, gender, and cultural tradition. Thus the potential meanings of this image derive from real social practices, social relationships and social structures to which this image refers. Yet in stressing the relationship between the image and society, are we not in danger of losing sight of the image as construct? Is it not now simply a transparent window onto those social practices? No, we can avoid a collapse back into the mimetic tradition if we remember that the meanings or potential meanings of this image are structurally related to what has been excluded from the image by the active process of selection in each paradigm. Further, as the category selected in each paradigm comes into contact with the selected categories from other paradigms, the possible meanings of the image shimmer, mutate and take shape as the exclusions and inclusions in each paradigm register in the consciousness of the viewer.

They do not, however, coalesce into a rigid or fixed set of meanings. For signs, as Voloshinov, the marxist philosopher of language argued, are always in a state of flux, subject to having their meanings refracted in a variety of ways according to the real practical struggles in which they are embedded.[18] Take for example the sign of bullfighting as a site of conflict between bullfighting's promotion of itself as heroic theatre, national culture, affirmation of masculine prowess, etc. and contesting definitions such as the animal rights argument against cruel sports. (Other, less literal interpretations of bullfighting are also possible, as we shall see below, and these would also take us into contested meanings around, for example, gender). The sign as a site of struggle will be variously acknowledged by both audiences and the texts in which the signs are constructed. Whatever image you construct, and whatever sequence of images you forge, this basic question is always there: how does this image relate to others of the same subject? What is your relationship to the meanings of those images?

According to Voloshinov's close associate Mikhail Bakhtin, no matter how resistant the sign is to acknowledging this struggle over meaning, the sign is always conducting some kind of dialogue with or making rejoinders (sometimes openly, sometimes surreptitiously) to other representations which seek nuanced or radically different interpretations of the same object or referent.

> ...no living word relates to its object in a singular way: between the word and its object, between the word and the speaking subject, there exists an elastic environment of other alien words about the same object, the

> same theme ... any concrete discourse (utterance) finds the object at which it was directed already as it were overlain with qualifications, open to dispute, charged with value ... It is entangled, shot through with shared thoughts, points of view, alien value judgments and accents. The word, directed towards its object, enters a dialogically agitated and tension filled environment of alien words, value judgments and accents, weaves in and out of complex interrelationships, merges with some, recoils from others, intersects with yet a third group: and all this may crucially shape discourse, may leave a trace in all its semantic layers, may complicate its expression and influence its entire stylistic profile.[19]

All this suggests a very complex dialogue in any specific utterance or representation between the meanings asserted by the signs used and, within a continuum of contesting possibilities, other meanings asserted by similar and different signs which converge on the same object or referent in other acts of representation. However, there are yet more things to take account of in understanding how meaning(s) are generated. This is hinted at in Bakhtin's reference to the 'stylistic profile' of an utterance or representation. Returning our attention to Fig 4.1. we can note that the examples from the fourth paradigm are all concerned with the relationship between subject and camera position and thus constitute an example of a sign (figure/camera arrangements) specific to the medium in which representation is taking place. There are in fact other specifically imagistic elements contributing to the possible meanings of the image, such as the skewed framing. However, the concepts of paradigm and syntagm are clumsy instruments when it comes to exploring the subtlety of meaning production via the image. We will need to use other concepts and vocabularies in order to draw out the interaction between those signs in general social and cultural circulation and those which the medium, with its own specific history of production and consumption, has developed.

Metaphor, metonym, symbol

Before we do that in any detail it is worth just commenting on the relationship between the image and the succession of images of which it is part, and how this may affect both the artistic process of selection and combination, and the act of interpretation. While a single image may emit what Christian Metz calls a micro-narrative, it is also shaped by the macro-context formed by the accummulation of each image. Micro and macro narratives are in constant interaction with each other. The evidence for this can be found in Fig 4.1 which may be said to emit faint signals for a number of possible narrative frameworks into which it could be inserted. Perhaps we may imagine Fig 4.1. is from an account (fictional or documentary) of a woman who campaigns against bullfighting, or perhaps this is the mother of a bullfighter who is unhappy that her son has such a dangerous occupation. In these hypothetical narrative frameworks we continue to read the posters as literally indicating 'bullfighting', and that wherever this women goes, this subject looms large in her life. But note what happens to the nature of the poster if we imagine a different narrative framework. Perhaps the narrative concerns a woman under pressure from her husband in some way. Now we no longer read the poster as indicating 'bullfighting' but rather it becomes a metaphor for the way the husband is menacing and toying with her. A metaphor can be defined as a sign (aggressive, manipulative husband) which is substituted for another (matador and bull) because there is a similarity or equivalence between the two (the husband is like a matador).

But what if the narrative has stressed how sexist our imaginary husband is? Perhaps he will not allow his wife to do certain things because she is a woman. In this case we may read the poster not as a metaphor but as a metonymy. A metonymic sign is one which is in some contact with or 'adjacent' to that which it is standing in for, as when journalists use the phrase 'the White House' to mean the president and his officials.[20] In our new narrative framework the poster and bullfighting becomes metonymic of Hispanic machismo: the poster is a part of and stands in for a larger cultural whole.

A third type of sign, the symbol, may be defined as any object or thing into which a whole set of values and beliefs are invested by a group, organisation or institution. The object is not selected on the grounds that it may be said to resemble or share qualities with whatever it signifies – for this is what defines the metaphor. Nor is the object selected on the grounds that it is a component of a larger whole – that is what defines the metonym. Rather the object/thing is selected largely for 'arbitrary' reasons and accepted by insiders of the group/movement/organisation, as well as outsiders, as its 'badge'. Obvious examples of this might be the dove standing in as a symbol for peace, or it may be highly generic such as the sheriff's 'tin star' standing for such abstract qualities as justice, law and order. Yet while symbols are often defined as signs which mean what they do for entirely arbitrary reasons, there are different gradations of arbitrariness. A dove for example makes more sense as a symbol of peace than a predatory bird, but it is also large enough to be depicted with some sense of grace. Within the world of genres, the badge rather than the gun or handcuffs is the appropriate symbol for a justice system that perceives itself as resting on the consent of the people. The gun and handcuffs would have to be disarticulated from their associations with force and incarceration to be appropriate symbols for the social democratic view of justice, law and order. For some communities of course the more coercive symbols of the gun, etc, do more accurately describe the principles of 'justice' within a racist, sexist and class-divided society, thus raising the possibility of using symbols to subvert an institution's perception of itself. Yet other kinds of symbols, such as colours (white for purity, red for danger, passion, etc.) are much more arbitrary (why these colours for these meanings?), and the values and beliefs they articulate are perhaps less easily identified as belonging to a particular group/organisation/institution, because they seem more diffusely shared and circulated within a given culture and society.

What should be clear is that the power and appropriateness of metaphors, metonyms and symbols depends very much on the overall artistic context in which they are placed. These types of signs help to 'thicken' out a text by reinforcing and elaborating meanings and making connections between different meanings within the text. Needless to say these concepts again contribute to making Bazin's window on the world more and more opaque, more and more a dense constellation of signs which are the outcome of choices and decisions made, whether self-consciously or 'spontaneously', as in the Gramscian sense discussed in chapter one.

Variables of the image

We now need to discuss in further detail the variety of signs which constitute the image, and in order to do so, it is worth drawing on a distinction common in film criticism between two kinds of variables that coalesce to produce meaning. The term mise-en-scène (meaning to stage an action) refers to all those performance signs that one would expect to find on the stage, in the theatre: setting, costume, props, lighting, gesture, movement and so on. The term cinematography refers to all those elements of the image that are specifically cinematic, such as: camera movement and its positioning in terms of distance, angle, height, as well as the type of lens employed, and such special effects as you may have available 'in camera' or in the editing suite. The meaning(s) of an image derives in part from the ensemble interaction of these theatrical and cinematic/videographic elements.

Long shot, medium shot, close-up

One basic decision you have to make with regard to the image is about the distance between the camera and the subject. Bazin preferred the long shot because it appeared to preserve the unity of the world recorded, while the medium and close up shot carved into that world suggesting the overly interpretative and guiding presence of the filmmaker(s). Yet as Trinh T. Minh-Ha points out, the idea that 'wider framing is less a framing than tighter shots' is difficult to sustain.[21] Certainly the 'unity' which the long shot preserves is the relationships between characters or other subject material and their environment. The long shot contextualises your subject, perhaps explaining or offering clues as to character behaviour and motivation. Raymond Williams has suggested that forging links between environment and behaviour was one of the key contributions to representation which naturalist aesthetics made in the nineteenth century.

> Characters and action were seen as affected or determined by environment, which especially in a social and social-physical sense then had to be accurately described as an essential element of any account of a life.[22]

If you do have locations available to you which could function in this way, then the long shot is a useful visual strategy. Throughout a student video called *Halt*[23] the long shot is used to contrast the rural and urban locations in which a war is unfolding. The rural locations, which are shown in flashbacks in the video, look peaceful but are eventually revealed to have suffered the incursions of war. In the present-day urban locations, two characters previously seen separately in rural settings are brought together. The long shot of Fig. 4. 3 brings the past and the present, the rural (left foreground) and the urban (large brick background) together in the single image. The woman in the middle background appears to be holding a baby. In fact she has been transformed from a mother who has lost her child because of the war, into a participant in the war: the 'baby' turns out to be a bomb. Dressing the bomb as a baby is a symbol of her loss and the particular trajectory that sucks her into the war.

The videomaker was fortunate enough to be able to use a building site for the scenes of urban devastation, and thus contextualise character action in relation to their environment. Fig. 4.4 shows the other character, the border guard, pissing like an animal marking out his territory. Through this metaphor the video hints at the territorial disputes that cause war. Finally, Fig. 4.5 shows the guard and woman

Fig. 4.3

Fig. 4.4

Fig. 4.5

in an environment which, with the houses in the background and the wasteground separating the two figures, seems to capture exactly one facet of war which images from the former Yugoslavia have hammered home: the slide from normal, civilised living to chaos.

Yet your locations may be full of things that are inappropriate, distracting or undermining of the scene you are trying to construct. In such circumstances you might need to primarily use close to medium close-up shots. While this may discard the long shot that Bazin thought essential and the establishing shot so beloved of dominant cinema, what you are rejecting is not some timeless, universally valid measure of 'quality', but simply the subjective criteria which do not fit your needs and circumstances. Tom Kalin's film *Swoon*, part of the new 'queer cinema', concerns the sexual and criminal relationship between two wealthy Jewish lovers who set out to kidnap and subsequently murder a 14-year-old boy. This story, without heroes and villains, had to make a virtue out of what was necessarily a low-budget production. For example, there was not enough money to fill the room, where the two gay men planned the kidnapping, with many props. The look of the interior scenes, then, was built up around tight close-ups, which in turn directed attention to the details of the crime: fingers on the typewriter keyboard; the keys punching out the ransom note, etc. Similarly, a video called *Drip*[24] was shot in an unexciting interior location. The narrative turns on a series of interruptions – including a dripping tap – which prevent a man from falling asleep. The video thus makes plenty of use of extreme close-ups to advance the simple narrative (see Figs. 4. 6 and 4.7).

Camera height

What about the height of the camera in relation to the action? The dominant convention is to place the camera at eye level. There are good reasons for this. The human face is very expressive, as the early film theorist Bela Balazs argued. Even as a 'mute soliloquy' a face 'can speak with the subtlest shades of meaning.'[25] Indeed Balazs argued that in the absence of speech, the silent film was forced to explore the 'polyphonic' qualities of the face, by which he meant its capacity to articulate multiple and even contradictory meanings. Best of all the camera could move in close to explore the microphysiognomic details of a face.

> In one of Eisenstein's films there is a priest, a handsome, fine figure of a man. His noble features, his inspired eyes are made even more radiant by a glorious voice. He is like the sublime image of a saint. But then the camera gives an isolated big close-up of one eye; and a cunningly

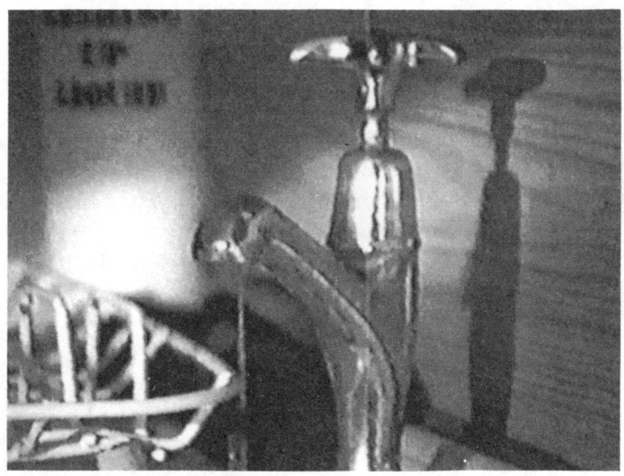

Fig. 4.6

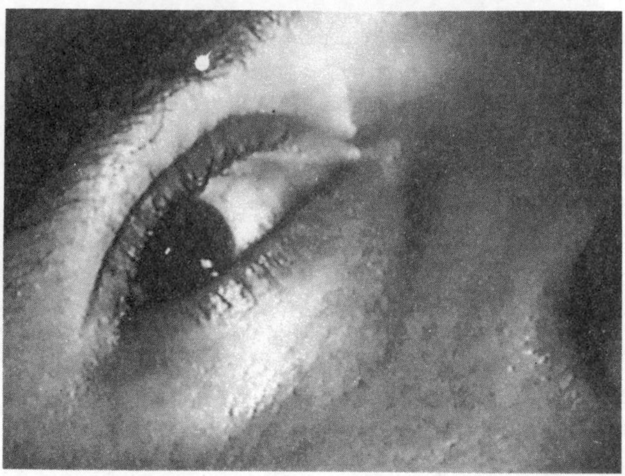

Fig. 4.7

> watchful furtive glance slinks out from under his beautiful silky eyelashes like an ugly caterpillar out of a delicate flower. … when the noble face reappears, it is like a deceptive screen concealing a dangerous enemy.[26]

Having said that, however, it is also worth lowering the level of the camera to see what might otherwise drop out of the bottom of the frame or go unnoticed; other parts of the body can be just as expressive as the face. Use of a tripod will help to encourage your own exploration of the full range of settings for camera height. Without the tripod, your first response would be to rest the camera on your shoulder as you stand. The tripod, however, physically forces you to think about height. Fig 4.8, again taken from *Drip*, shows our irritated would-be sleeper getting out of bed to turn the tap off. But instead of staying with a medium waist high shot of him getting out of bed, the video cuts to a level 'ground floor' shot of his feet hitting the floor. In this shot the feet have become transformed into a metonym. They are the expressive part of the character's whole bodily determination to shut the tap off, and indeed the shot is probably more expressive of that meaning than the more obvious alternative which would frame the whole body getting out of bed.

Camera angle

Along with the height at which you set your camera, another variable to be considered is the angle at which the camera is set on the mise-

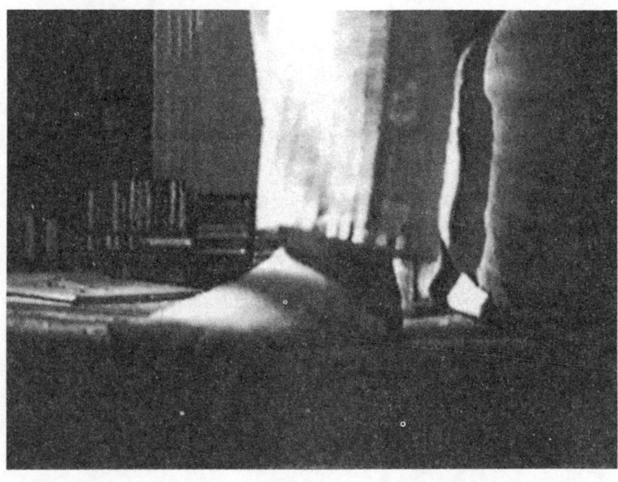

Fig. 4.8

en-scène. The camera may be set straight onto the action or have a tilted purchase on the scene. Two common uses of camera angles immediately spring to mind. The low angle shot is often used to infuse the subject with a sense of power, while the overhead shot angled downwards often suggests diminished power. These meanings have become attached to these camera angles by custom and habitual use, but it is important to stress that the readings are not intrinsic to these visual strategies. Instead, the meaning(s) of one element in the image (say, camera angle) will crystallise around its interaction with other elements within and between images. Depending on the context of their use then, low angle or high angle shots can just as easily suggest other meanings. You may also decide to tilt or roll the camera to the left or right of a subject. Why you may do this depends entirely on your needs and intentions. The tilted framing of Fig 4.1, for example, attempts to bring the bullfighting posters and the passing woman into some kind of dynamic or conflictual relationship. Fig. 4.7 – achieved with the macro close-up facility on the video lens – also produces a dynamisation beween subject matter (the character's eye) and framing (slightly tilted) which indicates a conflict between the character's condition (being awake) and the character's desire (to be asleep). As with all these variables you need to think about what you are trying to achieve before finally opting for one particular strategy over another.

Camera movement

Dominant cinema has evolved a number of ways of using camera movement. While these are likely to be useful to you they may not fully encompass your needs and so you should be aware that there is no need to restrict yourself to these common techniques. Camera movement in dominant cinema aims to do two things: be unobtrusive and contribute to the telling of the story in as clear and accessible a way as possible. Thus the main reason for camera movement is to keep characters in frame. This may require very slight movements to accommodate character movement (called reframes), particularly in the medium to close-up range, or more visible camera movement such as pans (where the camera is stationary but rotates in a degree arc,) or tracking shots (where the camera is actually mobile and able to follow the subject matter). In their dominant usage, both panning and tracking are motivated by the narrative: what they show (again usually characters doing something) unfolds the story. Some guides to filmmaking will even suggest that extensive camera movement should only travel from left to write, abiding by Western conventions of reading and writing, as if movement from right to left would somehow be 'unnatural'. Again what is meant by this is that such movement would draw attention to itself and infringe classical cinema's commitment to unobtrusive story telling. Clearly camera movement that allows you to follow character movement is useful – but why stop at that? For example, the camera can function autonomously from character(s), moving independently of them to explore space and setting. Or perhaps your camera movement can describe patterns which in themselves function to comment on the scene. One can imagine how triangular movements, circles, horizontal, vertical and diagonal movements could become part of the meaning(s) of a scene rather than simply recording it. In fact, in minor and low-key ways this is often the case with dominant cinema, but there is considerable scope for expanding the possible uses of this particular variable.

Mise-en-scène

Here we are concerned with the selection and arrangement of elements placed before the camera. More specifically we need to think of such things as figure movement and gesture, positioning, costume, props, setting and lighting as sign systems in their own right. As such you cannot afford to think of these variables as 'passive' or merely functional. For example, setting is not merely a convenient physical space in which to unfold the mise-en-scène in time. It also emits meanings which may either complement or contradict what you are trying to achieve. The meanings which signs produce are governed, albeit in a flexible and alterable manner, by codes. A number of signs such as a sofa and a television for example, are likely to be brought together under the code for domestic interior location. This code will be sustained by other additions to the mise-en-scène, such as a dining room table, while others, such as a motorbike, would strike us as rather odd (more on incongruous codes in a moment).

Recent attempts to develop a theoretical understanding of theatrical practice may provide a useful resource in understanding mise-en-scène codes. Theorists, for example, have explored the production of meanings produced by physical relations in space. Dubbed the proxemic code, there are two axes on which this functions: distance/closeness and high/low.[27] There can be no fixed meanings associated with these variables. Closeness between figures for example may indicate intimacy or hostility, while we may read the physical distance between figures as a sign of formality and social hierarchy, or (moving from the social to the personal) perhaps as a sign of an emotional vacuum between characters. In Fig. 4. 9 from *Halt*, the distance between the dead woman and her partner signifies the irretrievable loss of a loved one. At the level of the socio-political, the meaning of the image is that war results in separations of all kinds, and this meaning is here rendered in spatial terms. As this still indicates we must also consider not only the physical relationships between figures but also their relationship to the camera. Spatially this can be divided into foreground, middle ground and background areas. A strong line from bottom left to the top and middle part of the image moves the spectator's eye across and between the middle ground gap between the two figures. When composing figures and objects in these three planes of the image, it is precisely the question of the movement of the viewer's eye across various points of interest which you have to construct. Note too that our positioning next to the dead woman means that the viewer is very close to the man's expressed grief once he arrives at her side. A different camera position would have produced a different relationship to the action in the fore, middle and background.

The kinesic code refers to meanings produced by the body. As we have already noted, Balazs was one of the first theorists of film to recognise the potential which the camera had in isolating and foregrounding body movement, gesture or facial expression. The ability of the body to articulate what Elam calls attitudinal markers

Fig. 4.9

which indicate a figure's relationship towards others, an environment, the world, is an important component of low-budget work, characterised as it often is by sparse or even zero verbal communication.[28] The kinesic code in performance tends to draw heavily on body language recognisable from everyday life and whose meanings in a specific performance become clear by the presence of other mise-en-scène elements.

Vestmentary codes refer to meanings produced by costume. 'Costume', however, sounds as if it may refer to something rather more elaborate than a low-budget video could muster while 'clothes' sounds again very functional and perhaps something that you need pay little attention to. However vestments will emit meanings, and the more conscious you are of their potential to do this the more you will be able to mobilise them in accordance with, rather than in contradiction to, your intentions. Yet having coherent intentions does not neccesarily rule out utilising mise-en-scène codes which contradict one another. For example *Sarraounia* (Med Hondo, Fr./Burkina Faso, 1986) uses conflicting vestmentary codes at the film's conclusion. The narrative is set at the end of the nineteenth century and tells the story of western and in particular French imperialist adventures in Africa and the resistance to them symbolised by the warrior queen, Sarraounia. At the film's conclusion Sarraounia calls for unity and tolerance of religious differences amongst Africans. She then walks towards the camera followed by people from various tribes dressed in African garb of the period. As the rear of the procession comes into view, we see people wearing modern clothing: jeans, T-shirts, jackets, etc. Thus, by combining vestmentary codes from different periods, the film asks the audience to make connections between Sarraounia's call for black unity at the end of the nineteenth century with the present-day needs of the peoples of Africa. A similar strategy is used by the film *Edward II* (D. Jarman,GB, 1991), which uses props as well as costumes from different historical periods in order to suggest continuities about power, sexuality and the British state, across hundreds of years of history. Both these examples come from relatively high budget independent films, nevertheless the idea of using costume, props or other mise-en-scène codes incongruously, could be adopted and explored further.

Finally, lighting codes are perhaps the most difficult but, at one level, the most important to master (no light, no image). It is best to make use of instruction manuals which can give good advice and tips about positioning lights. There is only space here to note that the lighting codes associated with low-budget genres such as film noir and the horror genre, may also prove useful for you. These lighting codes were particularly useful for disguising poor quality sets, surrounding characters in darkness, relieved only by the odd shard or pool of light. If you can block out natural light by using blinds, curtains or black paper, some very striking effects can be achieved with one artificial light source. However, these codes carry with them sets of connotations (the supernatural for the horror genre, or psychological disorders for the film noir[29]) and you have to decide whether these meanings are appropriate to your purposes. If not, try experimenting with your own lighting patterns (an array of effects can be achieved with masks and gels).

Video: image of 'attractions'

I have already mentioned how the question of narrative context will determine the selection and combination of various elements of the image. But how exactly may we characterise the relationship between image and the narrative itself? I want to suggest that the low-budget videomaker may well need to think the relations between image and narrative in a different way to that of dominant cinema. I have hinted at this in my discussion of *Yellow* but I want to now briefly expand the argument by reference to early cinema.

Tom Gunning has argued that early cinema emphasises the spectacle and performance which the image displays, over and above the part played by the image in the flow of a narrative, in telling a story. This orientates the image towards an open acknowledgement of the spectator. In *How it Feels To Be Run Over* (C. Hepworth, 1900), for example, a car drives towards the spectator and appears to run over the camera. This interest in directing the mise-en-scène towards the camera and, by implication the spectator, suggests to Gunning a trace of the sort of concerns that were to preoccupy the avant-garde. For historically, as we have seen in the earlier discussion around modernism, the avant-garde have been interested in art that acknowledges the role of the spectator in interpreting cultural works, whether it's in film, theatre, painting or other mediums.

Gunning borrows the term 'cinema of attractions' from the radical avant-garde filmmaker Sergei Eisenstein, who used it to refer to the clash (the violent 'attraction') between various elements in an artwork, which then explode outwards in an 'aggressive' or direct impact on the spectator. An 'attraction', in short, is anything which stimulates forcefully. Marxist avant-garde practitioners such as Eisenstein and Brecht were drawn to popular entertainments such as the fairground, vaudeville and circus precisely because of the way their 'attractions' endeavoured to shock the spectator, pulling them up short, confronting and astonishing them with a particular spectacle. Left cultural workers saw in this a method for shocking audiences out of apathy and complacency for the purposes of social critique.

Eisenstein's main concern was with the 'attractions' between separate film shots, that is the process of editing (see chapter five). Gunning argues that the image in early cinema was similarly conscious of its relationship to the spectator. Like vaudeville theatre, which crucially was the place that most audiences saw films up until around 1905,[30] early cinema had a strong 'exhibitionist quality … [with] its accent on direct stimulation'.[31] Vaudeville, unlike bourgeois theatre, was not narrative orientated. Instead it consisted of a variety of unconnected acts directing their spectacle outwards towards an acknowledged spectator. The image of early cinema shows a like-minded awareness of its function to reveal something, to display or to show something to an implied viewer. As Gunning puts it:

> the cinema of attractions directly solicits spectator attention, inciting visual curiosity, and supplying pleasure through an exciting

> spectacle – a unique event, whether fictional or documentary, that is of interest in itself...[32]

After 1906, American cinema began to lose its links with vaudeville as the prime site of viewing. As its historical and spatial links with vaudeville were severed, a whole complex of forces were converging to ensure that cinema became increasingly dominated by narrative. While the cinema of attractions' emphasis on spectacle does not disappear entirely from the dominant cinema that was to develop, it came to occupy a subordinate place in a system geared towards narrative. Spectacle remains important for some genres such as the musical, and more recently in the special effects genres such as horror and science fiction. But even here, the spectacle is tightly integrated with the motor of narrative development. Thus, in the horror movie the monster's appearance always signifies danger for the human protagonists. As Gunning says, the cinema of special effects is the cinema of 'tamed attractions'.[33] Whereas in dominant cinema the tension between spectacle and narrative is resolved in favour of the latter, the scales are tipped more favourably towards the former in early cinema.

> ...a film like *The Bride Retires* (France, 1902) reveals a fundamental conflict between this exhibitionist tendency of early film and the creation of a fictional diegesis. A woman undresses for bed while her new husband peers at her from behind a screen. However, it is to the camera and the audience that the bride addresses her erotic striptease, winking at us as she faces us, smiling in erotic display.[34]

As we have seen, after 1906 such direct acknowledgement of the camera and the audience becomes increasingly prohibited as the function of the image turned inwards, integrating itself into the self-enclosed unfolding of the fictional world. But because of analogies in the working conditions and practices of early cinema filmmakers and independent videomaking, something of the former's 'exhibitionist tendency' comes through in the latter.

Firstly, low capital resources make single camera production the norm both for early cinema and videomaking today. In early cinema this is evident in the so called tableaux shot, where the scene unfolds from a single vantage point. Single camera production may be one factor encouraging or facilitating a more self conscious mise-en-scène, one aware of its status as a performance for the camera on behalf of a spectator. Tom Gunning has suggested that the filmmakers of the early period were less narrators of hermetically sealed stories (one indicator of a well capitalised industry) than showpeople, exhibiting what mise-en-scène their meagre resources could marshall, for the pleasure and delight of an audience which is acknowledged just as the camera is.[35] This proclivity for exhibitionism is further encouraged by another typical feature of low-budget drama: the stress on the relationship between the solitary performer and the camera, rather than relationships *between* performers. We have already seen how in *Yellow* the two gay protagonists perform (literally) in their separate spaces for the camera. This short circuits the construction of psychological motivation and individual personality, which interaction between performers requires and which is central to classical narrative. However, such narratives require considerable time and skills (script preparation, rehearsals with actors, etc.) and resources, all of which may be in short supply.

Beyond the pragmatic question of resources, the stress which the image of 'attractions' places on performance can help draw attention to the politics of images, as it does in *Yellow*. Performance is imbricated in questions of power, something illustrated by a student video called *Snuff*.[36] The Noirish, blacked out setting for the action contains only a television set (the only source of light), a VCR and a chair. It begins with a male character opening a package and finding a video tape and razor blade inside. He puts the tape into the VCR. A woman appears on screen, directly addressing the character as Graham. It transpires that this is not the first time he has received such a video and such a 'present' from her. Playing on those associations around video's capacity to operate beyond legal or official boundaries and in the realm of vigilantism, *Snuff* neatly reverses the infamous genre associated with the medium, so that now it is the watcher whom the video attacks. For the woman seeks revenge on Graham whose voyeurism and hounding of her sister, Olivier, led to her suicide. *Snuff* draws on and reworks elements of the film noir genre. The sister seeking revenge has some of the qualities of the femme fatale. Her large masculine shirt collars, her hair drawn up into a tight bun, her face half lit, half in shadow, all indicate the dual characteristics of menace and control which are usually reserved for male characters. Unlike the traditional femme fatale, however, this sister's motives are not self-serving, wanting as she does only what all male heroes of the western genre have always desired: justice. At this point, the sister lacks the femme fatale's sexuality. She is too hard, too phallicised to be able to tap into the voyeur's desires. The scene closes with Graham visibly disturbed by her accusations and her attempts to persuade him to take his own life. But he does manage to turn the video off without succumbing to her instructions to use the razor blades. In other words, the performance fails. The next scene opens with another package accompanied this time by pills. On tape, however, the sister has now dressed herself up as Olivier. 'It was insensitive of me to try and lock you out of my life the way I did', she says. 'You only wanted to be close'. And then she implores Graham, this time successfully, to join her in death. As Olivier, the sister has changed her performance, her character now draws on that other staple icon of the film noir, what Janey Place calls 'the nurturing woman'.[37] The nurturing woman stands for the femme fatale's opposite, since she is self-sacrificing and associated with domesticity, loyalty and the family, all of which seems, in the contradictory world of the film noir, to lead to her being a rather sexually repressed figure. In *Snuff* however, the sister/Olivier combines the figure of the nurturing woman with the sexuality typical of the femme fatale. Thus dressed only in a sheet, the sister/Olivier's invitation to Graham to join her in death is phrased in explicitly sexual language.

In many ways one can read *Snuff* as a metaphor of themes close to the heart of contemporary feminist film theory, in particular how women function as erotic spectacle for the 'male' gaze while men are accorded the active role of pushing the narrative along.[38] Significantly, narrative is largely suspended in *Snuff* while power flows from the woman's spectacle/performance on the television screen, which turns the once powerful compulsive act of looking (Olivier was driven to suicide by Graham's gaze) into an achilles' heel (Graham cannot stop watching the videos which lead to his death). It is also interesting how male silence, often a signifier of self-control and mastery of mise-en-scène in contemporary representations, is here inverted so that it is the woman who talks on tape who is powerful and it is the silent, watching Graham who bends to her will.

Ever since Norman Bates dressed up as 'mother' in *Psycho*, transvestism in popular cinema has figured as a convenient marker of 'deviancy', bordering on murderous behaviour. Like *Yellow* and *Snuff*, a student video called *T.V.*[39] makes an intervention into the politics of representation using the exhibitionist mode of 'attractions', although it also makes substantial use of narrative. As

Fig. 4.10

with the early cinema film *The Bride Retires*, this video is built around the tension between these two modes. The video begins in narrative mode with a sequence of domestic interior shots which introduce a heterosexual couple watching television. The woman then leaves and the man watches her from the window as she gets into a car. From a suitcase he then unpacks a dress, stockings, high heels. He puts on these clothes and begins to make up his face. The video then switches into a more display or direct address orientated mode of the cinema of attractions. The image, slowed by the stop-start quality of a strobe effect, has relocated to the exterior public space of the streets, the trains and so on. Our transvestite now performs for the camera rather than as part of a narrative flow (see Fig. 4.10). Again and again in low-budget video, 'spectacular' (in Gunning's sense of the word) poses are used in order to unravel dominant representations, of gender and sexuality in particular.

In *Trevor and Leonard*, for example, the heroes/heroines, dressed as both men and women, pose for the camera on a street corner before embarking on their (narrative) journey. In *Yellow*, the performance articulates an exuberant celebration of, and confidence in, another marginalised and misrepresented sexual identity. In

Bakhtin's words, *T.V.* provides a dialogic rejoinder to the dominant cinematic representation of transvestism.

As if sensing how compromised narrative is when it comes to such representations, *T.V.*'s centrepiece sequence finds affirmation of its subject through direct address. This celebration of the transvestite's identity is supported by passers by who express to camera their wonder at such a figure. This acknowledgement of the camera is central to the excessiveness which helps mark this sequence as a fantasy about and desire for social acceptance. Its fantasy status is confirmed by our return to the interior location in which our character is confined. The return of his partner raises the question about the acceptance/acknowledgement of his transvestism in the private sphere. For the purpose of generating suspense around this question, *T.V.* returns to a more conventional narrative mode. The partner enters the house unbeknown to the transvestite. She climbs the stairs, and prepares to enter the room where he is dressed up. The narrative twist is that his partner already knows about and accepts his transvestism. Thus not only has the cinema of attractions sequence celebrated his gender crossings, but it commits the subsequent return to narrative to retain the affirmation of that celebration. There is an implicit criticism that acceptance within the public spaces remains largely unachieved. As the partner undresses our transvestite protagonist, there is a return to the playful self-conscious cinematic tradition of *The Bride Retires* as a silk scarf drops over the front of the camera.

Conclusion

In this chapter I have discussed the image as a piece of symbolic material wrought out of the active process of selection and combination. Each image can be seen to a certain extent as a discrete product composed of mise-en-scène and videographic elements. However each image is also part of a series of images which have a mutually determining relationship with each other, something which I tried to illustrate in my discussion of metaphor, metonym and symbol. Further, I have suggested that for a mixture of pragmatic and political reasons, the low-budget video image is often inclined to be rather more self-consciously orientated towards the audience and towards the politics of the mise-en-scène, videography and performance, than in dominant film and television, where the image is generally fully subordinated into the flow of the narrative.

However, the politics of the image must also be grasped by understanding that the image also relates to other images of the same referent beyond the text; these images and indeed other symbolic materials (print, sound) are in general social circulation and the images you produce are, inescapably, in dialogue with them. Any reading of those images (say for example *T.V.'s* images of transvestism, or *Halt's* images of war and gender) in relation to the concept of realism is governed by three factors: a) the relationships of similarity and difference that your symbolic material has with other symbolic materials in circulation; b) the relationship between that symbolic material and the real world; and c), the politics of the producers and consumers of those images.

Practical exercises

- Set up a scene which can be framed with one shot, say someone at a table writing a letter, or working on a keyboard. Shoot the scene for about ten seconds, including camera movement if you wish. Think about how your framing has selected and emphasised particular mise-en-scène elements. Now shoot the scene again, but using a different set of videographic variables (framing, camera angle, distance, height, etc.). How has the different rendering of the mise-en-scène changed the shot? Does it draw your attention to different aspects and does this change the way one might potentially read the image?

- Try shooting the scene for a third time, now introducing a new prop into the scene. Again what differences can be noted? What three narrative contexts can you imagine that would make the new prop, a) a metaphor, b) a metonym, c) a symbol?

Notes

1 R. Williams, *Keywords*, Fontana, London 1983, pp.257-262.
2 B. Brecht, 'Against Georg Lukacs' in *Aesthetics and Politics*,Verso, London 1988, p.82.
3 See B. Henderson's 'Two Types of Film Theory' in *Movies and Methods*, vol. 1, University of California Press, London 1976, pp. 388-400. Henderson discusses the failure of Eisenstein and Bazin to develop their theories in relation to the formal organisation of entire films.
4 A. Bazin, *What Is Cinema?* vol 1, University of California Press, London 1967, p.12.
5 B. Nichols, *Ideology and the Image*, Indiana University Press, Bloomington, 1981, p.20.
6 R. Arnheim, *Film as Art*, University of California Press, Berkeley, 1971.

7 Nichols, *op. cit.*, p.20.
8 J. Berger, *Ways of Seeing*, BBC and Penguin Books, London 1972, pp.16-18.
9 Berger, *ibid*, p.18.
10 E.H. Gombrich, *Art and Illusion*, Phaidon Press, London 1962, pp. 179-181.
11 Quoted in J. Tulloch, *Television Drama*, Routledge, London 1990, p.161.
12 L. Masterman, *Teaching the Media*, Comedia, London 1986, p. 138.
13 D. Andrew, Concepts in Film Theory, OUP, Oxford 1984, p.21.
14 P. Gidal, *Materialist Film*, Routledge, London 1989, p.13, 15.
15 D. Hall,'Before the Concrete Sets' in London Video Access *Catalogue*, 1991, p.42.
16 J. Sturrock, *Structuralism and Since: From Levi-Strauss to Derrida*, OUP, London 1979, p.9.
17 See E. P. Thompson's critique of Althusser's brand of conventionalism in *The Poverty of Theory and Other Essays*, London 1978, p.18.
18 V. N. Voloshinov, *Marxism and the Philosophy of Language*, Seminar Press, New York 1973.
19 M. M. Bakhtin, *The Dialogic Imagination*, University of Texas Press, Austin 1992, p.276.
20 T. Hawkes, *Structuralism and Semiotics*, Methuen, 1977, p.77.
21 T. T. Minh-Ha, 'The Totalising Quest for Meaning' in *When the Moon Waxes Red*, Routledge, London 1991, p.34.
22 R. Williams, *op. cit.*, p.217.
23 Made by Tim Hicks (Brunel University College, 1994).
24 Made by Paul Lawes (Brunel University College, 1994).
25 B. Balazs, *Theory of Film: Character and Growth of a New Art*, Dover Publications, New York 1970, P.63.
26 Balazs, *ibid*, P.75.
27 E. Aston and G. Savona, *Theatre as Sign System: A Semiotics of Text and Performance*, Routledge, London 1991, p.154.
28 K. Elam, *The Semiotics of Theatre and Drama*, Methuen, London 1980, p.76
29 J. A. Place and L. S. Peterson, 'Some Visual Motifs of Film Noir' in *Movies and Methods* vol. 1, California Press, London 1976, pp.325-338.
30 D. Bordwell et al, *The Classical Hollywood Cinema*, Routledge, London 1988, p.113.
31 T. Gunning, 'The Cinema of Attractions, Early Film, Its Spectator and the Avant-Garde' in *Early Cinema: Space, Frame, Narrative*, BFI, 1990, p.59.
32 Gunning, *ibid*, p.58 (my emphasis).
33 Gunning, *ibid*, p.61.
34 Gunning, *ibid*, p.57.
35 T. Gunning, 'Primitive Cinema: A Frame Up? or The Trick's On Us' in *Early Cinema, op. cit.*, p.100.
36 Made by Karen Thrussell (Brunel University College, 1995).
37 J. Place, 'Women in Film Noir' in *Women in Film Noir*, BFI, 1978, p.50
38 L. Mulvey, 'Visual Pleasure and Narrative Cinema' in *Screen*, vol 16, no. 3, Autumn 1975.
39 Made by Clare Burgess, Leigh Butler, Andy Fairbairn, Kendra Pertott, Gareth Thomas, Nicola Willats (Brunel University College, 1994).

Chapter Five

Editing

We began the last chapter with a discussion and critique of a theory, articulated most cogently by Andre Bazin, that tried to suggest affinities between the camera and the images it produces, and everyday seeing. Here is Dziga Vertov writing in the context of the revolutionary upheavals and artistic experiments in the early years of the Soviet Union, outlining a rather different conception of the camera, the images it produces and the implications of combining those images into sequences:

> I am an eye. A mechanical eye. I, the machine, show you a world the way only I can see it. I free myself for today and forever from human immobility. I'm in constant movement. I approach and pull away from objects. I creep under them. I move alongside a running horse's mouth. I fall and rise with the falling and rising bodies. This is I, the machine, manoeuvring in the chaotic movements, recording one movement after another in the most complex combinations. Freed from the boundaries of time and space, I co-ordinate any and all points of the universe, wherever I want them to be. My way leads towards the creation of a fresh perception of the world. Thus I explain in a new way the world unknown to you.[1]

What is stressed here is the radically dissimilar nature of the 'mechanical' eye to the human eye. In particular, Vertov – with a characteristically modernist stress on the medium's own 'ways of seeing' – identifies editing as centrally important in constructing fresh perspectives on the world. Editing is the means by which the visual images you construct are organised into certain kinds of relationships with one another. Bordwell and Thompson define editing simply as the co-ordination of one shot with the next. To be able to 'cut' (an anachronistic word for video editing where images are manipulated electronically rather than by hand) from one scene to another, or from one part of a scene to another angle or vantage point within the same scene, opens up enormous creative possibilities. But it also raises the question of how to 'move' the spectator around in space and time in a way that is meaningful to them. The issue here is what kind of 'meanings' you are trying to construct. There are different traditions of editing but there is no 'right' or 'wrong' way of co-ordinating the visuals. It all depends on what you are trying to achieve and what is suitable for you. However, I will be suggesting that your position as a low-budget videomaker does have certain implications for the way you use the dominant system for constructing time and space: continuity editing. After outlining the conventions of continuity editing we will look at the different degrees to which continuity of time and space can be sustained and transgressed. We will also look at the principal editing alternative to continuity editing, known as montage. What must be stressed, however, is that whatever editing strategies you deploy, editing is not to be thought of as merely a convenient technical processes, onto which you then map the more interesting possibilities of narrative, sound, genre, etc. More than a technical necessity, editing is central to the processes by which you produce meanings.

Invisible continuity editing

Hollywood became famous for its invisible editing. This meshed together so smoothly, so neatly and so seamlessly the different shots, that the fact that the audience were being 'moved' about in time and space, was almost imperceptible to them. The editing joins became invisible. This effect is achieved by making sure that the spatial and temporal relationships are absolutely clear and without ambiguity, and that complete continuity is maintained through a whole ensemble of strategies. These are as follows:

a) the long shot, sometimes known as the establishing shot because it establishes for the viewer, the overall space in which the action is going to unfold.

b) medium shots and close-ups, the mainstay of what is sometimes called analytical editing, because they allow for more detailed examination of a scene and any important action that takes place within it. While continuity editing requires moving from establishing shots to mid and close-up shots, invisible continuity editing will strive to keep the number of camera positions, and relationships between shots, as simple as possible. So for example typically there will be one position which will function as the 'master' establishing shot. There is no intrinsic reason why there needs to be only one, but to have two or three different positions would prompt the audience to start comparing these long shots and questioning what is at stake in these different overall viewpoints on the action. In other words, the audiences' attention would be drawn to the editing and its invisibility would be shattered. But with invisible editing the one position for the establishing shot will probably be used more than once. The editing moves continually from close-ups, back out to medium shots, and if it is necessary, to the long shot once more to re-establish the overall space of the action in the mind of the audience. Edits from long shot to close-up are prohibited since invisible continuity editing strives to keep the graphics (the size and shape of people and objects in shot) relatively similar from shot to shot.

c) match on action establishes a continuity of movement across the break between shots. If you want to shoot a character getting up out of a chair from one position, then film them leaving the room from another camera position, a match on action will ensure that after the shot in which the character stands up, we 'rejoin' the scene from the other viewpoint while they are still beside the chair, or even still in the process of getting up. It would be a break in the continuity of action if from the shot when they stood up, we jumped to a shot of the character half way through the door.

d) the 180° rule is an imaginary line which guides the placement of the cameras within a semi-circular space so that when the footage is edited spatial continuity between characters will be maintained. Diagram 5.1 demonstrates the space that the camera can occupy when shooting two characters in conversation. If the camera was placed in the space beyond the 180° line, continuity could not be preserved at the editing stage. If A and B were both in shot then the two characters would have inexplicably swapped positions within the frame. But if only one of the characters, say A, was in shot then he would now be looking in the same direction (right to left) which B had occupied in previous shots. Character A would then appear (again inexplicably) to have turned his back on B. If the 180° rule is obeyed then typically two people talking would be constructed through the use of shot / reverse / shot. Here the camera observes the person talking from a position close to the character listening, but at about 45° off the 180° line. Although the listener does not occupy onscreen space, it is understood by the viewer that it is the listener to whom the speaker is addressing themselves. When the listener becomes the talker, the shot construction can be reversed.

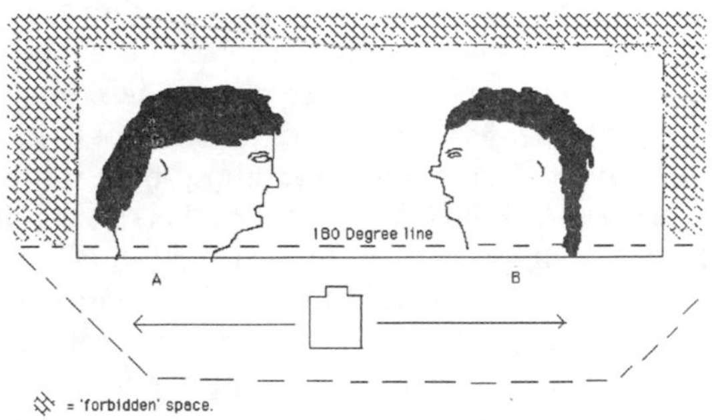

Fig. 5.1

e) the eyeline match 'matches' the continuity of onscreen and off-screen space as indicated by the direction of the character's gaze or glance. Of course editing can only do this if the 180° rule is obeyed.

Together, this ensemble of strategies ensured that the process of editing remained as imperceptible as possible. Its job was to subordinate itself to the telling of the story. As Hollywood formed itself into the powerful industry that would dominate world film markets, the criteria for invisible editing became the accepted norm for filmmakers within the industry and around the world. It is important then to bear in mind that continuity is a product of quite specific historical circumstances. There may be times when it suits your purposes to draw on this still dominant style. However, it is not a norm to which all film or videomakers need to adhere to if they feel their circumstances and their priorities are different from the dominant film and television organisations.

If we look at two early Russian filmmakers, Lev Kuleshov and V.I. Pudovkin, we can begin to distinguish between Hollywood's invisible style of continuity editing and alternative styles of what is still, broadly, continuity editing. Unlike their compatriot, Sergei Eisenstein, Kuleshov and Pudovkin were interested in continuity editing but their technique is looser, more flexible, more expressive than their Hollywood contemporaries. From a Hollywood point of view, their editing would be seen as flawed and rough. But it is not because these editors were inept that their editing differed from Hollywood's invisible style.

Kuleshov and Pudovkin are exemplary figures for a number of reasons. Firstly, they were theorists as well as practitioners – an integration this book advocates. They experimented with the possibilities of cinema and then integrated their experiments into films. They would then reflect on these possibilities, categorise them and suggest the best ways of maximising these possibilities further. One does not have to agree with everything they write to see the fruitfulness of this for themselves and for others. Secondly, reading their work at the other end of the century, the sense of their excitement at the possibilities of filmic representation has obvious parallels with the experience of the aspirant videomaker. Thirdly, their conditions of work – which had implications for what they produced – were more analogous to some of the features of low-budget videomaking than those of filmmakers working in Hollywood, now or in the past. It could be argued that Hollywood institutionalised invisible continuity editing because it assumed that audience pleasure was derived from concentrating on the content of what is shot. And of course it is in the content of what is shot (sets, costume, stars, lighting) that Hollywood movies spend a lot of their budgets on.

Obviously, as a low-budget videomaker on the margins of the audiovisual industry the huge capital resources available to Hollywood are not accessible to you. This may require you to think about whether the invisible style of editing is always appropriate for you. Your lack of a capital base should not necessarily be seen as a disadvantage. Since profitability is not the driving force of your work, it means that there is a greater opportunity for you to explore the boundaries of continuity editing, to develop a more varied and expressive style of continuity editing by exploring where the rules can be bent, and where they can be broken, while still maintaining a more or less coherent story world. This is exactly what Kuleshov and Pudovkin did. But if they were to develop a more central and experimental role for editing than their Hollywood counterparts, like you today, it was Hollywood that formed their initial point of reference when it came to exploring their new medium.

Kuleshov and Pudovkin

In the pre-Revolutionary days Kuleshov was working as part of a group of filmmakers exploring this new medium of film. What interested them in particular was the question: what made film different from theatre, from photography? Did film have qualities that were specific to it alone? Kuleshov tells how his group shot a scene, with, as he puts it 'superb actors, with superb scenes in superb settings'.[3] Yet when they studied the results, they concluded that what they had shot was not cinema. It was simply a record of a theatrical performance. Having filmed something but finding that what they had filmed was not 'cinema', they decided to go to the cinemas to observe what audiences were watching and how they responded to the moving image. In those days of 'silent' cinema (though the cinema was rarely silent, there was almost always some form of verbal or musical accompaniment), audiences watched cinema in a very vocal way, particularly according to Kuleshov, the Russian working classes:

> if the public was pleased by a particular scene in the picture, it applauded, shouting its approval; whereas if something in particular displeased it, it whistled and demonstrated its indignation unmistakeably.[4]

Kuleshov and company noticed that the American films were the most popular. They drew the loudest responses and this suggested that they had the biggest impact on the audience. So Kuleshov and his colleagues went back to their workshop and studied American movies. Comparing them with Russian films, they noticed that their dynamicism lay in 'a whole series of very short shots, of whole series of brief sequences … [whereas Russian films at that time had] a few very long scenes, one after the other.'[5]

To compare the lack of editing and reliance on the long shot within Russian films at that time, with the dynamic editing of the American films, Kuleshov came up with an analogy of a painted fence. If you are walking along a fence and for five miles it is red and then for five miles it is blue and then for five miles it is green, then the shifts from one colour to another will hardly be very exciting. But if the colour of the fence changes every few paces or so, then the alternation of the colours and the vibrancy of their contrasts will be all the more striking. Kuleshov writes:

> we became convinced that the fundamental source of the film's impact on the viewer – a source present only in cinema – was not simply to show the content of certain shots, but the organisation of certain shots among

> themselves, their combination and construction, that is the interrelationships between shots, the replacement of one shot by another. This is the basic means that produces the impact of cinematography on the viewer … the joining of two shots of different content and the method of their alternation.[6]

As I have suggested, what was subsequently to distinguish the Russians' interest in continuity editing from the American style, was their concern to keep the organisation and interrelationships of shots at the forefront of the viewer's perception. Hollywood by contrast developed a style that allowed it to use the benefits of continuity editing, while at the same time minimising its presence for the viewer.

Having found in editing what they thought to be the specificity of cinema, Kuleshov's group set about experimenting with editing's capacity to construct relations of time and space. Recalling one such experiment, Kuleshov describes how they filmed two actors:

> Khokhlova is walking along Petrov street in Moscow … Obolensky is walking along … the Moscow River … about two miles away. [This appears to be an exercise in cutting between two spatially separate events happening at the same time – but in fact it becomes clear that Kuleshov is showing how editing manipulates time and space and that these shots, in the context of Kuleshov's experiment, function as establishing shots.] They see each other, smile [eyeline match] and begin to walk toward one another [providing that one is walking to the left and one is walking to the right of the screen, this is a match on action]. Their meeting is filmed at the Boulevard Prechistensk [establishing shot]. This boulevard is in an entirely different section of the city. They clasp hands [match on action] … and look at the White House! [eyeline match].[7]

This is a good example of the attitude the Russians maintained towards film which they saw as a medium whose capacities and potentialities could not be assumed but needed to be explored. For American filmmakers, the possibility of having film workshops and laboratories diminished as the medium became commodified as a profitable mass entertainment industry. The example set here by Kuleshov certainly seems to strike more of a chord with the structural position of the videomaker on the margins of the corporate media industries, than with the working practices which ossified into unchallengeable norms in Hollywood. Kuleshov's experiment demonstrates the constructedness of meaning when one shot is joined with the next. And this construction does not begin at the end of the shooting process, in the editing room, but at the beginning, when you first conceive of a scene and how you are going to 'cut' that scene up into little fragments and re-assemble them in a particular order. When you first start thinking in terms of scenes you will probably be inclined to think of scenes as a whole, as a more or less complete unrolling of action. The frame of mind you need to think yourself into is one more attuned to the choices and decisions that go into building a scene step by step. As Kuleshov's experiment demonstrates, what you are working with is editing's powers of suggestion. Take for example, as a simple exercise, a car accident involving a pedestrian. You do not have the resources to film this sort of scene 'realistically', so what you would need to do is think how editing could construct an accident without it ever happening in reality, just as Kuleshov constructed an entirely imaginative meeting between two people.

Another famous Kuleshov experiment prompted thoughts about the role of the actor in cinema. This experiment was recounted by Pudovkin who was a member of the Kuleshov group. They filmed the facial expression of a well known Russian actor. They then cut this shot of the actor's face against a bowl of soup; then against a woman in a coffin; and then again with a child playing. According to Pudovkin when audiences watched this they read the face as meaning different things (hunger, pity, love) because they were constructing the meaning of the face by its juxtaposition with the other shots. Yet it was the same facial expression. Thus the argument went, the meaning(s) of the face did not reside in the acting, but in the editing.[8]

This led Kuleshov and Pudovkin to theorise the role of the actor in cinema as different from the theatre. Both directors declared themselves to be against psychologism. Kuleshov quotes a director as saying to him: 'cinema is not when the hero loses at cards, but when, standing by a window, he looks at the street and thinks about having lost'. Thus, psychologism requires the suspension of editing in favour of the camera humbly recording the actor's articulation of their role. Kuleshov and Pudovkin thought that the actor in cinema must be defined by their actions, by their physical movements, and by their physical appearance. They called for types, that is characters which, according to Kuleshov, 'physically present some kind of interest for cinematic treatment'.[9]

This is absolutely consistent with the Kuleshov group's earlier argument that film does not begin when actors act, but when the director begins to combine and join together in various combinations what is shot. The preference for types was to further affect the style of editing that was to develop. For these directors were interested in the movement and expression of the type, and capturing this was more important than always precisely and invisibly placing the actor in time and space. In other words, their interest in movement and the expressiveness of the body, means producing a loose, flexible and perceptible editing style. Of course today the notion that acting involves expressing inner feelings based on a detailed psychological profile, is not only familiar, but remains one of the dominant, and certainly one of the most prestigious traditions of acting. Kuleshov and Pudovkin's thinking about the role of the actor in relation to cinema is again strikingly useful for the videomaker. It is very likely that you may be using people who have little or no training in what most people take to be 'acting'. Yet acting need not be confined to the expression of psychology. Think about how you can use movement, expression, and the physical features of the body to articulate meanings in conjunction with editing. Thought of in these terms, acting becomes rather less mysterious and daunting.

The Mother

Let us take Pudovkin's *The Mother* (USSR, 1926) in order to investigate this editing style in more detail. The mother is first introduced in an interior long shot. She is busy in the kitchen: pots and pans occupy the foreground, she is hanging up a tunic in the mid-ground, slightly left of centre. We then cut to a close-up shot of her adult son, asleep. If you were to study the shot which introduces the mother without being distracted by the busy movements of this new character, you would just spot her son's legs in the background. But in terms of classical Hollywood editing this introduction to the two characters would be impermissible. The close-up on the son might be said to leave audiences wondering (needlessly) about the spatial relationships between the mother and the son. But from the point of view of the Russian tradition, such confusion would be beside the point, since the significance of this sequence lies in the juxtaposition of the mother busily working and the son peacefully sleeping. The film then cuts to an exterior shot of the father arriving home, drunk. We then cut to a medium close-up of him from behind, opening the door of the house and standing in the doorway. Next, an interior medium shot of the mother (Fig. 5.2). She is hunched, almost doubled over her tasks, as if her oppression were an invisible weight pushing down on her. She looks screen right, responding presumably to the

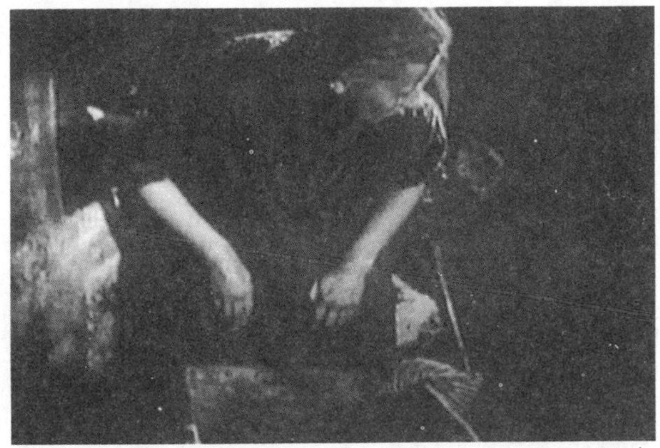

Fig. 5.2

Fig. 5.3

Fig. 5.4

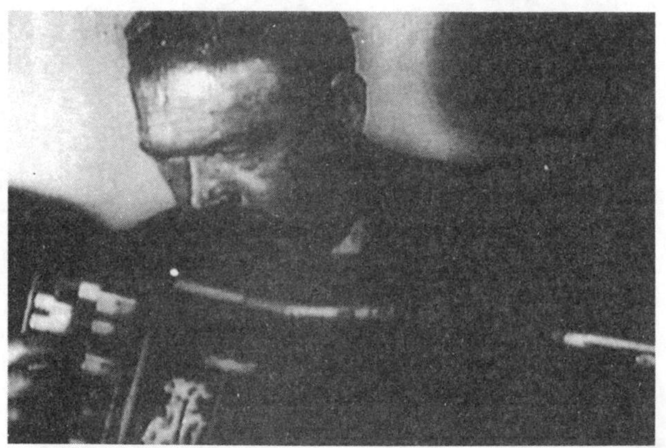

Fig. 5.5

entrance of the father, but note that her look does not function as a strong eyeline match. Her hunched position means her look is angled more towards the floor rather than giving any definite sense of offscreen space. The look is indicative of the father's presence, but that is all it needs to do and indeed a stronger eyeline match would contradict the meaning of the mother in this scene: oppressed, browbeaten. The scene then proceeds as follows:

6. Long Shot (L.S.) of father in the doorway, looking towards the camera. He staggers three paces forward.
7. Medium close-up (M.C.U.) of upper chest and face.
8. Medium Shot (M.S.) of the son, still asleep.
9. M.C.U of the father.
10. Fuzzy Point of View shot (P.O.V.) from the father, of the clock on the wall.

Shot 6 would be unusual although not impermissible within Hollywood's invisible style of editing. It is unusual because the camera is placed on the 180° line and so the father is looking into the camera. From a Hollywood point of view, this risks drawing the audiences' attention to the camera and the editing. However, it would be permissible if the audience could now read this shot as occupying the physical location of the mother. This would help give some narrative motivation for the cutaway, and therefore make it a little less 'intrusive' as far as the classical Hollywood style is concerned. Yet by the time we get to the point of view shot of the father (Shot 10), it becomes clear that he is not looking at the mother at all, but the clock on the wall. While the viewer's sense of spatial relationships is disturbed by this, our surprise to find that the father is not even looking at the mother, serves to underline to emptiness of their relationship. (The father will attempt to sell bits of the clock to buy more vodka). The transition from Shot 6 to 7 also transgresses the rules of invisible editing. The cut is very noticeable because we have simply moved down the 180° line. To make this cut less visible, a Hollywood film would have cut to a shot of the father from an angle with at least 45° difference from the preceding shot. Pudovkin, however, is not concerned with making the shots invisible, but rather with the impact of the editing on the viewer. Thus the 'jump' in the image from Shot 6 to Shot 7 underlines the threatening presence of the father.

In the scenes that follow, Pudovkin refrains from giving us a long shot that would establish the exact spatial relationships between the mother and the father and the position of thewallclock within the kitchen. Instead the shots cut back from one protagonist to the other. By refusing to place them in the same shot, our attention is focused on their particular body movements and expressions. Only when the father attempts to take the clock down from the wall, do the two protagonists share the same shot. For now the mother rushes into the frame and struggles with the father, who is standing on a stool. But even now the shot construction that follows is characterised by a concentration on one or the other of the two protagonists, even though they are next to each other. Thus we get:

C.U. of the mother's hands on the father.

High angle M.C.U. on the mother struggling.

C.U. of the mother's hands on the father.

Low angle M.C.U. of the father, swaying.

C.U. of the stool falling.

C.U. of clock being ripped from the wall.

M.S. of the father falling to the floor.

C.U. on the clock smashing on the floor.

The editing here is primarily concerned to highlight and contrast the actions and movements of the two characters, bringing out the features which have cinematic interest, as well as following separately the fall of the father and the fall of the clock. We can also see in this sequence of shots the imprint of Pudovkin's working practices. For he insisted that '[s]eparate, interrupted shooting is indispensable' if any film is to construct, through its editing, the multi-faceted nuances of a scene.[10]

In the scene which follows, we are introduced to the local bar. The scene begins with an interior long shot of the bar. As we see from Fig. 5.3, it is crowded. During the shot, one or two characters stagger around drunk. In Fig. 5.3, a well-lit bartender stands out in mid-background, to the right of the frame. He stands listlessly. This shot is then contrasted with a side-on medium shot of three accordion players (Fig. 5.4). We then jump back to the initial long shot (Fig. 5.3), and sure enough two of the three accordion players are just visible to the left in the extreme background of the shot. From a Hollywood point of view, this long shot fails to adequately establish the locations and the spatial relationships of the characters who are going to figure in the subsequent shots.

But again it is all relative. Pudovkin is concerned to establish continuity of spatial and temporal relations, but only loosely, especially the spatial relations. Thus the opening three shots, released from the injunction to be invisible, use editing to bring out the different nuances of life in the bar. In this example, the drunken listlessness of the bar is juxtaposed with the energy of the three accordion players. The fourth shot reintroduces us to the musicians. Then there is a sequence of three shots between the three players. A medium close-up of one, a low-angle, side on view, shows him sweating and agonising over his instrument. A level close-up of a second shows him to be a sombre and steady player (Fig. 5.5). Then we cut to a big close-up of the third, smiling happily into the camera. Again, the meaning of each of these shots of the three accordion players is built up through mutual interaction and contrast with one another. The editing is deliberately obvious in order to emphasise these contrasts.

Pudovkin's fascination with the way editing constructs meaning is evident in the smallest details. A medium shot of a stout barman looking bottom left (Fig. 5.6) is followed by a big close-up of a half eaten piece of fish on a plate (Fig. 5.7). We then cut to the barman scratching his face and looking from bottom left to the right of the frame. The plate of fish could have been placed in the initial shot of the barman and indeed would have been in a classical Hollywood film just to reinforce the spectator's absolute command over and anticipation of the flow of shots and the spatial relationships they construct. But for this film, to place the plate in the same shot as the barman would make the big close-up of the fish redundant since the viewer would already know what the barman is looking at. Watching *The Mother*, one is very aware of the capacity of editing to surprise the viewer and to keep demanding that we construct the spatial relations and the subsequent meanings between shots. The film then introduces the Black Hundred: strike breakers. As with the previous scene between the mother and father, a long shot establishing the spatial relationships between the various members of the Black Hundred is withheld until very late in the sequence. Again, as with the representation of the accordion players, the editing cuts rapidly between the various characters, bringing out the nuanced differences of their character types. These range from the ugly, violent types tearing into their food while their leader talks to

Fig. 5.6

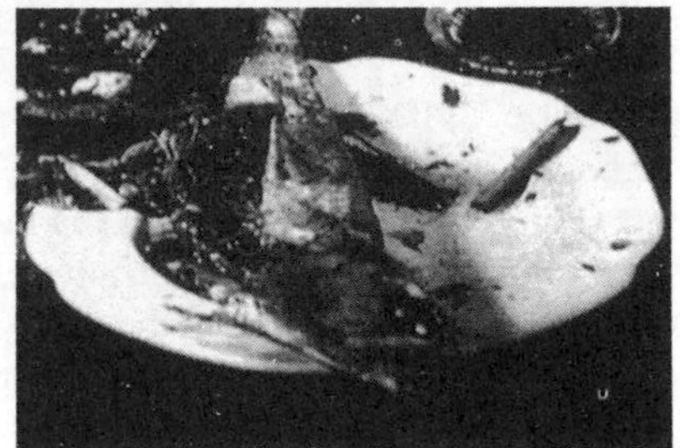

Fig. 5.7

Fig. 5.8

them, to the type represented in Fig. 5.8: heavy set, dependable, listening attentively, intelligent and with a semblance of being well-groomed. It is only when their leader has united them in their purpose to break the strike, that Pudovkin uses a long shot to confirm their close spatial proximity. But this is not some belated gesture towards continuity editing, rather the all inclusive shot functions symbolically to represent them as a united force about to make its intervention into the class struggle.

An example of a similar strategy from a more contemporary film underlines Pudovkin's relevance to the present. Med Hondo's film *Sarraounia*, already mentioned in chapter four, is a story about the Western European drive to colonise Africa. In an early sequence the film shows the military conflicts between different African tribes. The editing shows two armies appearing to share the same space and engaged in conflict. As with Pudovkin, however, the film deliberately witholds the kind of classical establishing shot that would unambiguously locate the two tribes in the same space. For this would encourage the spectator to concentrate on the action and excitement of the battle. Rather than offering the spectator a vicarious experience, *Sarraounia* wants us to understand the historical significance and political implications of the battle in relation to the coming white colonialist expansion. Cutting between the two tribes but refusing a unified view of the event underscores the point that what is important here is that already established conflicts between the African tribes undermined unified black resistance against the Europeans. A representation of conflict between Africans is also articulated by mise-en-scene and by cinematic elements, such as the contrasting colours of the combatants (orange and white) , the choice of lens selected for shooting each tribe (wide angle for one, telephoto for another) and the direction of the figure movement in relation to the camera (one tribe is shown moving rapidly left to right across the screen, the other is shot on horseback, moving at a leisurely pace towards the camera). It is important to remember how editing works in conjunction with the elements discussed in relation to the image.

Pudovkin's five modes of editing

Pudovkin identifies five ways of mobilising editing for different effects. We can illustrate three of these modes operating towards the end of the Hollywood film *High Noon* (Fred Zinnemann, USA 1952). I am thinking of the sequence of shots which juxtaposes the sheriff writing his will, the men on the outskirts of town who have come to kill him, and various members of the town who have in one way or another abandoned the sheriff to his fate. The editing here is perceptible and expressive and so would seem to contradict the claim that Hollywood developed an invisible style of editing. Indeed Hollywood films are a good resource for examples of just such expressive editing. But the Hollywood film can only sustain such a foregrounding of the editing for short bursts and, crucially, this expressivity must be motivated by the narrative. The momentary foregrounding of editing in *High Noon* is motivated by the fact that the gunfight is about to commence and that the sheriff has exhausted all the avenues for help. After this brief flourish, the editing then subsides back into the narrative flow of the film.

i) Contrast

In *High Noon* the film juxtaposes three shots (shots with three people in them), two shots and one shots and mixes these as close-ups, medium shots and long shots of the various characters that the film has previously introduced us to. The nature of the contrasts at work here is largely stylistic. Pudovkin had in mind contrasts that brought out thematic and conceptual meanings as well:

> the miserable situation of a starving man ... will impress the more vividly if associated with mention of the senseless gluttony of a well-to-do man.[11]

Pudovkin does not mention it, but editing might also work to establish similarities between shots. For example, shots juxtaposing objects with people may signify similarities (metaphors) at the level of position, physique or character/psychology. Alternatively, two or more subjects of a similar shape but contrasting or opposing meanings may be juxtaposed.

ii) Simultaneity

This involves crosscutting between two or more narrative strands, with the understanding that the events are taking place simultaneously and that the narrative strands are converging and therefore are going to have an impact on one another. This, of course, is a classic device of Hollywood films and is at work in *High Noon*. Indeed, the momentary expressivity of the editing is permitted precisely because it signifies the point of convergence between the pardoned outlaws seeking to avenge themselves on the sheriff, the collective cowardice of the town, and the subsequent isolation of the sheriff. The message of this expressive editing is that the gunfight is imminent.

iii) Leitmotif

This involves the reiteration of a theme through the visual repetition of shots. In *High Noon* the repeated shots of the clock ticking its way to the time appointed for the gunfight, signifies that time has run out for the sheriff. There are also shots of the chair in which the leading villain once promised to return to the town, thus the motif of revenge – central to the western genre – is signalled. Note how the motif can only be accommodated within dominant cinema, if it underlines and drives that plot onwards. We will see later in the chapter on narrative that there are possibilities for allowing motifs a more independent role.

iv) Parallelism

As Pudovkin notes, the contrast mode of editing may well overlap and work within the parallel mode, but the latter has considerably wider structural implications for a text. It has some affiliation with simultaneity in that parallel editing weaves two or more distinct narrative strands. Where it differs is that the narrative strands are not necessarily to be read as happening at the same time, but even if they are – and this is the key feature of parallelism – the narrative strands remain separate from one another and do not converge or run into one another. The viewer is thus invited to construct conceptual links between the narrative strands but not cause and effect links between the narrative strands. Parallelism is a key editing strategy for the low-budget videomaker and is explored in more detail in the chapter on narrative.

v) Symbolism

This is a rather vague catch-all term. Pudovkin gives as an example of this kind of editing: the famous juxtaposition in Sergei Eisenstein's film *Strike* (USSR, 1924). Here, shots of the workers being fired upon by the army are cut against a bull having its throat slit. In fact Pudovkin uses a similar editing strategy at the end of *Mother*, when shots of the workers demonstrating are cut against the lyrical image of the ice thawing on the river. Such editing tries to heighten an emotional response on the part of a viewer by constructing associative links between different events. Indeed, Eisenstein called this example of editing emotional or associative editing. In Eisenstein's film the slaughter of the workers is underlined and emphasised by the Grand Guignol juxtaposition with the slaughtering of the bull. In

Pudovkin's film the thawing of the ice underlines the emergence of the workers' militance and class consciousness. In both these examples, the images do not come together with an equal weighting. One is dominant, while the other, in a subordinate position, functions to emphasise and foreground meanings already implicit in the dominant image. Thus Eisenstein is not suggesting that the shooting down of the workers and the killing of the bull are directly comparable; nor is Pudovkin suggesting that nature has a role to play in revolutionary struggles. The images of both the bull and the thawing river are essentially used metaphorically, to give a shocking quality to events in Eisenstein's film and an epic quality to events in Pudovkin's. However, this hardly exhausts the possibilities of this kind of editing, its general cultural implications or its relevance to the videomaker. But in order to explore this mode of editing further we need to turn our attention to Sergei Eisenstein, one of the Soviet film-makers who explored in theory and practice the multi-dimensional possibilities of what he called montage.

Montage and Eisenstein

A French word, literally meaning assemblage, montage was at the centre of a debate between Eisenstein and Pudovkin which occurred during the 1920s. Like Kuleshov and Pudovkin, Eisenstein believed that editing was the essence of cinema. Thus like Kuleshov and Pudovkin he was not interested in the 'content' of shots for their own sake, but rather with the way shots (and their content) were 'assembled'. However, Eisenstein disagreed with Kuleshov and Pudovkin over the way this assemblage was to be conceived. Eisenstein quoted with dismay Kuleshov's statement that the editor's job of joining shots together was like the bricklayer's job of placing bricks end to end. This analogy may indeed over-emphasise the smoothness of the editing of Kuleshov and, in particular, Pudovkin. However, Eisenstein's objection was more that, as he shrewdly pointed out, if this was the principle underlying the development of editing, it would lead to 'mere evolutionary "perfecting"' where the style would aspire to become increasingly polished and invisible in the manner of Hollywood.[12]

We have seen how Pudovkin remained loosely concerned with spatial continuity, while remaining more closely bound to temporal continuity. Eisenstein, however, while retaining an interest in constructing narratives, wanted to continue to push and explore the possibilities of assembling shots in a variety of combinations. Thus he regarded Kuleshov and Pudovkin's conception of editing as 'linkage' as only one form of montage, neither to be rejected outright nor raised as a standard to which filmmaking should aspire. For Eisenstein such a standard would merely call an arbitrary halt to what he saw as an ongoing endeavour. He was ready to sacrifice spatial continuity to a considerable degree in order to explore 'the potentialities of formal development'.[13] His films also played with temporal relations to a much greater degree than either Kuleshov or Pudovkin were prepared to do. Indeed, while they worked, albeit loosely within the conventions of continuity editing, Eisenstein developed a much more 'aggressive' theory of editing, one that stressed the discontinuities between shots. For him montage referred to the collision, the conflict, the clash between shots. Here is Eisenstein discussing a familiar scene:

> '1. A hand lifts a knife.
>
> 2. The eyes of the victim open suddenly.
>
> 3. His hands clutch the table.
>
> 4. The knife is jerked up.
>
> 5. The eyes blink involuntarily.
>
> 6. Blood gushes
>
> 7. A mouth shrieks.
>
> 8. Something drips onto a shoe…
>
> and similar film cliches. Nevertheless, in regard to the action as a whole, each fragment-piece is almost abstract.'[14]

For Eisenstein, plot only provides the rationale to communicate something to an audience, but notions of spatial and temporal unity should not be allowed to determine the method of communication. Thus the idea of murder which this hypothetical plot requires, could be constructed by assembling 'each fragment-piece' in any number of different orders and with any number of repetitions. Each version would then generate different associations according to the chosen collisions between the shots. Eisenstein's tabulation of this typical murder scene interestingly brings out the differences between himself and Pudovkin as well as the way Pudovkin's editing strategies departed from Hollywood's continuity style. With its sustained use of the close-up and attention to so many various parts of the body, the scene as tabulated corresponds closely to the way

Pudovkin might have edited it whereas the socialised reflexes of a Hollywood filmmaker would probably have inserted more medium and long shots to frame both participants, and to emphasise what Eisenstein calls 'the action as a whole' over and above 'each fragment piece'.

For Eisenstein conflict was a general artistic principle. He did not see the notion of a collision between elements as peculiar to film editing. He could point to the way Japanese haiku poetry works by constructing 'montage phrases', or the way, when scanning a painting, the eye is confronted with a plethora of conflicting elements (colour, brush stroke) which comprise the painting's dynamism.[15] The centrality of an aesthetics based on conflict and juxtaposition links Eisenstein to a wave of modernist-inspired theories and cultural practices, whose attacks on the bastions of established art intensified as the horrors of the first world war unfolded. Dadaism and Surrealism both used the method of juxtaposition to shock and unsettle their audiences' preconceptions. The link with Eisenstein could not be clearer for he preferred to describe montage editing as a series of shocks jolting the viewer. The aesthetic justification for this assault on the audience can be found articulated in the Russian Formalist school of thought. This grouping of largely literary artists argued that established art was composed of tired and worn conventions which the reader passively used just to get them through a book or poem. Such art was unable to articulate any fresh perspectives on life. The Formalists advocated the formal strategy of *Ostrananie* – meaning literally, 'making strange' – as a means by which culture could regenerate itself. This required culture to become self conscious, to reflect upon and pay attention to its own language, so that instead of consuming art in the familiar and expected way, the reader's relationship with the book or poem is made unfamiliar and strange, in order to open up consciousness to new possibilities. Thus when Eisenstein writes of art as the site of 'conflict between customary conception and particular representation', and sees customary perception requiring 'dynamisation of the inertia of perception'[16] his aesthetic links with the Formalists and modernism could not be clearer.

It should be pointed out that the Formalist attack on conventional means of expression and perception, has its roots in the Romantic period of the eighteenth century. However, with revolutions and Fascism sweeping across a crisis torn Europe from the end of the first world war to the beginning of the second, the notion of making strange became more than a rehash of Romantic yearnings to transcend all forms of social and cultural influence. In the works of the photographer John Heartfield as much as Eisenstein, making strange by means of montage, acquired a decisive political purpose. It urged (shocked) the audience into re-evaluating social relationships in the light of the juxtapositions and collisions of disparate elements which the work offered. Making strange also laid the basis of Brecht's defamiliarising or alienation techniques.

Eisenstein identified three levels of film form where conflict and collision could be generated:

i) Graphic conflicts

Classical continuity editing will strive for graphic matches between shots. This requires a similarity between shots of compositional elements such as shape, size, volume, depth, lighting, and colour. Graphic matches would also include smooth transitions in terms of the camera's vantage point on the action (long and medium shot, close-up, low and high angle, level shot, etc). Montage editing is not a pure negation of graphic continuity, but it opens up a whole spectrum of possibility by allowing graphics to stress contrasts and dissimilarity between shots. Eisenstein also stressed the importance of generating graphic conflicts and tensions within the shot.

ii) Temporal conflicts

Temporal relations can be subdivided into three levels. Order refers to the 'when' of an event/action. Montage editing need not be a pure negation of sequential order, but sequential order can be sacrificed to open up other kinds of relations between shots other than 'X is followed by Y'. Duration refers to the length of an event/action. Eisenstein points out that there can be a conflict between an event and its screen duration (through slow or fast motion for example).[17] Frequency refers to how often an event/action occurs. Most obviously a tension can be set up between the single event or moment and its repeated showing.

iii) Spatial conflicts

We have seen how continuity of space is constructed by a variety of editing strategies: establishing shots, the 180° line of action, and so on. This orientates the viewer to the totality of the space in which the action takes place and how that space is being used by the characters moving within it. Thus, even when – as is the norm – the totality of space is not in view, the spectator still retains a sense of the spatial relationships existing beyond the perimeter of any particular shot. With montage editing this sense of offscreen space can disappear entirely. This is because meaning is generated by the juxtaposition between different spaces or different perspectives within the same spatial location, rather than continuity of space.

Montage: emotion and intellect

We have already discussed the way one shot can give an emotional charge to another shot — what Eisenstein called emotional montage, which he saw as distinct from what he called intellectual montage. Emotional montage seeks to intensify the impact of a concept or meaning contained in an image or series of images by calling up an emotional response in the audience (e.g. the workers being fired upon by soldiers is associated with the slaughter of the bull in *Strike*). The meaning of the first set of images can only be intensified because it is already evident. This, as we have seen, is what makes those images 'dominant' in the montage construction. Intellectual montage, on the other hand, attempts to make concrete an idea or set of thought processes which are not already evident within the shots themselves but exist only in the juxtaposition of the shots. The sense of a 'dominant' image often disappears in intellectual montage because the meaning or concept has not already been crystallised pictorially. The meaning exists only in the synthesis between shots.

In the 1970s, re-readings of Brecht's defamiliarisation strategies tried, in both theory and cultural practice, to evacuate any emotional charge between the 'spectacle' and the spectator. What was stressed instead was a highly intellectualised experience of cultural consumption, one which eschewed identification and other 'traditional' pleasures, as mystificatory. Sue Aspinal has cautioned against this reading of Brecht, and argues that we should be interested in 'where emotions come from, how they are influenced by social structures, and how to put emotional energy to better use'.[18] Moreover, the binary opposition between emotion and intellect which underpinned the 1970s readings of Brecht, can be deconstructed. In terms of Eisenstein's work, the slaughter of the workers juxtaposed with the slaughter of the bull in *Strike* both moves us emotionally and simultaneously distances us from this particular slaughter, suggesting in the methodical work of the butcher, a more abstract, structural relationship between workers in general and the capitalist state. Brechtian defamiliarisation is at its best when what is illuminated, with a shock, is this dynamic between the particular and the general, the individual and the social. Thus there is, in Eisenstein's example of 'emotional' montage, a latent intellectual process being urged.

Intellectual montage has been central to photomontage. For example Peter Kennard's *Tanks into Ploughshares* (1982) shows a sequence of six photos in which a tank becomes progressively transformed into a mechanical plough.[19] What is being proposed here is an argument about the priorities with which society distributes its resources. Klaus Staeck's photomontage titled *The Individual is Always at the Centre of Things* shows a picture of a person from the chest up, whose face has been obliterated by a montage insertion of a large bar code.[20] This example of intellectual montage makes pictorially concrete a whole set of arguments around the contradiction between the centrality of the individual in bourgeois ideology (at least in the west) and the displacement of the individual through the anonymous, automated production of commodities and the centralisation of information demanded by capitalist economics. There is no absolute gulf between emotional and intellectual montage, it is just that with intellectual montage we are encouraged to make connections between apparently disparate phenomena on the basis of our knowledge about social relationships in the world.

Eisenstein discusses a number of cinematic examples of intellectual montage from *October* (1927, USSR), an account of the bourgeois and communist revolutions in Russia, 1917. One not particularly persuasive example he gives is his juxtaposition of Kerensky (the prime minister for the first bourgeois government established after the overthrow of the Tsar) with a peacock. The juxtaposition suggests Kerensky's strutting self-importance, but seems to me more an example of emotional montage. One could hardly sustain an argument in written or verbal discourse for a comparison between the two on the basis of any knowledge about social relationships. The Kerensky/peacock juxtaposition works primarily at an affective level.

An example of a moment in which emotional and intellectual components seem equally weighted, is the sequence in *October* where shots of soldiers in the trenches are under mortar fire, and are juxtaposed with shots of a weapons factory, which are in turn montaged with Russian civilians standing in long queues for food. Here there is a clear, sustainable proposition being forwarded about the bourgeois government's priorities: production for war is more important to it than peace and bread. But while this is clear from the content of the images being juxtaposed, there is also a strong emotional charge generated by the precise editing in this sequence. The large mortars being lowered to the factory floor are juxtaposed with the soldiers in the trench, who, by a false eyeline match appear to be looking up at the mortar being lowered in the factory as if it were about to crush them. This spatial conflict is affective in a way which a straightforward juxtaposition between factory and trenches would not be. Similarly, when the mortar in the factory is finally lowered to the factory floor, its heavy, cold qualities (emphasised through montage repetition) are brought out by the juxtaposition with the bare feet of starving people standing in the snow. The viewer, then, is invited not only to think about the indifference of the war machine to the needs of the people, but also, as we look into the upturned face of the young soldier in the trenches and the vulnerable bare feet in the snow (and not just a long shot of the queue of people), to feel that tragedy, to be stirred by it.

Finally, Eisenstein gives another example of intellectual montage which is much more convincing than his Kerensky example, and in which the weighting between intellectual proposition and emotional charge favours the former. At one point the narrative deals with the attempts by the Generals still loyal to the Tsar to organise a counter revolution under the slogan of 'For God and Country'. Eisenstein explains his intentions:

> A number of religious images , from a magnificent Baroque Christ to an Eskimo idol, were cut together. The conflict in this case was between the concept and the symbolisation of God. While idea and image appear to accord completely in the first statue shown, the two elements move further from each other with each successive image. Maintaining the denotation of 'God', the images increasingly disagree with our concept of God, inevitably leading to individual conclusions about the true nature of all deities. [21]

These attempts at intellectual montage were criticised at the time from some quarters within Russia as being too abstract. One could argue that, on the contrary, Eisenstein was trying to make abstract ideas perceptible and concrete. However, the film/videomaker needs to recognise that it is clearly a form of editing which makes great demands on the audience.

The 1960s and Pop Art editing

Just as filmmakers like Pudovkin, Vertov and Eisenstein were influenced by the Dadaist and Surrealist experiments in defamiliarisation by juxtaposition, so filmmakers in the 1960s were influenced by Pop Art, or at least caught up in the cultural shifts of which Pop Art was symptomatic. Although there were diverse practitioners in Europe, Britain and America, one typical feature of Pop Art was the extension of Dadaist assemblage to the object world of mass culture: its media, its advertising, its fashions and mass consumption goods.[22] For example Richard Hamilton's parody/homage to this consumerist universe in the photomontage piece *Just What is it that Makes Today's Homes so Different, so Appealing?*, sets various mass culture icons in bizarre juxtaposition against the background of a domestic interior.

French New Wave Cinema emerged at around the same time as Pop Art, with its parodies/homages to the components of genre cinema. Dadaist assemblage, extended to new content, manifested itself in the more dynamic and surprising editing style pioneered by filmmakers like Jean Luc Godard and Francois Truffaut. It was through innovations at the level of editing that the brashness and directness of the gangster movie or the musical were to be reinvented and communicated to a new cine-literate generation of film goers.

As we have seen, Hollywood perfected the steady, smooth, seamless style of editing designed to move the spectator around the fictional world in an imperceptible way. Pop Art editing tends to 'leap' around space and time thus making the editing 'joins' that much more perceptible. Godard's 1959 film *A bout de souffle* (Fr, 1959) opens with a scene which both alludes to the continuity conventions of the eyeline match, while playfully disregarding them. We find Jean Paul Belmondo in gangster mode reading his newspaper in a port town. He looks up and appears to signal someone. Cut to his 'moll' who looks offscreen in two directions, preventing us from constructing any coherent spatial relationship between her and Belmondo (is he standing off to her left or right?) while on cutting back to Belmondo we find he too is now looking in various offscreen directions signalling to her. While this scene plays around with space, *A bout de souffle* also popularised the 'jump cut'. In this strategy, portions of time are lost between edits as we follow the action within a scene. If you wish to shoot a scene as a broadly continuous unfolding of action you may find jump cuts a more useful visual grammar than the strict rules of continuity editing. Jump cuts immediately declare a scene's construction according to principles other than that of a seamless flow. Typically the camera goes on the shoulder rather than a tripod, so that it is mobile and can follow the action as it unfolds. This in turn frees performers from having to worry about the position of the camera. Irrelevant or unexpectedly interesting action can be easily discarded or included as required at the editing stage. Above all, if your performers have had pre-shooting preparation, this can be a remarkably quick form of image production. Time, remember, is often the scarcest of the low-budget videomaker's resources. The jump cut is ideally suited for shooting scenes fast and without lots of retakes. It allows the filmmaker to select whatever material worked in a scene without having to worry about the gaps between actions which have been left out.

Less well known than Godard, Truffaut et al, the Japanese filmmaker Suzuki Seijum deployed other Pop Art editing techniques in *Tokyo Drifter*, made in 1966. In this film Seijun regularly leaps from a long shot of characters to extreme close-ups of their facial expressions. Another tactic is to orientate the spectator to the spatial relations of a particular scene and then suddenly cut to a hitherto unknown space adjacent to the action we were just watching and were comfortable with. For example, two men in an interior scene are discussing business; then we cut to the secretary in the outer office laughing at something she is reading. We can still see one of the men in the background so we know that we are still in the same location, but with Pudovkinesque delight Seijun's editing reveals new and unexpected details of a scene. *Tokyo Drifter* also uses editing to underline contrasts between character movement and the sort of statuesque mid-action pose of the comic book drawing. For example, we may see a character turn violently in one shot, but instead of a match on action whereby the character would still be moving in the next shot, we cut to an image of them standing perfectly still. Once again we find editing being used expressively in its own right and this potential may provide you with a range of strategies to stimulate your audiences in the absence of high production values.

The videomaker and Montage

We now need to consider how the theory and practice of montage editing is relevant to the low-budget videomaker's practical needs and creative potentialities. Dramatic material generated by the video-maker may acquire a number of advantages and possibilities if organised in part, or even entirely, according to the principles of montage. For example, montage generally requires shot lengths of a fairly short duration, thus the staging of dramatic acting is easier to film because it is captured in short segments. Acting is one of the key components of the way mise-en-scène unfolds in time. It is also, if you are going to get it right, one of the most difficult and time consuming components, involving dialogue, physical movement and facial expressions. Montage can minimise and even dispense with dialogue, thus cutting out one dimension of pre-shooting preparation and one factor that contributes to multiple takes. And because of the short duration of shots it is easier to set up and record the movement, position, posture or expression required. Montage may also legitimately allow you to repeat shots, something which is particularly easy when, as with video, your original material is not used up when you are assembling your master tape. Thus, 'an image, a gesture, a movement can be repeated in absolutely identical form'.[23] In this way you can make maximum use of your strong images.

Finally montage is more familiar to audiences today than it was in Eisenstein's time. Yet that familiarity comes largely from the consumption of advertisements and pop videos. Thus audiences are both competent readers of montage which is an advantage, but also largely unfamiliar with its use in dramatic fiction, which is also an advantage since you are trying to engage their attention and interest. The video, *Yellow*, which we have already discussed in chapter three, while looking like a pop video, also opens up a textual space for representations around masculinity and gay sexuality that would rarely be open to pop videos proper. None of this is to suggest that montage is an easy option. One can produce a video that looks like a poor imitation of the pop video just as easily as producing a video that looks like a poor cousin to a dominant cinema film. It is just to say that montage may provide one way of negotiating the contradiction between your economic resources and the cultural resources of both yourself and your audiences.

In my dicussion of modernism in chapter two, I argued that between the two poles of determinate, unequivocal meaning and indeterminate plurality of meaning possibilities, modernism gravitates towards the latter. Certainly one difficulty with using montage as an organising principle, is that you have to resolve the tension between an aesthetic built around fragmentation, plurality and collision, while maintaining enough 'unity' and coherence to be able to tell a story. A student video, *In Private* [24] resolves this by juxtaposing three locations in order to illustrate the contradictions between the public persona of a (fictional) well known author and his private life. The three locations are: the author at a book signing session; the author in a taxi cab; and the author arriving home, intercut with shots of his partner in a bedroom. Beyond the explicitly revolutionary preoccupations of the Russian masters we have looked at, montage is often associated with films in which the central protagonist has a disturbed state of mind. Pasolini noted Godard's use of this strategy back in 1965: Godard's characters have a 'neurotic and scandalous' relationship to reality, something conveyed very often precisely through montage repetition.[25]

An analysis of the editing in *In Private* allows us to recap some of the possibilities of editing already theorised. Firstly, graphic conflicts are used in the way the author is presented from the front, at the booksigning session, then from the side in the cab, and then from behind in a corridor leading to the room where his partner is waiting for him. There are also graphic juxtapositions between these corridor shots of the author in low angle and close-up (suggesting perhaps a threatening intrusion) and shots of the partner from behind looking isolated and vulnerable in a level long shot. There are temporal disruptions in the video, which locate it more in the tradition of Eisensteinian montage than Pudovkin's. Is the book signing session happening before or after the events that unfold in the author's private life? Is the cab shuttling the author from his private life to his public life (the bookstore) or vice versa? Dislocations of temporal order are also suggested when we see the partner, first from behind with a packed suitcase on the bed, then subsequently juxtaposed with shots of her packing the suitcase. There are also conflicts at the level of frequency: the repetition of shots, such as the author entering the private space and shutting the door on the outside world, displays something of that 'obsessive attachment to a detail or a gesture' which Pasolini thought characteristic of Godard's 'neurotic' characters.[26]

The temporal dislocations and spatial collisions which *In Private* weaves, lend it an economy and power very suitable to a short low-budget video. For example, it allows the videomaker to make maximum use of only three locations. In another video, the cab journey might have a merely descriptive function, providing the bridge between two scenes. We would have seen the journey only once. But here, whether the cab is going to or from the book signing session is less important than the significance of the cab as an intermediate zone between private and public spaces. The montage construction also facilitates economy in the sense that it circumvents the need to know details about the author's public life, as well as the details of the conflict within his private life. In the exchange of dialogue at the end of the video, the partner throws the author the packed suitcase, tells him he is leaving and that he knows what he has done wrong. This is all the detail we learn, yet the video can get away with this sketch of personal relations because its power resides primarily in its formal construction.

Through montage, the video obeys Eisenstein's injunction that art should stir up 'contradictions in the spectator's mind ... from the dynamic clash of opposing passions'. [27] By controlling and gradually increasing the tempo of the montage, the video acquires a force and impact in ten minutes that many feature films fail to achieve over two hours. Finally, it should be noted that the penultimate scene in which the author's partner tells him to leave is presented in more or less classical shot reverse shot editing. The sudden shift from image juxtaposition to ('rough') continuity editing and dialogue-led story only heightens the precarious equilibrium of the scene. Thus the very contrast between montage and continuity editing can be part of the meaning of the text.

Like *In Private*, the video *240* [28] deploys the convention of using a central character's psychological distress as a way of establishing liberty of technique. In this case the psychological crisis is caused by the prospect of imminent mass destruction: *240* being the number of seconds in the four minute warning. This provides the trigger for a series of memories and fantasies. Unlike *In Private*, this video organises its fragmentary aesthetic not around the spaces and locations of the action, but around thematic categories, specifically: love, fear, anger and self-destruction. The video begins in the present with a swish pan from the television set (which has presumably just delivered the devastating news) to our central character. The first set of memories triggered in the character's mind revolve around familial and sexual love. The setting is a dinner table where the character's father, brother and girlfriend are present. Jump cuts are used to present snatches of scenes: the character hugging his father, conversing with his brother and then kissing his girlfriend. These images are rendered with surrealism's characteristic juxtaposition of elements within the image: various moments of intimacy are played out on the table while other characters appear to carry on eating apparently oblivious to this disruption of social conventions (see Fig. 5.9).

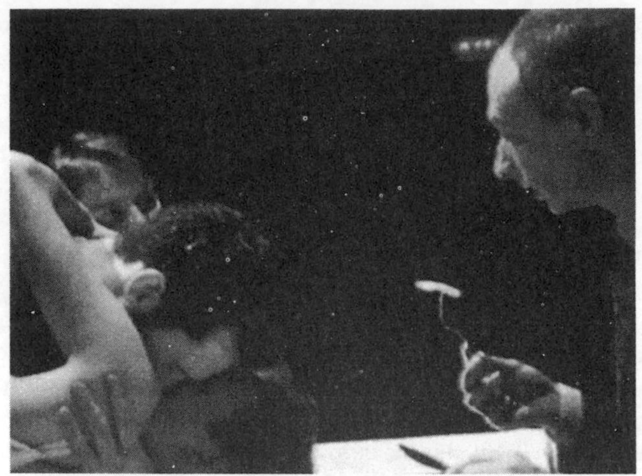

Fig. 5.9

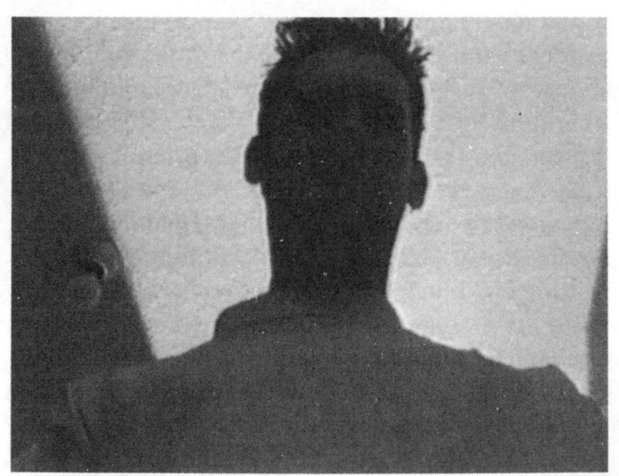

Fig. 5.10

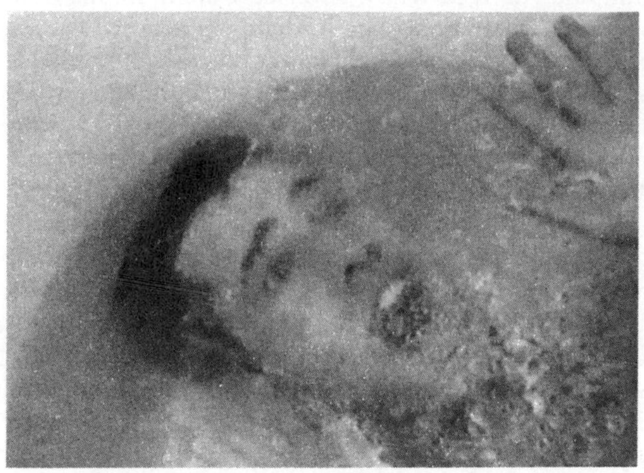

Fig. 5.11

We then return to what appears to be the present to find the character entering his bathroom. Now there is a shift to continuity editing. There is an eyeline match to the bath. Cut to a point of view shot of the bath. A towel is lying across the top of it. A hand pulls the towel away and to our surprise there is our character now in the bath and apparently trapped behind some transparent material (see Fig. 5.10). A Kuleshov style editing trick has been used to manipulate our character's presence in time and space to explore the theme of the second category – the fear generated from a claustrophobic sense of being trapped. As with the first images of love, the acting techniques being mobilised here are not naturalistic and do not aspire to lay bare individual psychology. Meaning (love or fear) is articulated in the way the elements of physical movement, gesture, action and expression perform for the camera, and are subsequently juxtaposed in the editing process.

Video in the age of reproduction

In Private and *240* demonstrate what can be done with montage in conjunction with dramatic material which you yourself generate. But montage intersects with the position of the low-budget videomaker and a wider historical context in another way altogether. In his article 'The Work of Art in The Age of Mechanical Reproduction', Walter Benjamin attempted to sketch how the production and consumption of culture had changed with the onset of modern, mass industrial society. Rather than being an in-depth argument buttressed by detailed empirical evidence, Benjamin's analysis is epochal in scope. It is also modernist in many of its themes and, though written before video technology existed, nevertheless it speaks to the position of the contemporary videomaker. Benjamin's interest is in the reproduction of art, the scientific possibility of which has 'advanced intermittently' across history. But from the Greeks' abilities to reproduce bronze, terracottas and coins, to the reproduction of writing through the printing press, to the development of photography and then film, reproducibility has advanced quantitively and qualitatively. Mechanical reproduction opens up the possibility of a multiplication of sites for the consumption of culture, thus: 'the choral production, performed in an auditorium or in the open air, resounds in the drawing room.'[29]

This enables art to 'meet the beholder halfway'. In other words, art is prised out of any exclusive venue for its consumption and is brought closer to the mass of people in their everyday lives. Mechanical reproduction 'substitutes a plurality of copies for unique existence'.[30] This notion of a plurality of copies also encompasses the possibility of constructing multiple versions, of reassembling art in new combinations and new contexts. Theoretically this brings audiences closer to art by abolishing all reverence for art as a singular otherworldly thing. Benjamin suggests that that which 'withers' in the age of mechanical reproduction is the 'aura' of art. This aura is the product of fetishism, the investing of art with magical powers in primitive times, with religious power in feudal times or more recently, under capitalism, with a secular metaphysical power emanating from the unique vision of the individual author. All such 'auratic' art tries to interpose a barrier between art and life by elevating the former to a pedestal high above the latter. Reproducibility offers the chance to sweep the pedestal aside and bring the work of art tumbling into the hands of anyone who has the desire to reshape it. A whole host of technological developments in photography and film made this desire practically possible at the time of Benjamin's writing.

Benjamin's optimism makes a refreshing change from the pessimistic responses which mass production and consumption usually provokes from intellectuals. However, Benjamin was not naively optimistic. At the time of writing this article he was strongly influenced by marxism, and in particular, by his contemporary, Bertold Brecht. He understood that the potential democratisation of culture which the mass media offered, could be horribly inverted under the pressures of class society. In his famous diagnosis, he pointed out how fascism attempted to aestheticise politics using the mass media. [31] This of course is the exact reversal of the avante-garde or radical modernist project to politicise aesthetics. Using all the resources of mechanical reproduction, fascism organises and disseminates spectacles of itself (marches, parades, celebrations) to which the audience is invited to bow down. This aestheticising of politics attempts to persuade people to invest heavily in the destructive aura constructed around the 'great leader'. It is a costly investment, as Benjamin notes:

> All efforts to render politics aesthetic culminate in one thing: war. War and war only can set a goal for mass movements on the largest scale while respecting the traditional property system ... Only war makes it possible to mobilise all of today's technical resources while maintaining the property system. [32]

Benjamin's prognosis seems particularly apt in the aftermath of the Gulf War. For here the sophistication of military technology (so called 'smart' bombs) and media technology (see the war live on CNN!) interlocked, presenting what unfolded as a dramatic spectacle, before which we were invited to suspend our critical faculties.

Some two decades after Benjamin wrote his article, the Situationists were mining, in theory and practice, similar terrain. A loose international grouping of radical artists, the Situationists argued that capitalist economic relations had so penetrated society from top to bottom, that everything had been transformed into a commodity. They renamed the consumer society – a vacuous term which suggests society is controlled by the consumer – as the society of the spectacle.[33] This more aptly captures the condition of life under capitalism. The vast majority of people are turned into spectators, passively, and unless they assert themselves, powerlessly watching social processes unfold without their active participation. The mass media were obviously regarded as key propagators of the specularisation of society. The notion of the spectacle clearly has affinities with Benjamin's notion of the aura. Both suggest the subordination of humanity to that which they could and should control. Despite the expansion of the mass media since Benjamin's time, and despite the amplification of what Benjamin warned against – the aestheticisation not only of politics but society in general – the Situationists did not collapse into pessimism. They argued for example that if radical practices could be co-opted (in the way that advertising had absorbed surrealism) then the products of the mass media could also be appropriated for radical use. Their notion of detournement meant literally to re-route the dominant meanings which the system produces, to take them on a detour for radical ends. *Yellow*, as we have seen, extracts the utopian energies of mass culture and presses it into the service of progressive representation. Thus it provides a good example of detournement.

Benjamin's discussion of the impact of mechanical reproduction on the production and consumption of culture and the Situationists' notion of detournement are both extremely relevant for the videomaker. Video is the medium of reproduction par excellence. The possibility exists for the videomaker to collect, store and easily access a vast range of media material whose meanings can then be re-routed by placing them (montaging them) in new combinations and contexts. The interface of video with computer technology and software packages further expands the possibilities of production, reproduction and processing. Both film and video are forms of analogue recording. That is to say, they use tangible, mechanical processeses (chemical and electro magnetic respectively) to record phenomena. The fact that the image's film and video records have a physical basis means that the image has certain obdurate qualities. Its physicality presents difficulties and limitations when it comes to manipulating, reproducing and preserving those images. The work of art in the age of digital reproduction, however, further extends the possibilities for democratising culture which Benjamin anticipated in relation to the mass media. When an image or sequence of images is digitised it no longer has a physical form. It has been turned into numbers and so reproduction can be accomplished infinitely, without degrading the image. Moreover, as numbers, the image has been transformed into discrete units of information. This means that any part of a single image or set of images can be subjected to the arsenal of image processing, manipulation and assemblage which software packages are constantly developing.

However, in classical marxist terms, there is a major contradiction between the productive forces of capitalism – in this instance capitalism's tendency to increase access to the means of production and reproduction through technological innovation – and the social relations of capitalism which act as 'fetters' to that productive potential since they protect corporate power and profits.[34] For it is these social relations of production which explain the emergence and increasing importance of copyright law.[35] While technically access to information goods becomes ever easier, software owners are increasingly concerned to keep track of the flow of their sounds and images and extract royalties for their use under copyright law. Not only does copyright act as a censor by making economic demands on cultural producers, it can also function to give copyright holders political power. The video group Gorilla Tapes experienced this in relation to their montage piece *Death Valley Days* (GB, 1984). Made originally with no regard for copyright clearance on 'stolen' tv footage, once Channel Four planned to broadcast it the text became subject to the legal system which frames commodities. As Jon Dovey of Gorilla Tapes recalls:

> Any footage of the Right Honourable M. Thatcher proved conspicuously difficult to clear. London Weekend Television refused to release footage of her from a recent chat show which we'd used in the programme's original version ... independent producers have difficulty getting access to news footage unless they can convince the copyright holders that the material will be used in the original 'spirit' in which it was transmitted, rather than as comedy or satire. [36]

Leaving aside the question of access, there is also the question of evaluating what is produced once access is achieved. Access does not automatically lead to challenges to dominant cultural forms. We find, for example, the debate between subversion and incorporation at play in the phenomenon of Scratch video, which blossomed in the early 1980s. Scratch worked by raiding and remixing television's images (including its film images). While some argued that Scratch represented a form of 'popular deconstruction', others argued that Scratch amounted to no more than a 'souped up' celebration and maximisation of the visual pleasures television already offers.[37] Clearly, Scratch, like modernism itself, can politically face more than one way.

Conclusion

The technological process of editing film has been very different to editing video (although films are increasingly being edited in part or totally on videotape before being transferred back to celluloid). However, it seems to me that there is very little in the respective technologies of film and video which insists that you must edit in one way and not another. As a language, film and video have much in common, and so it seems to me that the way you edit videos depends upon choices made from a range of cultural influences rather than technological determinants. Thus I make no apologies for locating this discussion of editing within the rich history of film culture.Indeed, developments in digital non-linear editing make the theory and practice of film montage more, rather than less, relevant. I have tried to make that history relevant to the reader as an independent videomaker. In the course of the last two chapters we have moved from a consideration of the image itself to looking at the way images are coordinated with each other. We must now turn to the larger formal structures within which considerations of the image and editing must work.

Practical Exercises

The following editing exercises can all be done 'in camera'.

- Storyboard and shoot a scene with no more than eight shots, using classical continuity editing strategies. Try and build it around a definite piece of action and include at least one establishing shot, match on action, shot-reverse-shot, eyeline match. How does the editing piece together the shots and make the action intelligible? How is the 180° rule built into the piece? Could you have broken the 180°rule while still preserving intelligibility of the action?

- Bearing in mind Kuleshov's experiments in constructing entirely fictional spaces, storyboard and edit together a scene in which a character appears to be having a conversation with their twin. This exercise should indicate just how much editing conventions work by suggestion rather than literal showing. How else might this understanding be useful for a low-budget videomaker?

- Storyboard and shoot a simple scene – say two or more people talking, eating, playing cards, etc. – but in a Pudovkinesque manner: witholding the establishing shot (completely or until late into the shot sequence) and focusing on character movement, action, physical qualities, etc. What are the strengths of this looser construction of spatial relations? When might it not be appropriate to use?

- Working in groups, each person takes a turn to go out with the camera and shoot eight to ten seconds of an image.

Then return, hand over the camera to the next person who, not knowing what the previous person has shot, goes out and records their own image. Remember to think imaginatively about all the videographic variables that need to be selected. When you have between six to twelve shots, play back the tape and see if any sense can be made of the image juxtapositions. What does this exercise tell you about the role of the audience in generating meaning?

- Shoot between six and twelve images which are linked not by continuity, but by some graphic and/or thematic link. What does your audience make of the sequence? Do they 'get it' too quickly in your opinion? Partially? Not at all? What problems does this raise for the use of montage?

Notes

1 Quoted in J. Berger, *Ways of Seeing*, British Broadcasting Corporation/Penguin Books, London 1972, p.17.
2 D. Bordwell and K. Thompson, *Film Art: An Introduction*, McGraw-Hill Inc., London 1993, p.247.
3 L. Kuleshov, *Kuleshov On Film*, University of California Press, London 1974, p.44.
4 Kuleshov, *ibid*, p.45.
5 Kuleshov, *ibid*, p.46.
6 Kuleshov, *ibid*, pp.46-47.
7 Kuleshov, *ibid*, p.52.
8 V.I. Pudovkin, *Film Technique and Film Acting*, Vision Press Ltd, London 1958, p.168.
9 Kuleshov, *op. cit.*, p.64.
10 Pudovkin, *op. cit.*, p.269.
11 Pudovkin, *op.cit.*, p.75.
12 S. Eisenstein, *Essays in Film Form*, Harcourt Brace Jovanovich, London 1977, p.37.
13 Eisenstein, *ibid*, pp.36-37.
14 Eisenstein, *ibid*, p.61.
15 Eisenstein, *ibid*, p. 32.
16 Eisenstein, *ibid*, p.47.
17 Eisenstein, *ibid*, p.39.
18 S. Aspinal, 'The Space for Innovation and Experimentation' in *Screen* vol.25, no. 6, 1984, p.85.
19 D. Evans and S. Gohl, *Photomontage: a political weapon*, Gordon Fraser, London 1986, p.97.
20 Evans and Gohl, *ibid*, p.107.
21 Eisenstein, *op.cit.*, p.62.
22 N. Stangos, *Concepts of Modern Art*, Thames and Hudson Ltd., London 1994, p.227.
23 R. Armes, *On Video*, Routledge, London 1988, p.205.
24 Made by Mick McAloon.

25 P.P. Pasolini, 'The Cinema of Poetry"'in *Movies and Methods* Vol 1, University of California Press, London 1976, p.554.
26 Pasolini, *ibid*.
27 Eisenstein, *op. cit.*, p.46.
28 Made by Clare Andrews, Nick Erskine, Paul Hutchison, Stuart Sinclair, Neil Webster.
29 W. Benjamin, 'The Work of Art in The Age of Mechanical Reproduction' in *Mass Communication and Society*, Edward Arnold/O.U. Press, London 1977, p. 387.
30 Benjamin, *ibid*.
31 Benjamin, *ibid*, p.407.
32 Benjamin, *ibid*.
33 G. Debord, *The Society of the Spectacle*, Detroit 1970.
34 K. Marx and F. Engels, *The Communist Manifesto*, Penguin Books, Harmondsworth 1967.
35 N. Garnham, *Capitalism and Communication*, Sage, London 1990, p.40.
36 J. Dovey, 'Copyright as Censorship: Notes on Death Valley Days' in *Screen* vol.27, no.2, 1986, p.54-55.
37 S. Marshall, 'Artist's Tapes' in *ICA Video Library Guide*, ICA, 1986, p.7.

Chapter Six

Narrative

Having discussed the image and the various kinds of rationale that may animate the editing of images into sequences, we need now to turn our attention to the question of narrative. In doing so we will be exploring the different kinds of rationale by which images and sequences can be organised into an overarching structure, something which moves us from the opening titles to the end credits in a way that tells a story or makes sense according to some other (non-narrative) logic. As with the image and as with editing there is no one right way of 'making sense' of your material narratively. However, to continue my general approach, I will suggest that there are pragmatic and political implications and consequences to be considered when it comes to the question of narrative construction for the low-budget videomaker. I will also consider modes of organising your material that more or less dispense with narratives entirely.

Structuralism and narrative

Structuralist enquiries into storytelling are premised on the idea that, while individual stories may look utterly different from each other on the surface, they may in fact share certain basic structures and common arrangements in their internal organisation. This commonality means that while the director(s) make important decisions and choices and exercise a number of options in relation to a particular project, these choices/options interact with and are framed by larger rule-governed systems of storytelling. It is interesting that intellectual work in this field has percolated beyond the rarefied world of academia and into the film industry, where this knowledge has become part of the means of (film) production.

In 1985 a film school graduate called Christopher Vogler, while working for the Disney studios as a story analyst, wrote a long memo proposing the existence of a universal story structure. The memo was later expanded into a book called *The Winter's Journey*, which essentially translated work done by earlier writers into a language that movie executives could understand. The book has subsequently provided the basis for software packages designed to help writers craft stories in the desired mould. Vogler's book illustrates both the strengths and weaknesses of the structuralist method. The strength is its ability to make links in the formal structure of apparently quite different works. In Vogler's version, the universal form involves disrupting the hero/heroine's Ordinary World and setting them on a journey or Call To Adventure. Often, the central character's first reaction is to Refuse The Call (or others suggest they should Refuse The Call). The Mentor figure will encourage them to undertake their 'journey' where they encounter Tests, Allies and Enemies. After many adventures they arrive at the threshold of achievement, or in Vogler's terms, they reach the Approach To The Inmost Cave. Here they encounter a Supreme Ordeal before seizing their Reward. However, their enemies regroup, endangering the Road Back. One more ordeal must be endured (a Resurrection) before the transformed hero/heroine can Return With Elixir. In all Vogler identifies twelve stages in the narrative process. [1]

The weakness in the structuralist method is that it can quickly become insensitive to questions of historical context and cultural specificity. To take the question of historical context first, the fairytale qualities inherent in Vogler's narrative categories, suggest that Hollywood, an industry with a specific history, emerging and changing for historically determined reasons, is after all merely expressing timeless storytelling strategies. Such a method offers little in the way of a critical purchase on the output of Hollywood, or any other audiovisual industry. Then there is the question of cultural specificity. Structuralism's insensitivity to cultural difference also disempowers those who are struggling to contest Hollywood's global hegemony and protect and foster cultural diversity. Diversity of storytelling strategies can quickly become lost to a method as indifferent to cultural nuances and inflections as structuralism. For example, a *Sunday Times* report on Vogler's book applied his categories to four films. These were the mainstream British film, *Four Weddings and a Funeral* (M. Newell, GB, 1994) and three Hollywood films, *The Wizard of Oz*, (V. Fleming, 1939) *Star Wars* (G. Lucas, USA, 1977) and *Romancing The Stone* (R. Zemeckis, USA, 1984). The analysis mapped out a similar narrative trajectory for the hero in the British film as for the heroes in the American films.[2] Yet what this glossed over is that even *Four Weddings and a Funeral,* a film which is very consciously pitched at the American market, seems, with its episodic and even 'repetitive' scenarios (the four weddings of the title), significantly different from the more linear narrative structures of the other Hollywood films. All this is not to reject structuralist inspired analysis (still less to hold *Four Weddings and a Funeral* up as a radical example of cultural diversity), but rather to keep in check structuralism's tendency to find universal models and smooth over difference. I want to start with a structuralist account of the dominant Hollywood version of the classical narrative, because its dominance tends to define our thinking about what a story 'is'.

Classical narrative

Fig. 6.1 maps out the narrative structure of *Trading Places* (J. Landis, USA, 1983) and identifies five stages in the classic narrative's underlying structure. The first stage, the exposition (close to Vogler's category of Ordinary World) establishes the fictional world in terms of its norms. It tells us something about those norms or the central character's(s') place within them, which will be transformed in the course of the unfolding narrative. The conflict stage provides the trigger for the action(s) by which those norms will be transformed. There may already be dramatic conflict established in the exposition, but the conflict stage is that event or happening which changes the norms, which defines the first important goal of the central character(s). The conflict stage may bring latent conflicts or problems established in the exposition, to the surface. As Fig. 6.1 indicates, the fictional world established in the exposition of *Trading Places* is a society of class differences. The conflict is set in motion by the Duke brothers who bet on whether they can make their pampered, upper-class protege (Dan Aykroyd) into a criminal, and conversely, whether they can make a small-time con artist (Eddie Murphy) into an honest stockbroker. We know that the bet constitutes the conflict because it produces the sudden upward and downward social mobility at odds with the stable society of class differences established at the beginning of the film.

Trading Places : A Diagram of Narrative

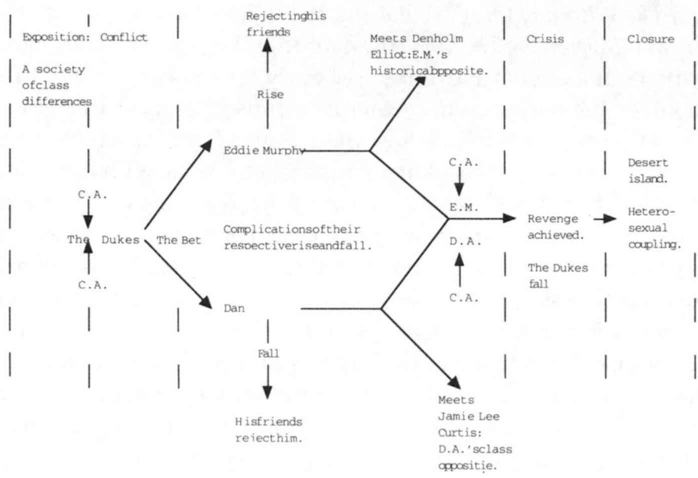

Key

C.A. = Causal Agent.

Fig. 6.1

Trading Places is a good example of both a classical narrative film, but also of the variables that can exist within that model of storytelling. A particularly strong feature of the classical narrative is the way it locates causal agency (the 'because' principle of why things happen) at the level of individual characters. In a classical narrative the characters with the most strongly defined goals are the characters who are charged with the causal principle of making things happen, of pushing the narrative along. *Trading Places* has such characters, but perhaps a little unusually, for at least half the film causal agency is located with the Dukes, who are the film's villains. It is unusual for a classical film to keep its heroes so powerless for as long as this one does. Yet that is what is required if the Dukes are to engineer and direct the respective rise and fall of the Eddie Murphy and Dan Aykroyd characters. Crucial to the unusual centrality of the villains as causal agents, is the fact that the Eddie Murphy and Dan Aykroyd 'stories' are separated into parallel narrative strands. Such extensive use of parallelism is in itself rather unusual in a classical narrative film, which usually aims to bring the main stars' stories together as rapidly as possible. However, although separated by parallel narratives, the film creates a lot of correlations and links by the use of 'negative' symmetry. This is apparent, not only in the reversal of fortunes of the two characters, but the inversions that take place with regard to their respective friends. Eddie Murphy rejects his working-class friends as he becomes increasingly concerned with wealth and property, while Dan Aykroyd is rejected by his upper-class friends when he is set up as a drug dealer and pimp by the Dukes. It is through the use of such patterning that the meanings and pleasures of whole sequences add up to a coherent narrative structure.

Yet that 'coherence' may also function strategically at an ideological level, for it may be the means by which the classical narrative smooths over the social contradictions which the story itself is stirring up. For example, at one level *Trading Places* appears to be about class differences and how circumstances influence behaviour and attitudes. At a deeper level, however, the film could be read as trying to conceal class differences. For both Eddie Murphy and Dan Aykroyd are prised out of their respective class communities vis-a-vis their friends, so that the narrative can bring the two together in order to resolve their problems as individuals. This allows the Aykroyd character's racism (established in an early scene where he interprets a poor black man automatically as a mugger) to disappear and also 'true love' to blossom as his expulsion from the elites introduces him to Jamie Lee Curtis who plays the 'whore with a heart of gold'. Again there is a neat symmetry here between Eddie Murphy's character and Denholm Elliott who, as Aykroyd's former servant, is, in an echo of the slave trade, Eddie Murphy's historical opposite. Just as Curtis will achieve her aspirations to escape her class origins through her meeting with Aykroyd, so Elliott regains the pride which his servile status had robbed him of.

In the narrative, Curtis and Elliott function as Allies and Mentors in Vogler's terms, helping our heroes to clarify and achieve their goals. At the point where the two parallel narratives converge, causal agency shifts rapidly over to the heroes. The classical narrative is usually characterised by a ruthlessly efficient regulation of 'knowledge'.

The point at which what we the audience 'know' converges with what the heroes/heroines know, is always a key moment in the narrative. In *Trading Places* the shift in causal agency requires the two heroes to understand what the Dukes have been up to, and plot their revenge. From this point the audience and the heroes 'know' more than the Dukes. Causal agency flows irrevocably away from them because they are unaware of this new alliance and unaware of the plans being hatched for their own downward social mobility.

All this, the bulk of the film, occurs in the complications phase. The film reaches a climax at the crisis stage where the goals of the main characters (revenge in this case) are achieved. This stage often turns on a rapid reversal of fortunes for the villains and so it proves in *Trading Places*. The final stage, the film's closure, makes it clear that the narrative has exhausted itself of the potential for any further development. The closure attempts to persuade the audience that all the questions raised by the narrative have been answered, and at the level of plot, this is usually true. But the sociopolitical embers which have been stirred by the narrative (in this case, about class differences, class snobbery and racism) are also snuffed out in a final image of harmony, achievement and success; this closure can also be achieved without a 'happy' ending, such as in *Thelma and Louise* where the two protagonists choose to die rather than to be arrested.

To summarise the main points so far, we can note the use of parallelism, of symmetry, inversion and reversal as ways of patterning sequences into a coherent story. Certainly these are useful strategies for making connections between disparate narrative elements. We also need to acknowledge the intensity of this patterning and the purpose to which it is put in the classical narrative. For the classical narrative is an extraordinarily 'closed' structure. Everything feeds directly into the unfolding story; no characters or actions can have autonomy from the main causal chain. There is a strict hierarchy of who has the most causal power in the narrative, although this can shift. There is a careful regulation of what the audience can know and when. Everything must serve the motor, the narrative drive towards resolving all the problems within the fictional world. With this drive towards closure the classical narrative has difficulty in keeping some of the interesting questions which it may touch upon, alive in the mind of the audience after the film has finished. And it has to be stressed that, in order for the closure to be convincing at the end of the narrative, a form of closure is operating throughout the course of the narrative, not just at the end. For while new meanings and possibilities must be generated in order to advance the narrative, there is also a strong movement towards the control and containment of those meanings in ways that can be resolved in time for the final credits. These, then, are the grounds on which theorists have been critical of the politics of the classical narrative and have advocated one form or another of modernist film practices.

Narrative and Barthes' five codes

Fig. 6.2, which can be transposed onto Fig. 6.1, draws on the concepts developed by Roland Barthes. In his book *S/Z*, Barthes develops his argument through an analysis of a short story written by the nineteenth century French writer, Balzac. The relevance of this to our understanding of contemporary storytelling lies in the suggestion that nineteenth century literary developments in narrative techniques were to subsequently become dominant in many areas of mass culture, including film. The term 'classical narrative' has been used to describe this dominant form of storytelling, although the word classical is misleading since this form of storytelling does not have a particularly long historical pedigree. (For instance, the picaresque technique, which tells stories through a succession of more or less unrelated episodes, is much older, dating back to Spanish literature of the sixteenth century.) The defining feature of the classical narrative is that it is underpinned by an aesthetic devoted to unifying all its elements into a tightly woven whole. Certainly the concept of the 'classical narrative' is open to criticism since it can all too easily smooth over and ignore very important differences between the specific elements within it. I have already indicated that this is also an inbuilt tendency of structuralism.

The Barthes of *S/Z* avoids some of these problems since (influenced by post-structuralism) it is precisely the apparent unity and integrated quality of the classical narrative that he is trying to unpick and unravel. In order to do so, Barthes identifies five codes at work in the classical narrative. He defines the codes very loosely as 'voices'. However, these voices do not belong to the author, but rather to the social and cultural context of the author and the text. What defines the classical narrative is the importance that it allots in the sequencing of material, to enigma/resolution codes and action codes. These are the codes whose task it is to construct a unified, integrated text. The classical narrative's method of engaging audiences is to constantly get us to ask questions about the plot and it does this by carefully regulating information about particular events and

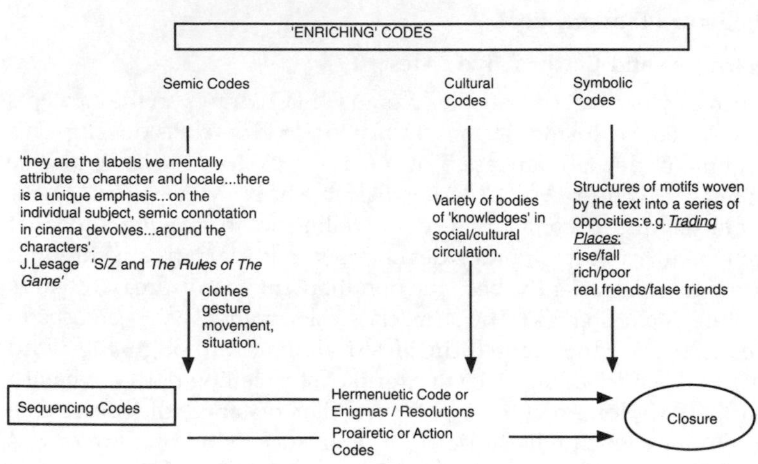
'ENRICHING' CODES
Semic Codes
Cultural Codes
Symbolic Codes
'they are the labels we mentally attribute to character and locale...there is a unique emphasis...on the individual subject, semic connotation in cinema devolves...around the characters'.
J.Lesage 'S/Z and The Rules of The Game'
clothes
gesture
movement,
situation.
Variety of bodies of 'knowledges' in social/cultural circulation.
Structures of motifs woven by the text into a series of opposities:e.g. Trading Places:
rise/fall
rich/poor
real friends/false friends
Sequencing Codes
Hermenuetic Code or Enigmas / Resolutions
Proairetic or Action Codes
Closure

Fig. 6.2

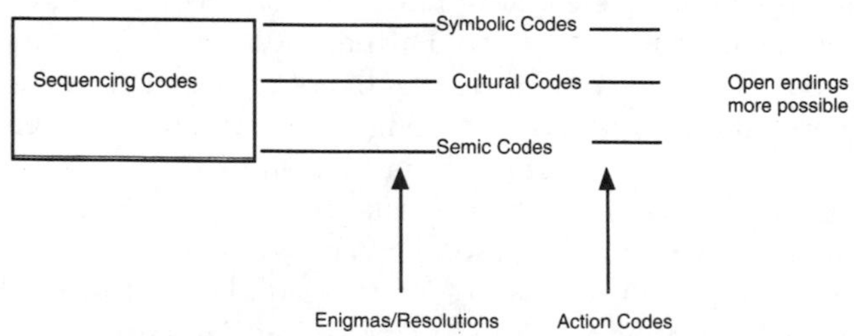
Sequencing Codes
Symbolic Codes
Cultural Codes
Semic Codes
Open endings more possible
Enigmas/Resolutions
Action Codes

Fig. 6.3

characters (how their goals are going to be achieved, what 'really' motivates them, etc.). As enigmas are answered, the narrative is pushed in certain directions (and not others), and new enigmas are generated (or important, primary enigmas are withheld until later).

Much of the craft of the classical narrative lies in the way that it can unfold the story rapidly, without sacrificing intelligibility. Contemporary Hollywood cinema in particular has achieved high velocity pace without sacrificing audience comprehension. This paradox can be understood by the work of the action codes, which function to enable the story to develop in ways that 'make sense'. This is often shaped by generic conventions and/or star image(s). When, for example, we are introduced to Eddie Murphy in the beginning of *Trading Places*, his character appears to be that of a blind, legless Vietnam war veteran reduced to begging for money. But – given that impersonations are central to Eddie Murphy's star image, and that this film belongs to the genre of comedy (rather than social drama), and given that two policemen are seen approaching Eddie Murphy and viewing this character with some suspicion – it is the action code which is at work when it is revealed (and we are not surprised) that the blind crippled character we have before us is in fact a small-time con artist. It should be noted that to tap into such audience expectations in an effective and systematic way requires resources to build up the generic world that are quite out of reach of the low-budget/no-budget videomaker. Thus the already indicated political objections to the classical narrative are reinforced by pragmatic ones.

It is perfectly possible to begin to dismantle the classical narrative by working within the enigma and action codes, but loosening them with regard to the use of these two codes to sequence the narrative. For example, one may pose enigmas but never answer them, or only answer them ambiguously, or more radically, offer several mutually conflicting answers. Whereas the action codes of the classical narrative tend to ensure that each sequence has fairly direct cause-effect implications on the next sequence, it is possible to loosen these codes as well. For example, a video called *Clangers*,[3] a deftly jaundiced view of the student experience, works in part by constructing a series of unconnected comic episodes of a character's time at university: we have a lecture scene, a bar scene, a scene in Camden Town (a metonym of trendiness), the flawed attempts at establishing relationships with the opposite sex. None of these episodes have any real knock-on effect in the narrative, which remains largely composed of a number of self-contained sketches. The beauty of sketches is that they do not have the complex demands of driving a plot forwards (something which usually involves resources) yet, without much 'happening', they can make a simple and effective point.

The problem with Christopher Vogler's motif of narrative as journey is that it leaves little room for thinking of the journey as anything other than driven by a tightly structured chain reaction of cause and effect which, as various critics have pointed out, is fairly ruthless in its prioritising of The Goal as the end point of the journey. But narrative journeys can be rather more picaresque affairs, accommodating a variety of experiences which are important in their own right rather than for what they contribute to making sense of the action that follows. The picaresque journey (metaphorically through a social institution such as in *Clangers*, or a literal physical journey) has indeed been appropriated by filmmakers as a vehicle for satire and critique. One thinks of Godard's *Pierrot le fou* (Fr., 1965) and *Weekend* (Godard, Fr., 1967) where couples journey through a social landscape encountering various manifestations of complacency and violence. In Fernando Solanas' *The Journey* (Argentina, 1991) a character searches for his father in an allegorical Argentina wrecked by political authoritarianism and absurd economic policies.

A student video, *The Box*,[4] is likewise structured largely around a journey. The central protagonist, Tosh, leaves his home only to stop, turn round and then reappear, through a jump cut, carrying a large box. In the journey that follows, street signs are used to comment on Tosh's circumstances. The sign for a crossroads ahead is inserted early on, functioning metaphorically to indicate that Tosh, too, is at a crossroads in his life. His physical journey is intercut with (and paralleled by) a psychological one where he is in session with his (unseen, but heard) therapist. Georgina, Tosh's girlfriend, and his therapist, are both trying to encourage Tosh to overcome his feelings of guilt. The sources of these feelings reside both in his personal biography (guilt about the death of his father who committed suicide) and in history. The latter is represented in an encounter which is familiar to anyone making a journey in 1990s Britain: Tosh comes across a young homeless woman, wrapped in a sleeping bag. With an intertextual link to a similar scene in Godard's *Weekend*, where an Arab and African discuss to camera the struggle against imperialism in the third world, the woman stares back at the audience while a voice-over offers an analysis of the capitalist society she lives in, which has, absurdly, pushed her to the margins of life:

> The basic economic unit in capitalist society is the individual family, and it is held to be sacred – particularly by the political guardians of the system. Indeed, so deeply held is the belief in the family, that conservative politicians such as Cecil Parkinson and Timothy Yeo, have had more than one…

The voice-over may be hers but there is no necessary link between the voice that speaks and the face that looks back at the audience. The discourse of the voice-over remains at an impersonal level of analysis, which suggests that the homeless woman functions very much as a metonym, i.e. adjacent to the wider structural failures and injustices of capitalism as a social and economic system.

Later, complaining to his therapist that he thinks he is being followed, we cut back to the physical journey and the resolution of this enigma, which is constructed through classical suspense/action codes (close-ups of the feet of the mysterious follower, exaggerated sounds of footsteps). He is in fact being followed by himself, dressed up as the Italian filmmaker Antonioni, who, complete with crew, is filming him. Just as *240* uses Kuleshov-style fabrication when the protagonist apparently discovers himself trapped in the bath, so this scene uses the shot-reverse-shot convention to construct a discussion between Tosh and himself as Antonioni. Antonioni/Tosh, tells him (in Italian) that by confronting him, he shows he has the courage to go forward and liberate himself from his personal demons. The journey also raises questions about the relationship between how one feels about oneself and more general beliefs concerning 'the meaning of life'. In therapy, Tosh rejects religious beliefs as a way of making his own life meaningful, but he rejects them in very stark and dogmatic terms (as a 'confidence trick'). Later, back on the road, Tosh as Antonioni plays a trick on himself: we hear a thunderclap and with an orchestral introduction a female voice announces: 'This is the voice of God, I know you can hear me Tosh'. Tosh, looking bewildered, turns round to find Antonioni and his crew laughing at their practical joke. The journey, and the device of splitting the character not only between two locations (the road and therapy) but also into different physical manifestations (Tosh, and Antonioni), is used to raise a number of issues around the problem of self-worth, society, and political and religious responses to the world.

Such questions, because they are raised in an episodic manner, are not definitively resolved by the end of the video, even though at a personal level Tosh does make some progress. In therapy Tosh tells us how his father died. He committed suicide one Saturday while Tosh was out shopping with his mother. Tosh describes how his father ran himself a bath and poured himself at large whisky. At this point we cut from a close-up of Tosh retelling the episode to an overhead shot of a full whisky glass on a blue background. As Tosh tells us that his father committed suicide, the liquid in the glass turns red (keyed in at the editing stage). Obviously then this image functions as a symbol of his father's suicide. But the image also returns later, and in a way that continues to make connections and add more layers to the text. In the final scene we find Tosh at the end of his journey, teetering on the verge of repeating his father's self-destruction as he sits on the edge of a bridge and stares into the river below. Georgina has also arrived: we hear a shout and cut from her to the river (classic action codes once again) but instead of throwing himself into the river, Tosh has thown his box, his symbol of insecurities, into the waters. At this point, as the box sinks, the image of the blood red whisky tumbler is mixed in to generate a set of connections between the images (the box linked to whisky, both as symbols of dependency, the red blood mixing with the blue waters, a symbolic mingling of life and death). One of the strengths of *The Box* is the way it manages to balance some sense of optimism with a narrative structure that refuses the typical classical narrative closure of the issues raised.

To return to our map of the classical narrative, the three other codes which Barthes discussed have a supportive but firmly subordinate role to play. The classical narrative does not allow these other codes to organise the narrative material – it leaves that to the enigma and action codes – rather their function in the text is to 'enrich' the classical narrative structure, layering it with the potential for some complexity of meanings, but never allowing these codes to interrupt the causal drive and structure already discussed. The semic code allows us to label attributes of characters and locations. It functions by association, or as Barthes describes it, 'flickers of meaning'. Cultural codes are those by which the text most recognisably saturates itself with signs of the real world. These codes refer out beyond the text and draw their authority from the bodies of accepted 'knowledge' or 'wisdom' in society at large. For example, *Trading Places* draws on popular assumptions that the aspiration to be wealthy is a natural and desirable core of human motivation. Yet the film also suggests that being rich involves surrounding oneself with crooks and fair weather friends. For this reason the newly enriched protagonists at the end of the film must be withdrawn from the urban context and isolated from their fellow human beings in an island paradise so that the film can suggest wealth without the negative connotations which it has attached to that condition in the course of the film. We have here then a closure which tries to mask an ideological contradiction at the heart of the film. Finally, the symbolic code (close to the notion of thematic structures) is responsible for spinning and weaving a set of motifs throughout the narrative. In the classical narrative these motifs tend to be organised into a series of binary oppositions, as indicated in Fig. 6.2. This is because the binary oppositions can be easily grafted onto the dramatic clash between opposing forces: heroes vs villains, goals vs obstacles, and so on.

Fig. 6.3 suggests other non-classical ways of sequencing narrative by displacing the centrality of the enigma/resolution and action codes and promoting one or more of the semic, cultural and symbolic codes in their place. We have seen, in the analysis of *Trading Places*, how a classical narrative makes use of parallel strands to its narrative. A parallel narrative is one which makes use of two or more narrative strands unfolding in different places at the same or different times. The classical narrative constructs parallels that are taken to be happening more or less simultaneously, so that the strands can be easily brought together in the interests of achieving narrative closure. I want to indicate while discussing semic, cultural and symbolic codes, how parallel narratives can function in non-classical modes as well.

A student video called *Pissing in the Wind* [5] opens with a good example of how semic codes can be put 'in charge' of sequencing material. The video begins with a hand-held shot travelling up a staircase, then entering a room. The camera then proceeds to survey the room's contents. Various props, in particular books and magazines shot with the macro lens facility, tell us something about the character whose room it is (Fig. 6.4). However, this camera activity is not given a narrative explanation: it is not another character's point of view, nor does the character whose room we are in appear to be present (thus justifying, in classical narrative terms, the camera's presence). In fact, the video cuts from exploring character through props, to the character in person as he travels by train to some (unknown) destination. Thus another narrative strand has been set up. Enigma codes are faintly detectable (where is this character going?) but they are hardly very central. Whereas in the classical narrative cinema, information about characters forms part of the narrative drive (the enigmas and action codes), here the information is the narrative. There is no other explanation of our presence in the room other than the information we glean about the character from the room. The second narrative strand, the train journey gives the audience a figure with which to link the exploration of the room. The text makes explicit connections between the two, for example cutting from a tortured-looking expressionist painting in the room (Fig. 6.5) to a close-up of the character with a red gel over the lens, suggesting his emotional state.

As *Pissing In The Wind* develops, the camera in the room does 'find' the character we observed travelling, now painstakingly building a model aeroplane (Fig. 6.6). The other narrative strand continues as well, until we discover the destination of the character's journey to be the airport. Thus, as with *The Box*, we have the parallel narratives splitting the same character between two different locations. The temporal relationships between the two strands (as with *In Private*) are ambiguous (does the visit to the airport precede the building of the model, happen at same time or after?), and in this case unimportant. What is important is the way the symbolic codes are also being enlisted as the rationale for sequencing the material. What is being explored, as the making of the model and the flight of actual planes are cut against each other, are popular associations around masculine creativity: its version of freedom ('cutting loose', taking off, leaving all constraints behind), the linked tendency towards isolationism, obsessiveness, and finally, in a fantasy sequence which sees a failed attempt to fly the model plane, masculinity's self-destructive qualities. Significantly, the symbolic codes are not articulated as a set of binary oppositions that can be resolved by individual causal agency. Rather, the codes are deployed and the viewer is asked to interpret them instead of leaving the unfolding of narrative plot to do it for them.

Chronotopes

It was Mikhail Bakhtin who developed the concept of the chronotope and deployed it in his analysis of literature. The concept refers literally to the way texts organise their narratives around time–space relationships. Bakhtin encourages us to think of the artistic work as giving time an almost tangible, pliable quality. In his analysis of ancient literature he discerns a number of different conceptualisations of time. For example, adventure time refers to the unexpected and unforseen turning of events; the rupturing of the expected flow of events in time by chance and fortune. Clearly, the

Fig. 6.4

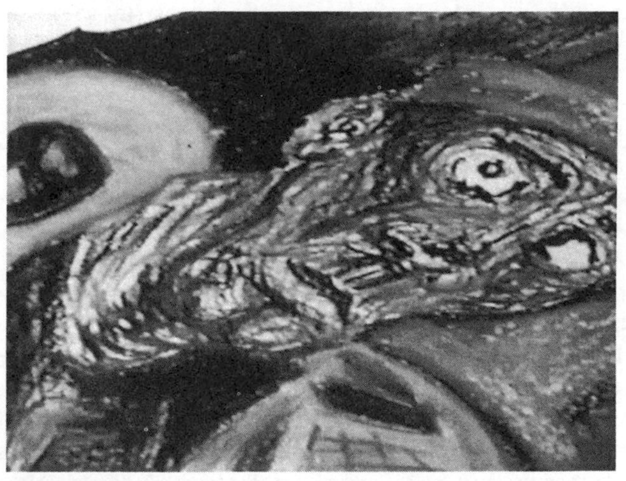

Fig. 6.5

classical narrative film also deploys adventure time to some extent, but with a significant difference from its earliest manifestations. Discussing the hero in Greek romances, Bakhtin notes that while they,

> act in adventure time – they escape, defend themselves, engage in battle, save themselves ... they act, as it were, as merely physical persons, and the initiative does not belong to them. Even love is unexpectedly sent to them by all-powerful Eros. In this time, persons are forever having things happen to them (they might even 'happen' to win a kingdom); a purely adventuristic person is a person of chance. He enters adventuristic time as a person to whom something happens. But the initiative in this time does not belong to human beings. [6]

As we have seen classical narrative does stress the central characters' ability to initiate action and not simply be subject to chance, only ever extricating themselves from bad fortune and/or happening to come across good fortune. This is because the classical narrative draws upon a conceptualisation of time only really developed towards the end of the middle ages: biographical time. This conceptualisation of time directs our attention to the way characters grow and develop and change as a result of their interaction with adventure time. Without a concept of biographical time, characters remain fixed, already defined 'physical persons'. Indeed, in the classical narrative only the central characters are given biographical temporal indicators, while the other characters function more or less to initiate adventure time. Another category of time is that of historical time: the unfolding of events which are the product of collective humanity. The highly individualistic stress of the classical narrative means that historical time is usually subordinate to biographical time. Bakhtin notes the importance of the picaresque novel in integrating an emerging awareness of historical time into adventure time: 'it is the sociohistorical heterogeneity of one's own country that is revealed and depicted' in the adventure time 'encounters' which the picaresque journey deals with.[7]

If biographical time refers to the psychological and emotional life of characters, body time refers to the temporal processes which the physical body itself undergoes. Bakhtin discusses body time in relation to the medieval writer, Rabelais. Bakhtin argues that the stress on the imagery and anatomy of the body in Rabelais' work, is an attempt to subvert the Christian world view which relegates the body to 'a sad necessity of the sinful flesh'[8] and privileges the spiritual, immaterial world. Rabelais inverts this world view choosing to celebrate and affirm the raucous, living, breathing, eating, drinking, defecating and dying body. The body remains an important motif in contemporary narratives. I have already discussed for example the gendered body in such videos as *Snuff*, *T.V.*, and *Yellow*.

This brief discussion certainly does not exhaust the list of chronotopes which Bakhtin discusses, or the further number of chronotopes that are conceivable. The concept, though, is a particularly useful way of thinking about ways in which texts may conceptualise time differently and indeed how different conceptualisations of time may be mobilised within a single text. This is particularly true of parallel narratives where different spaces and their temporal qualities may be juxtaposed quite explicitly. To return to *Pissing tn the Wind*, the interior scenes where we watch the character build the model plane may be characterised as labour time. Here we see time unfold through the progressive building up, bit by bit, of the model (Fig. 6.6). Labour time involves intense concentration on the work being done, as well as rest periods, which we also witness. This unfolding of time is contrasted with the shots of the character watching planes taking off, sitting in the airport cafe, wandering around the airport. This is leisure time. It is unstructured and, in contrast to the meticulous unfolding of labour time, it does not require anything to happen in any particular order. As well as contrast there is also continuity, in that both labour and leisure time unfold as isolated experiences. Finally, there is the fantasy sequence where the character attempts to fly the model plane but ends up destroying it. The setting for this scene is a hilltop in a rural setting. (Fig. 6.7). The character is dressed only in his underwear. This juxtaposition of figure and landscape is not only a physical juxtaposition; it also embodies two different conceptions of time in the same image. The half-dressed character evokes a domestic, private, transient and mortal time, set against the background of the vast cyclical time of nature which makes his efforts all the more tragic.

As we have seen, a text need not be composed of a single homogenous conceptualisation of time. This is true for *The Box*, which draws on biographical time (the character coming to terms with certain aspects of himself in the course of his journey); adventure time (unexpected meetings: the homeless woman, Tosh as Antonioni); historical time (use of news footage); and artistic time (the references to Antonioni and Godard's cultural practices). Thus

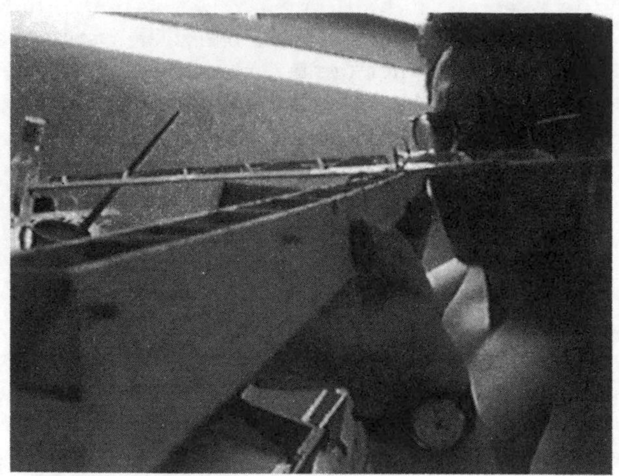

Fig. 6.6

Fig. 6.7

the concept of the chronotope allows you to dissect the particular qualities and types of time–space which you may mobilise, and the implications of combining these chronotopes in particular ways.

Categorical structures

I want to reintroduce another of Bakhtin's concepts as a way of feeding the discussion into ways of organising material into categories. Bakhtin's concept of dialogism, which I discussed first in relation to the image, is also relevant to the macro-structures of a text. *Yellow* for example is clearly a video dialogically aware of other images in circulation around its subject (gender and gay sexuality). And in terms of dismantling classical narrative structures, *Yellow* would be an example of a text organising its material primarily through the use of cultural codes. Notice that while it is easy for cultural codes to filter unchallenged into a classical narrative as 'accepted knowledge' and 'common sense', it is rather more difficult for them to do so when they are the prime means of organising the material. At this point, as *Yellow* demonstrates, cultural codes can become the subject of an investigation and critique. Yet while *Yellow* demonstrates a very acute self-awareness of how gender and sexuality are figured in representations outside its own boundaries, as it were, there could be more internal dialogue within the video on the meanings of being gay in a homophobic society. Likewise, *Pissing in the Wind* interrogates masculinity, but arguably only poses one version of it, implying perhaps that that version is inescapable, if lamentable. To be able to articulate a plurality of experiences, and perhaps conflicting arguments, propositions or positions remains one of the most difficult and ambitious of tasks at the level of form. Multiple character formation and interaction is no guarantee of achieving this, for, as we have seen, cast in the mould of the classical narrative, complexity is rapidly sacrificed to closure. The picaresque technique may be one strategy for resisting this, as *The Box* demonstrates, but others need to be developed.

I have already referred to the possibility of organising material into categories: for instance the way *240* used the four themes of love, fear, anger and self-destruction to chronicle the last minutes of a character's thoughts before nuclear annihilation (see chapter five). This video uses a single fictional proposition (the end of the world) and a single character, to provide the continuity and to link each category explored. There is a contradiction, though, between the subject matter, which affects all humanity, and the form, which allows only one identity and rationale (white, male, heterosexual) to organise the imagery. Now of course all texts are finite and all texts have boundaries established by the processes of including and excluding material. Nevertheless, there is a very long way to travel between privileging one perspective and coming up against those finite boundaries. If one relinquishes the unifying role of the central character, organising material via categories may prove a fruitful way of opening up a text and generating more extensive internal dialogue.

The video *True Identities* [9] edges us away from character-centred narrative, while making tongue-in-cheek use of the narrative propensity to ask 'what if?' in order to establish a proposition that can be explored. In this case the 'what if ?' being entertained is the idea that William Shakespeare may have been Willimena Shakespearella, a black woman forced to write under a pseudonym in order to get published. While a text may be organised around thematic categories, *True Identities* is structured around different kinds of formal strategies, which attempt to articulate a dialogue within the text around the 'what if?' scenario. Specifically, the video attempts a humorous exploration of the meanings invested in the sign 'Shakespeare'.

The first formal category the video uses to organise its material is that of the television studio discussion. Here the presenter/chair establishes the subject to be discussed and introduces her parodic panel of guests. These include the famed international medium, Doris Hoax; an Oxford professor of literature, Norman Higginbottom-Smith, a pompous Anglo-Saxon defender of the status quo; and (in an allusion to the anthropologist who challenged the conventions of western society) Myra Mead, a cultural historian specialising in recovering women from the margins of historiography. During the discussion, Doris Hoax is asked how Willimena revealed herself to the medium. Her description of the experience provides the link to the next sequence, in which shots of the black female Shakespearella strolling through gardens with classical columns, are accompanied on the soundtrack by bagpipes. We have seen that fantasy sequences are a recurrent feature of many of the texts discussed in this book. As Cherry Potter writes in her useful book on narrative:

> Many of us experience an excitement when we think about these three concepts [dreams, memories and fantasies], an excitement rooted in the prospect of breaking free from the confines of so-called reality and allowing our imagination to play with our own personal and long-nurtured imagery. [10]

I would only add the rider that all 'personal' imagery always has intertextual resonances with other discourses across various arenas. The social is always already installed in the most private and interior of thoughts, reflections and imagistic reflexes. This can often be obscured by fantasy sequences yoked to a single character. What marks the fantasy sequence in *True Identities* off from the norm, is that while the figure of Doris provides the rationale for the shift in register from studio 'reality' to supernatural communication, the fantasy does not belong to her as an individual character, but rather it functions as a cultural and political fantasy. In voice-over Willimena tells Doris not to disturb her as she is trying to 'get in touch with my African creative energy'. This provides the cue for the third category of formal technique, a montage sequence of African art and carvings accompanied now, not by the sounds of the Celtic fringe, but by African rhythms. In this way the links between an older black African culture and black western culture, links not articulated within the context of the all-white studio panel, here find some space in the text.

After a brief return to the studio, the convention of the studio link and vox pops (the fourth formal category) is used to bring in more 'voices' outside the panel. What follows is a series of short interviews in which respondents reveal what meanings are or might be invested in the sign 'Shakespeare' (as a body of texts and meanings) and how these function within a racist and patriarchal culture. Two white women disbelieve the possibility that Shakespeare could be anything other than the Shakespeare they 'know'. Another white woman sees the prospect of a female Shakespeare as very liberating for women while a black man hopes that it will force people to recognise the contribution black people have made to culture and history. Interestingly some of the actors are used in Brechtian fashion to present different characters/views. Thus the white woman who welcomes the notion of Shakespeare being rediscovered as a black woman, reappears in another role dismissing the idea and claiming that black women are illiterate and 'ponce off the social. Don't get me wrong,' she finishes, 'I'm not a racialist'. We then return to the studio where Professor Higginbottom-Smith argues that defending the Shakespeare that we all 'know' is a very different academic concern to the expressions of crude racism heard in some of the responses. However, the universal 'Shakespeare' that liberal discourse has constructed as a mouthpiece for all humanity, and who has dominated the curriculum and national culture, has certainly been held in place by the gendered and ethnic identity (white, male) of the now dead individual known as William Shakespeare. In other words, would Shakespeare have been installed in the heart of the literary canon and cultural summit if 'he' had been a 'black she'? *True Identities* can be seen as playfully swiming in the same stream as radical critical discourses that have attempted to contest the dominant liberal consensus on the meanings of 'Shakespeare'. Such interventions have sought to reconstruct 'Shakespeare' as a contradictory locus of power struggles around questions of class, colonialism, gender and ethnicity. [11]

Reframe [12] is our second example of a video using categorical structures, and here we move away from narrative structures altogether. In *Reframe* the categorical logic is thematic rather than formal and the theme being explored is video itself and its multiple manifestations within a media(ted) world. We came across these manifestations as a subject of a single text when I discussed *Homework* in chapter two. *Reframe* manages to discuss as many categories of video practice, more explicitly and arguably in a more complex web of associations and implications, despite the fact that *Homework* lasts an hour and a half and *Reframe* some ten minutes. Again this demonstrates that viewing time does not impose limits on what can be articulated. Rather it is a question of the formal strategies selected. *Reframe* does not organise its material into a set of self-contained categories which follow one after another. Indeed, no categories are explicitly announced. Rather the viewer has to work through a montage of sound and images, the underlying rationale for which may only become clear after several viewings. I have tabulated these categories and the means of their articulation (see Fig. 6.8) more or less in the order in which they first emerge in the video. Five of the categories are concerned with different media forms or genres, while the sixth category is more thematic.

Conclusion

I began this chapter by discussing how structuralism has been popularised and fed into the production of classical narratives at the scriptwriting stage. Thus not all examples of explicit theorising are necessarily liberating. However, I have tried to argue that structuralism and other theoretical traditions and concepts may equip you with the means to critique dominant models of organising material into overarching, macro structures and provide the resources and inclination to develop alternatives. The alternatives I have discussed may be of benefit at a pragmatic level, better suiting the

Fig. 6.8 *Reframe* Narrative

CATEGORIES	SOUND/IMAGE
1. Pop Video	1.This frames the opening and end of the video with two iconic images of the pop band. The beginning draws on the band as streetwise and cool as four figures (the videomakers) advance on the camera in long coats, with collars up, to a soul soundtrack. At the end of the video, the iconography of bands 'having fun' is deployed as the 'characters' run around the street.
2. Television Documentary	2.'Who defines the border between public and private?' asks a voice-over. Then cut to a woman talking to an offscreen interviewer (also unheard) confessing that she has never talked about sex to strangers before (including, by implication, the watching audience). She then proceeds to begin to talk about a boyfriend who wanted to be the woman in the relationship. The 'scene' then changes to another sequence of images before returning towards the end of the video (implying the passing of time) where the woman, having evidently completed her story is asking of the professionals: 'is that what you want, is that the sort of thing you wanted me to talk about?'
3. Family Video	3.Setting: a living room. A video of a family outing to the seaside is playing on the television. On the soundtrack we hear a woman talking to other people in the room (all of them unseen) about the various members of her family. Someone is rolling the video backwards and forwards as the woman's memories are stirred. The camera zooms in on a still image as the voice-over declares, 'that's me, there I am!'. The close-up shows us that the texture of the image suggests it is cine-film transferred to video: video, in other words, continuing in the tradition of personal archive. This setting and discussion returns later in the video.
4. Video as Surveillance	4.Various images of surveillance sprinkled throughout the video; plus a spoof Roger Cook type attempt to interview someone who does not wish to be interviewed – resulting in a fracas with the cameraperson – which has now become iconic of so-called investigative journalism.

5. Video as Production Process	5.Various fragments of the video can be collected into this category which essentially refers, often in an obviously staged way, to the making of *Reframe*. Examples of this are: a) Using the graphics of a Channel Four video box. Rachel complains that she has not been getting behind the camera enough and even now the others are 'pissing around outside'. b)A spoof news conference where another member of the production team, Louis de-Val, is asked questions about whether he is going to appear in the video. 'I will appear when I am ready,' he responds after checking with his publicity manager sitting next to him. c) Shots of the videomakers beside a camera, tripod and microphone, apparently recording something but also in rather bored poses (one of them is flicking through a magazine). This is intercut with images from other categories on several occasions. d) The points at which a voice-over asks a question to frame the next set of images, the process of construction and ordering on the part of the videomakers is illustrated by shots of an edit monitor being used to manipulate the first image, which leads into the next sequence. e) Soundtrack over the end credit titles reveals a snippet of a discussion amongst the videomakers.
6. Sex and Communication	6. This is framed by a larger question introduced by the voice-over, using the sound/image strategies referred to in 5, c). 'In the European Single Audiovisual Space', the voice-over asks, 'are we all speaking the same language?' This question refers both to Europe's multilingual character and the wider cultural question around values embedded in communication around sex generally. Cut to a man and a woman dancing coolly, but shot with a red gel over the camera lens

Fig. 6.8 cont.

giving a rather seamy quality to the image. On the soundtrack a man and a woman are speaking Italian. The image subtitles offer an interpretation in English: 'Let's make love. Here. Now.' says the woman. The titles tell us that the man's response is, 'Enter Semiotics or theories of the Subject'. Cut to a man performing fellatio on a high-heeled shoe. Cut to a scene where two women and a man sit at a long table in a spacious white room. After a while one of the women speaks in German. 'Hamlet,' she says to the man. Cut back to the dancing Italians. 'I'll get the yogurt, you get the rubbers. I've got the snorkel,' says the woman. 'I think I've got a clash … on my timetable' the titles translate the man's response. Cut back to the scene which began with 'Hamlet,' and the woman is confessing to having had an affair. Hamlet counters with his own declaration of an affair. The common theme here is the process of appropriating cultural resources from other countries and the necessary (re)interpretation of the material that is required.

low-budget audiovisual practitioner's resource base by breaking away from the particular verisimilitude which the classical narrative weaves. When we ask whether a classical narrative is 'realistic', we often mean whether the story world is convincing and persuasive in its own terms. The verisimilitude of the classical narrative is, as we have seen, built around a causal logic located in individual characters who are supported by continuity of formal characteristics (mise-en-scène, editing, linearity, etc.). Some dramatic situations may definitely benefit from such strategies. *Desperate Minutes* uses clear temporal progression and an entire story bounded by a temporally defined 'moment' (the ninety minutes of a football match) to good effect. This use of time (and suspense) is typical of the classical narrative.[13]

However, in many cases a looser organisation of story material, one with more gaps and dislocations, might open up more opportunities on a low-/no-budget production. But it is important to recognise that this pragmatic response is not a compromise, it is not a resort to flawed aesthetic strategies. Although no doubt from a classical narrative perspective such strategies would be viewed as 'flawed', they have their own logic, their own credibility and persuasiveness. Furthermore, as I have indicated, such aesthetic strategies have not at all been defensively deployed in the shadow of classical narratives. They have been implemented as, and bound up with, confident critiques of the political and artistic limitations of the classical narrative. Hopefully this chapter has given you some practical as well as theoretical inspiration to explore different ways of organising your material – narratively and non-narratively.

Practical Exercises

- Cut up a photo-love story from a teen magazine into single and two-frame pieces, mix these up and give them to someone else to reassemble into the original narrative order. They should do the same for you with another photo-love story. When you have all completed the reassemblage, compare notes on how the task was completed. What knowledge about classical narrative conventions were you drawing on to reconstruct the story? What similarities do the stories share as photo-love stories?

- Now try and combine the two different photo-love stories using parallel narrative strategies. Do such strategies alter the original stories in any way?

- Using a specific thematic category as your rationale (e.g. gender, wealth, the police, etc.) assemble on video between six and twelve images that have been produced by the media industries (film, television, advertising, photography, etc.). Does your assemblage critique, interrogate or reveal something about these representations? In what way might images you could produce yourself (dramatic or documentary) add to your commentary on these media images?

Notes

1 R. Widdicombe, 'Discovering Legends in his Own Lifetime' in the *Sunday Times Supplement* 4th September 1994, pp. 10-11.
2 Widdicombe, *op.cit.*
3 Made by Mike Latham (University of North London, 1993).
4 Made by Tony Holmwood (Brunel University College, 1995).
5 Made by David Gibson, Vanessa Hodge, Tim Hicks, Tim Sullivan, Alaistair Corlett (Brunel University College, 1993).
6 M.M. Bakhtin, *The Dialogic Imagination*, University of Texas Press, Austin 1992, p. 95.
7 Bakhtin, *ibid*, p.245.
8 Bakhtin, *ibid*, p.185.
9 Made by Askala McMorris, Myrad Todd, Anna Wilson, Jayne Rowe, Kalbir Dhillon, Harnake Hunspal, Fiona Morrissey (University of North London, 1993).
10 C. Potter, *Image, Sound and Story: the Art of Telling in Film*, Secker and Warburg, London 1990, p.39.
11 See J. Drakakis (ed), *Alternative Shakespeares*, Methuen, London 1985.
12 Made by Rachel Bell, Tony Cryer, Louis de-Val, Jackie Palmer (University of North London, 1993).
13 D. Bordwell, J. Staiger, K. Thompson, *The Classical Hollywood Cinema*, Routledge, London 1985, pp42-49.

Chapter Seven

Sound

One of the most evident differences between dominant audiovisual practices and low-budget work, turns on the question of sound. The concept of verisimilitude is as applicable here as it is in relation to narrative: sound is used to make the image 'credible' within a very narrow definition of 'realism'. A key feature of dominant cinema is the resources it puts into the post-production of sound. Next time you are watching a medium-budget mainstream movie, count how many people are credited at the end for producing the sound: two dozen or so would not be an unusual number. However, the dominant industry's definitions and practices of how sound 'should' be used are problematic for the videomaker since these narrow boundaries rule out a whole range of possibilities. Yet if you are working with relatively low-grade sound technology at the production and post-production stage, you may well find it necessary to adopt a critical position in relation to those stipulations, since they rule out strategies which could be useful to you in negotiating your skills and resource base. Once more, however, as we shall see, the question of devising aesthetics from necessity also glides into political questions about representation.

The dictatorship of the image

Cinema was never a medium of 'silent' moving images. The cinemas and other sites in which 'silent' film was exhibited, always employed musical accompaniment or even in the early days, the verbal accompaniment of commentators . However, many practitioners and theorists of the 'silent' cinema were hostile to the arrival of the soundtrack which would institutionalise sound as part of the production and post-production of film. In part, the roots of this hostility lay in the concern of early writers on film to identify the specificity of cinema. Some found that specificity in editing (which distinguished it from theatre), or in magical effects, or in the capacity of the image to register movement and time (which distiguished it from still photography). All such discussions though revolved around the imagistic qualities of the medium. Moreover, if the legitimacy of cinema as an art form rested on its differentiation from the other arts, the coming of 'talkies' threatened to drive cinema back towards 'wordy theatricalism'.

Altman claims that such opponents of sound, intent on 'preserving the purity of their "poetic" medium' crucially stalled the development of sound theory.[1] This seems a little unfair since many of these theorists were not against sound *per se*, but rather they made a distinction between the sound film (which many declared themselves to be interested in) and the 'talkie'. They feared, rightly as it turned out, that a very narrow repertoire of sound strategies would be implemented. Rene Clair recognised that the interlocking of the major film corporations with the banks and corporations developing sound technologies (the telephone and music recording companies) ensured that 'talkies' were going to become an entrenched and dominant part of film culture. '[S]ceptics who prophesy a short reign for it will die themselves long before it's over,' he declared.[2]

Specifically the 'talkie' meant dialogue synchronised with the image. For Eisenstein the 'illusion' of talking people, of audible objects went against every montage principle his work stood for.[3] The more sound interlocked smoothly with the image, the more the shot, the basic material of montage, would become inert and frozen into a set of naturalistic relations. But in rejecting the 'talkie' he conducted a polemic in favour of using sound as a montage element in itself. Similarly, for Pudovkin, 'talkies' represented an enormous missed opportunity. 'The role which sound is to play in film' he argued, 'is much more significant than a slavish imitation of naturalism'.[4] His position was similar to that of René Clair, who made a distinction between the limited and disappointing use of sound to imitate real noises and the use of sound to interpret the image, bringing out meanings not evident in the images alone.[5] Thus when Altman complains that such resistances to the 'talkie' laid the basis for the 'ontological fallacy regularly applied to cinema ... that film is a visual medium and that the images must be/are the primary carriers of the film's meaning,' he misses the mark.[6] On the contrary, many opponents of the 'talkie' wanted to expand the possibilities of what one could do with sound far beyond that of synchronised dialogue and synchronised audible objects. Would that such individuals had had the influence Altman implies, but as Clair more realistically acknowledged, such voices of dissent were mere straws in the wind of multinational corporate forces. In fact, if we want to understand why sound theory has developed so slowly and why sound is so routinely marginalised in the educational curriculum, then one need look no further than the 'talkies' themselves. Although the possibilities of using the three components of sound – dialogue, music, and noise/sound effects – have certainly expanded within dominant cinema since the 1950s (listen, for example, to Scorsese's 1976 film, *Taxi Driver*), fundamentally, the principles governing sound–image relations, established during the 1930s, have remained intact for most dominant cinema films.

The conventions of dominant cinema require the soundtrack to be integrated with and subordinate to the image track, which is privileged as the dominant carrier of meanings. The task of sound in this conception is to support the 'reality' or more accurately, enhance the verisimilitude of the image and narrative. As Mary Ann Doane notes, sound practitioners working within the dominant industry are usually complicit in this subordination of the sound since they tend to be uncritically locked into aesthetics which stress a unity of textual elements above all else. This stress on the 'ideal' text being fashioned into organic wholes,[7] rules out any use of sound that is independent of the image track. For, by definition, aesthetics shaped into organic wholes are always hierarchical structures. The organic whole requires that each element finds its place and its place appears predetermined almost – as the term organic implies – by nature. Far from being natural, however, the organic text is persuasive in its verisimilitude simply because it sticks to a narrow and hierarchised set of signifying strategies. In this way convention becomes invisible, the signifier transparent. This is the criterion on which elements are judged to 'fit' within the whole or not. Other kinds of 'fits' between elements (conceptual, thematic, categorical) are only admissible insofar as they are subordinate in their function to the whole, and guarantee narrative verisimilitude.

The empirical aesthetics which govern the image (discussed in chapter two) are thus also imposed on sound: the more invisibly sound accompanies the image, the better, as far as this ideology is concerned. Doane notes that empiricism customarily makes a highly ideological distinction between fact (evidence which appears unmediated by human motives) and value or interpretation (evidence that is recognised as having a source, coming from a position). The empiricist's neat, binary view of the world is often superimposed over image and sound, particularly music and noise. For empiricism, as an ideology of the visible, of immediate appearances, must somehow come to terms with sound even though sound lacks the tangible qualities of the visible. Confronted with something which resists its logic, an empiricist aesthetic must banish music and sound effects to another realm, one that is important in so far as it has qualities that are usefully different to the image, but firmly subordinate to the realm of the image. As Doane argues:

> If the ideology of the visible demands that the spectator understand the image as a truthful representation of reality, the ideology of the audible demands that there exist simultaneously a different order of reality for the subject to grasp.[8]

This different order of reality is that of intuition, emotion, feeling. Empiricism then reproduces the binary world of patriarchal ideology in so far as sound is to the image what woman is to man (valued for her different qualities, but those qualities are less powerful, important, reliable, etc., than those qualities associated with the male): the image is aligned with an unproblematic, 'factual', i.e. verisimilar rendering of reality in the same way that man is aligned with practical, scientific, factual knowledge. We have indicated already in relation to the earlier discussion of *Snuff* how looking is associated with male power in the cinema. Within patriarchal thinking, the construction of women in terms of intuition often has the effect of locating them in the realm of the mysterious, the ineffable. Sound and its effects are often accorded a similar status. We can acknowledge that sound produces a certain *je ne sais quoi* but that is as far as we can go within this ideology. By locating its effects as somehow outside language, beyond anything so rational as analysis, this ideology of the audible frustrates and hinders our understanding of precisely how sound works in relation to the image.[9]

While music and atmospheric noise are consigned to the realm of feeling, the ideological role of the voice in dominant cinema, underpins another tradition of thought often associated with western bourgeois ideology: individualism. As Doane notes:

> The addition of sound to the cinema introduces the possibility of representing a fuller (and organically unified) body, and of confirming the status of speech as an individual property right.[10]

Just as there is a strict hierarchy between the image and sound, so there is a hierarchy within sound in relation to the image. Synchronised dialogue is the sound which best conveys the body as fully in touch with its needs, feelings and wants, thus allowing it to function as the site of causal agency in the classical narrative. Music and sound effects then must not be foregrounded in the sense of cutting across, interrupting or commenting on the dialogue (at least not without narrative explanation). Doane again notes that all traces of production and post-production manipulation and construction of speech must be effaced even more ruthlessly than is the case with music and sound effects. If, for example, characters' dialogue was subject to fades and dissolves in the way that music is, the spectator's sense of the character within the film as being in command of their own destiny would be radically disrupted.[11] The spectator would be reminded forcibly of the character's functional, conventional role within the narrative structure.

The political question which organic aesthetics poses is indicated in Doane's reference to the way sound strategies in dominant cinema (and television) offer us an image of the unified body. Implicitly Doane is drawing on psychoanalytic discourses which have, since Freud, critiqued the view of the human subject as unified, coherent and transparent to themselves. Psychoanalysis understands the subject to be traversed by contradictory drives and desires. It locates these contradictions in the clash between sexual desire and the socio-cultural and institutional constraints within which sexuality and desire is channelled in bourgeois society. At a more mundane, quotidian level we can all no doubt identify shifting, multiple and contradictory thoughts and feelings which we have everyday across a whole range of subjects. Are organic aesthetics capable of representing such a fluctuating experience? Can alternative uses of sound perhaps make a contribution and access this inner world?

Like psychoanalysis, marxism similarly views the individual's identity as fissured, although the cause here is located in the social relationships of capitalism and the effects are also differently conceived. For marxism, the individual is fissured by: the divisions within the labour process, in which a narrow selection of skills and aptitudes get overdeveloped (specialisation) while others are stunted and underdeveloped; by the divisions between work and play, necessity and creativity; by being alienated from control and enjoyment of the social wealth labour produces; by being thrown into competition with fellow humanity; by the struggle to reconcile the rhetoric of bourgeois society (that for example the individual is at the centre of things) with the reality (that the individual is valuable only so far as they can be pressed into the service of capital); by the conflict with the oppressive dimensions of civil life (e.g. the family) to which we remain necessarily attached because, impoverished as they are, they are the only shreds of solidarity and community on offer in an atomised and competitive society. The list could be extended considerably, but the point is made I think. Can organic aesthetics access such contradictory aspects of the individual's fissured life and external world? The debate and the evidence for and against is an ongoing one, and of course there are various gradations within what one may call an organic, or classical narrative text. But if you decide to operate on the margins of or outside those aesthetic rules, then a whole range of other sound/image relationships may be explored. This has the pragmatic benefit of asking audiences to find ways of relating to your work other than comparing them to the well-resourced products of the dominant audiovisual industries and it may open up new possibilities in the representation of life.

Defining sound/image relationships

Before I discuss the three components of sound (dialogue, music and noise) in any detail, we need to define the kinds of relationships which any of those components can have in relation to the image. There are four defining types of relations and most descriptions of sound/image relations requires a pairing of two of the four categories. The first of these pairs is: diegetic and non diegetic sound, which refers to the spatial relationships pertaining between sound and image. As Bordwell and Thompson explain:

> Sound has a spatial dimension because it comes from a source, and that source may be characterised by the space it occupies. If the source of a sound is a character or object in the story space of the film, we call the sound diegetic ... On the other hand there is non diegetic sound, which does not come from a source in the story space.[12]

The other two terms are synchronous and asynchronous sound, which refers to the temporal relationships between sound and image. Independently of where the sounds come from (within or outside the world established on the image track), sound may be matched exactly in time with the image (synchronous sound). If it is not exactly matched, it may have one of three temporal relationships with the image: the sound may constitute the past in relation to the image; the sound may constitute the present in relation to the image (which may be located in the past); or the sound may be located in the future in relation to the image. In all such cases the sound is 'out of sync' with the image and this temporal slippage therefore constitutes asynchronous sound.

i) Synchronic Diegetic Sound: This is the most widespread and dominant use of sound in fiction, i.e., it has its source in the world of the image track and there is an exact temporal match between sound and image. Thus it is any sound (dialogue, music or noise) which characters make and/or can potentially hear and respond to. The sound does not have to be 'in shot' however, and can be used to simply and economically extend the fictional world without the aid of the image. For example, in *Drip* one of the sounds which continually frustrates the protagonist's attempts to get to sleep, is the noise of a party (which we never see) going on next door. *Drip* uses diegetic synchronised sound throughout, such as the dripping tap, the snoring man or the party sounds. But *Drip* casts itself in the genre of the 'silent' comedy and in order for this effect to be achieved, the synchronised sounds are not absorbed naturalistically into the diegesis, but are clearly and self-consciously dubbed over at the post-production stage. For example, when we hear the dripping tap, that is all we hear and the volume is amplified. When we hear the man snoring, that is all we hear, there is not even any room tone, that faint but detectable hum 'created by the movement of air particles'.[13] Thus, in order to recreate a video as parodic 'silent' film, *Drip* must acknowledge the gap between image track and soundtrack, and this in turn allows a simple but effective use of sound appropriate to the videomaker's skills and resource base. *Drip* is an excellent example of a text thinking strategically about the relationship between its resources and its audiences. Such playful appropriations of the silent cinema and the comedy genre in particular, offer possibilities for the videomaker to negotiate some of the problems of using sound in an economical and controlled manner.

However, you may want to use diegetic synchronised sound in a more naturalistic manner in parts of or throughout the video. In this case you will need to think about how the environment will affect the sounds. Different interiors, for example, will produce different kinds of sound and different kinds of problems for sound recording. Environments with lots of hard surfaces like metal and glass will give off bright and sharp sounds, while a room with lots of soft materials (carpets, curtains, upholstered furniture, etc.) absorbs and deadens sound.[14] You will need to think not only about the type of sound you will be dealing with, but the simultaneous mix of sounds there will be at any one moment and the volume you want from each sound. In terms of dialogue you will need to think about whether your characters are moving around and talking, or stationary (obviously it is easier to maintain steady volume levels with the latter). You ought to shoot cutaway shots whenever you think the sound quality of speech might be suffering (competing for example with other noises) so that you can dub dialogue on at post-production without the difficulty of trying to match dialogue with lip movement. While lip-synching requires special technology, cutaways to a character's hands, a shot from behind, a long shot, a cut to another person listening, or to other parts of the mise-en-scene, make post-production dubbing much easier. The question of the long shot being combined with 'close-up' sound poses an interesting point of tension within the classical narrative. A close-up of an object emitting a noise, say a piano, will be louder in a classical film than if it was viewed in long shot, thus preserving some verisimilitude with regard to sound 'perspective'.

However, as Doane notes, when it comes to dialogue, classical narrative will change the rules in order to ensure the privileged role of dialogue within the narrative. Thus we are perfectly familiar with long shots of characters walking along a beach, or through a crowd of people, but we hear their conversation as if we were right next to them.[15] Here verisimilitude is in conflict with narrative intelligibility. Because of this, the paradox of the long shot with 'close-up' sound, is usually used only briefly, perhaps as an introduction to a scene, or to conclude a scene. Extended use throughout a conversation risks drawing the audience's attention to the constructed nature of the sound/image relationship and therefore risks the rupture of verisimilitude. One question you have to address when using synchronic diegetic sound is this: to what extent are you committed to maintaining verisimilitude? This is the sort of question you must resolve at the initial stage of conceptualising your project, otherwise, unplanned or forced breaks in verisimilitude simply look like incompetence. But if it is built into your project from the beginning and used systematically, then a strategy for resolving practical problems looks, rightly, like innovative daring rather than failure. For example, if you have a scene where two characters are conversing outdoors, then you have to negotiate the problem of getting steady volume levels as your characters compete with the wind, cars, aeroplanes, other people, etc. However, you may choose to shoot the scene entirely in long shot (while recording ambient noise) and dub the dialogue over at the post-production stage. The long shots could alternate with moments of silence or pauses between the characters, which would be shown in close-up. Such a stylised use of sound/image would hardly conform to classical verisimilitude, but if used in a planned way this would be its strength at an aesthetic level, while it would resolve certain problems with sound recording at a practical level.

ii) Asynchronic Diegetic Sound: These, then, are sounds which belong to the world of the image track, but which have a dislocated temporal relationship to the image track. As already noted, there are three kinds of asynchronic relationship that can pertain between sound and image. We also need to make a further subdivision as to whether the asynchronism is motivated by the subjective, psychological world of characters, as part of their story space, or whether it exists as a narrator's comment on the characters and/or the world they occupy.

a) The sound may constitute **the past** in relation to the image. As motivated by individual character this may typically take the form of the image constituting the present with the character recalling a sound from the past (whether noise(s), a piece of music or part of a conversation). But it is not essential for character subjectivity to motivate such asynchronous relations. It may also be used as direct commentary on the characters and/or their world, by the narrator. In the case of the documentary, an example of asynchronic diegetic sound would be a sequence in which shots of the subject 'in the present' were overlaid with, for example, the soundtrack from an interview we have already heard the subject give at an earlier point in the text.

b) The sound may constitute **the present** in relation to the image. As motivated by individual character this may typically take the form of a voice-over located in the present, introducing us to a flashback from the past. In the classical narrative the voice-over quickly recedes and synchronic diegetic sound takes over, as in *Double Indemnity* (B. Wilder, USA, 1944). Or perhaps the voice-over is reading a letter that the character is writing to someone telling them what a wonderful time they are having on holiday. We hear them say, 'Dear X…' while the image track reveals the wonderful (or, if the letter is ironic, dreadful) time they have been having. Perhaps these images will be mixed in with one or two shots of the person writing the letter (just to confirm to the audience who is writing and locate the voice firmly as 'the present') and the sequence might easily conclude with image and sound gliding together as the character finishes the letter reading it out aloud.

It is easier to give a brief recognisable example of asynchronic diegetic sound motivated by individual character than it is to suggest an example of the kind which deploys 'external' commentary without extensive explanation/contextualising. However, imagine we have come to the conclusion of a narrative. The image and soundtrack are synchronised: then, with a fade out/fade in, or mix, there is a switch to images we saw earlier but the sound which marks 'the present', say two characters talking, continues over the images. Such a disjunction between sound and image may point up differences between the past and the present vis-a-vis the two characters. An example in the documentary mode would be a simple reversal of the sound image relations given for the example in category a): i.e. images of the subject 'in the past' dubbed with them talking 'in the present'.

c) The sound may be located in **the future** in relation to the image. This is a rather unusual type of asynchronism, although the classical narrative may make momentary use of this sound/image discrepancy as a bridge to the next scene. Here the sound from the next scene 'bleeds' momentarily into the image of the scene we are stiil watching, just as it is closing. In such examples, the act of narration is again foregrounded in so far as an organising force is declaring that it 'knows' what is coming next. Precisely because it is not motivated by individual characters, the classical narrative uses such strategies only briefly. It might indeed be interesting to expand this bridging strategy into a more extensive interpenetration of future sound with images located in the diegetic present. A subjective example of this type of sound/image relationship requires the character to have an auditory premonition of the future, while the image stays in the present. Bordwell and Thompson give the example of Marion in *Psycho* (A. Hitchcock, USA, 1960) who, while driving her car, imagines what her boss will say when he discovers that she has stolen money from him.[16] This type of sound/image relationship is not realisable in the documentary format unless it deliberately constructs the sound as a fictional future set against documentary images.

iii) Non Diegetic Sound: This is sound which does not have a source in the world of the images. In the classical narrative, the largest role for non diegetic sound is reserved for mood music. The characters cannot hear non diegetic music, for it does not belong to their world but is directed at the audience alone. Non diegetic dialogue and noise in a fiction film is unusual (although not unheard of) because of the tendency to absorb everything into the narrative flow, yet by definition, non diegetic sound stands outside the narrativised image. An example of non diegetic dialogue can be found in *Yellow*. What is interesting about the documentary voice used in that video is that it is has no temporal relationship with the image track whatsoever. In this sense, we need a fifth category to define this non relationship since it is neither synchronised with anything going on in the image, nor can it be said to be asynchronic since that presumes that there is a temporal relationship that has been skewed. Thus it is an example of what we might call non synchronic and non diegetic sound.

There are, on the other hand, plenty of examples of non diegetic sound being synchronised with the image for comic and/or polemical purposes. It may seem paradoxical to talk of non diegetic sound being synchronised with the images if the sound by definition comes from elsewhere, but in fact we can talk of a broad synchronisation of non diegetic sound in many cases. Numerous comedy films have employed the device whereby the 'natural' sounds of a scene, action or prop are replaced by synchronised non diegetic sound. Here are Bordwell and Thompson discussing a René Clair film:

> In *Le Million* various characters all pursue an old coat with a winning lottery ticket in its pocket. They converge backstage at the opera and begin racing and dodging around one another, tossing the coat to their accomplices. But instead of putting in the sounds from the actual space of the chase, Clair fades in the sounds of a football game; because the manoeuvres of the chase do look like a football game, with the coat as ball, this enhances the comedy of the sequence. We hear a crowd cheering and a whistle's sound; yet we don't assume that the characters present are making these sounds (so this is not a manipulation of fidelity, as with the earlier examples from *Le Million*).[17]

For some reason Bordwell and Thompson make a distinction between this example of non diegetic sound and the notion of manipulating the expected fidelity of the sound/image relationship. The examples they give of this use of sound from *Le Million* include the clash of symbols played over an image of a plate being dropped, and the sound of a heavy bass drumbeat when the characters collide with each other during a chase sequence.[18] I cannot personally see the difference between these examples and the use of football sounds quoted above. They all seem to me to fall under the category of non diegetic sounds synchronised with the image. However, I raise the point because it illustrates that, while there is a broad consensus when it comes to defining and applying sound concepts, as with the use of any concepts, there are also differences in the way theorists and practitioners define and apply the vocabulary of sound, particularly as it is used in relationship to the image.

I want to conclude this section by fine tuning the definitions and applications of the concepts discussed so far. I have defined synchronous diegetic sound and asynchronous diegetic sound, of which we saw there are three types, which can be further subdivided into psychologically or individually motivated temporal slippage, and temporal slippage which allows the text to comment directly on the event, action, character or situation. Further I have discussed nonsynchronic, non diegetic sound and synchronic, non diegetic sound. But under these definitions is there such a thing as asynchronic, non diegetic sound? The answer must be no. Non diegetic sound can either be manipulated to match the image as in the comic examples given above, or its relation is non temporal rather than asynchronic as in the example from *Yellow*. By definition, asynchronic sound refers to a set of dislocated temporal relationships which requires a sense of the 'now' , a sense of 'before' in relation to the now, and a sense of 'later' or yet to be in relation to the now. Non synchronous sound cannot function in this way since there are no temporal relationships, even ambiguous ones, between sound and image. Fig. 7.1 summarises the permutations discussed so far. It is now time to consider some of the ways in which noise, dialogue and music may be used.

Noise

In his discussion of asynchronic sound Pudovkin locates the motivation for such a formal strategy firmly in our natural subjective life. Pudovkin argues that asynchronic sound is far more common to our aural perceptions of the world as lived than synchronic diegetic sound. What we hear is as much a product of our constantly shifting and fluctuating attention and thoughts as it is of the sounds existing to be heard in the first place. Here is his hypothetical example, drawn from 'actual life':

> the reader, may suddenly hear a cry for help: you see only the window; you then look out and at first see nothing but the moving traffic. But you do not hear the sound natural to these cars and buses; instead you hear still only the cry that first startled you...now watching the [injured] man, you become aware of the din of traffic passsing, and in the midst of its noise there gradually grows the piercing signal of the ambulance. At this your attention is caught by the clothes of the injured man: his suit is like that of your brother, who, you now recall, was due to visit you at two o' clock ... all sound ceases and there exists for your perceptions total silence. Can it be two o' clock? You look at the clock and at the same time you hear its ticking.[19]

Pudovkin grounds his aesthetics by using 'natural' perception as a standard, but a much more 'subjective' version of seeing and hearing is manifest in his theory and practice (and in the above example) than say the 'objective' seeing and hearing that characterises dominant audiovisual texts. For the latter, natural perception means an invisible omniscient narrator organising everything we see and hear, in order for the spectator to have maximum control and mastery over the unfolding narrative. As we saw in relation to Pudovkin's editing and as we see in relation to the example given above, Pudovkin's spectator is invited into a world in which what is interesting and what is striking is in considerable (audiovisual) perceptual flux. Thus we can measure the distance between Pudovkin and the dominant cinema of his time.

	SYNCHRONOUS	ASYNCHRONOUS
DIEGETIC		**DIEGETIC**
	Eisenstein: 'the illusion of talking people, of audible objects'. Sound and image are meshed tightly together.	a) sound is located in the past vis-à-vis the image. b) sound constitutes the present in relation to the image which is located in the past. c) sound is located in the future in relation to the image. All three categories of asynchronous sound could be motivated by the perception of the individual character(s), or by the text itself commenting on the diegetic space.
NON DIEGETIC		**NON DIEGETIC**
	Comic example from *Le Million*. Or for polemical use in a documentary e.g. a politician found to have asked Parliamentary questions for cash might be synched with the noises of a pig on the soundtrack.	
NON DIEGETIC		
	E.g. *Yellow*	
	NON SYNCHHRONOUS	

Fig. 7.1

If that distance is measured, say in centimetres for Pudovkin, then for someone like Dziga Vertov, it must be measured in metres. For Vertov there is no question of grounding his aesthetics in a conception of 'natural' perception. Vertov's documentaries radically reorganise the materials they record precisely because, for him, ordinary perception has only a rather limited capacity to understand the world in all its chaotic, swirling movement. The Kino-Eye and Kino-Ear have 'objective' capacities built into them, which must be used to liberate the human senses from their temporal and spatial limitations. For Bazin, the 'objective' qualities of the cinematic apparatus function as part of a polemic on behalf of transparent technique. In his conception, cinema exists above and independently of human struggles, and thus is able to record them faithfully. For Vertov, on the other hand, the 'objective' qualities of the cinematic apparatus mean that it can be independent, not of human struggles *per se*, but of our ordinary perception of the world and our endeavours within it. This is why for Vertov, the notion of 'objectivity' can be reconciled with maximising and utilising all of cinema's formal powers and strategies in order to represent the world and enrich our ordinary human perceptual apparatus.

Jean Epstein's conception of slow motion sound runs along similarly Vertovian lines (although without the marxist politics). Just as the slow motion image can transform our ordinary perception of a boxer's jab from 'a single and rectilinear movement' into 'a combination of multiple and infinitely varied muscular movements', so sound can be slowed down, its various components separated out and magnified. In particular, Epstein had noises in mind:

> slow motion sound [can] discover, for example, that the monotonous and blurred howling of a storm breaks up, in a more refined reality, into a crowd of very different and never before heard sounds: an apocalypse of shouts, cooings, rumblings, squealings, boomings, tones and notes for most of which no name exists. A less rich example can just as well be chosen: the sound of a door opening and closing. Slowed down, this humble, ordinary sound reveals its complicated nature, its individual characteristics, its possibilities of dramatic, comic, poetic or musical meaning.[20]

Recording a sound such as a closing door at 'normal' speed produces sharp peaks and troughs in the sound waves. Rerecording the sound at a slower speed, the peaks and troughs become less acute, the wave is drawn out into little bumps and more gradual slopes as each of the elements which compose the sound of the door closing, extend their audio life. Just as Eisenstein could write about montage being the process where by the autonomy of the separate elements of the image are maintained, so too the single, unified, homogenous sound now becomes broken down into its separate components. Thus, the humble sound of the door closing turns into the creak of the hinges, the rattle of the door handle, the latch scraping across the metal plate before clicking into place, the door hitting the frame, etc. Once you start to break the world of noise down into its constituent components, it becomes a huge resource which can be tapped, sampled, and reworked. And as with the world of images, if you have access to digital reproduction, sound becomes as infinitely pliable as the image. But even without digital reproduction, sound is relatively easy to manipulate on videotape.

Let us now turn to a concrete example of noise being used non diegetically and asynchronically. My example is a sequence from *Hour of The Furnaces* (F. Solanas and O. Getino, Argentina, 1968), a film celebrated for its ability to combine formal innovation and daring with with radical politics.[21] Specifically the film attempts to situate what was then the contemporary social crisis of Argentina, in the context of neo-colonialism. Fig. 7.2 tabulates the sequence which begins with the title: 'The Daily Violence'. The film articulates a complex mix of noises and images in order to represent two distinct but interlocking kinds of violence which the people of Argentina have to contend with. The first kind has been written about extensively by, among others, Frantz Fanon. This is the role of physical, military violence directed at the colonised and neo-colonised people.[22] This kind of violence is easy enough to represent, and indeed there is an established iconography around street battles which does just that. However, sociologists and political philosophers have pondered about the way whole societies, though riddled with inequality, continue to reproduce themselves without direct coercion being exerted on a daily basis. A vast body of work on the role of ideas (ideology) in reconciling people to the status quo has been developed.[23] Other explanations emphasise less the role of ideas than material factors, or what Marx called the 'dull compulsion of economics'.[24] Among the material explanations for social cohesion even in the teeth of inequality, are: the routinisation of work, and the necessity to earn a wage; the threat of unemployment; the

Hour of The Furnaces

Image	Dialogue	Noise
Titles: 'The Daily Violence'		
Exterior shots of office windows; camera sweeps over roof tops of a city.		Humming of a machine, sirens.
Exterior shots of people running and on bicycles: right to left, left to right.		Machine making a punching sound: regular, systematic.
Title: 'The violence visited on the Latin American people is constant, planned, systematic.'		
Interior shots of factory workers	Voice 1 (male): 'I'm a worker, but I've been laid off. I've always worked, even on Sunday.'	Background noise of machines operating continues throughout this sequence: but periodically breaking through this is the sound of a machine making a high, rapid whirring sound. When it comes in, this sound is as loud as the dialogue.
	Voice 2 (m): 'There's no work now. Factories are closing.'	
	Voice 3 (female): 'We work hard, we behave ourselves. But we're paid very little.'	
	Voice 4 (m): 'The government told the police to surround the warehouse. We had to beg for food at the farms.'	
	Voice 5 (m): 'They found out I'd been a union official and wouldn't take me on.'	
Title: 'The Daily Violence'		
Interior shots of workers clocking in their time cards.	Voice 6 (m): 'Of course I'm afraid of losing my job. I Have to think of my family.'	The sound of the machine making a punching sound now returns, juxtaposed against the image; it is now confirmed as a time clock punching the workers cards. The punching sound increases in frequency then drops again. It is joined now by an intermittent drilling sound.
	Voice 7 (m): '3 of my friends were killed by police. I was fired because when Peron fell everyone was changed.'	
	Voice 8 (m): 'They didn't shoot in the air, they shot directly at us.'	
	Voice 9 (m): 'The police guarded the doors.	
	Voice 10 (f): 'There's repression in the factories.'	
Lights bobbing up and down in darkness – an almost abstract image. Then the lights are revealed as miners' lamps.		Babble of voices: growing in volume.
Title: 'Our war is the peace, the order, the normality of the system'		

Fig. 7.2

interdependence of social life, making integration into the system a material and contractual force which need have little ideological dimension. All exert strong pacifying and atomising forces on the exploited. It is this other daily coercion or violence which the sequence from *Hour of the Furnaces* also seeks to articulate, but outside any narrative framework.

After the titles we see several exterior shots of office windows: the image connotes the anonymity of daily life and/or perhaps its facade of 'normality'. The sound of a machine, the underlying motif of the sequence, is first heard at this point. Since the time of the Futurists' celebration of the machine, the imagery and sounds of industry and technology have percolated into popular culture, but rarely can they have been mobilised with such analytical precision as in this film. There is at this stage no dialogue. Then the sirens cut in to connote urgency, danger, the presence of the authorities. We see images of people running and these shots are cut against the punching sound of a machine. Alberto Cavalcanti suggested exploiting the ambiguous possibilities of noises, the fact that they 'do not inevitably suggest what made them'.[25] The punching sound, precisely because it is divorced from the image, starts to acquire metaphorical significance. Society is like a machine; oppressive, pummelling. Yet because the sound is divorced from the image and therefore cannot be definitely pinned down, the punching noise also doubles as a signifier of gun shots from which the people we watch could be fleeing. Thus the one sound intertwines the two types of daily violence: society as a dull compulsive machine and the coercive forces of the state.

The images then shift to interior shots of factory workers and non synchronised, non diegetic dialogue cuts in. Here noise begins to function almost classically as background, as ambient sound. However, the sounds remain constant even while the image track cuts around to various interior factory locations. Thus the sound appears to be functioning in a broadly synchronic diegetic way, but on the other hand it is clearly being manipulated at the post-production stage. This delicate ambivalence in the use of background sound is important because it signifies that the film is not really committed to verisimilitude. Thus it makes sense when the high whirring sound of a machine (completely divorced from the image) is periodically foregrounded, cutting across the dialogue of the workers. Here, noise moves from merely signifying the mood or feel of the environment (its dominant usage as Doane points out), to the status of something which has to be analysed and comprehended as much as the dialogue. What the sound 'means' is also tied up with the fact that 'noise' escapes from its usual low status in the hierarchy of volume, to actually compete with the dialogue of the workers. It is as if the machines are bolting on the walls of society's prison, fixing and locking people into the oppressed roles described by the voices.

Then we hear the punching sounds heard earlier over shots of workers clocking in their time cards. The sound is now retrospectively hooked up to its source so that it functions as more evidence of the way the working class suffer the daily violence of regulation and policing. Even now, sound and image remain in an asynchronic relationship, allowing the text to play with the rapidity of the noise, a sort of 'fast motion' sound (coupled with volume amplification). Thus the musical, expressive qualities of noise (in this case the rhythmic tempo) which Epstein was interested in, are brought to the fore. The time clock, a 'normal' feature of working life for many people, becomes connoted as sinister and oppressive, through these sound strategies. Finally, even the dialogue becomes a kind of noise as the voices run into each other. Where as before we heard snatches of dialogue linked thematically by their shared expression of anxiety, fear and passivity, now, as the voices merge into one another, it is if the clamour for change and for resistance is building, growing, and becoming more excited.

Dialogue

When the theorists and practitioners of silent cinema did think about the possibilities of sound in the cinema, they were inclined to think more positively and creatively about the use of noise than about dialogue. We have seen how effectively noises from an environment can be used to comment on it and our relationships to it. Yet Pudovkin's innovative thoughts on the asynchronous use of noise contrasts with the rather limited ambitions he has for asynchronous dialogue. Here he complains that films are in danger of reducing editing to 'no more than a cold verbatim report' [26]as the spectator's attention is switched neatly and mechanically from one character to the next. Pudovkin wants instead to open up the possibilities of cutting to a character before they begin to speak, still listening to another speaker, and vice versa, cutting to a character after they have begun talking. Such moments, in which sound and image lag behind or anticipate one another, are indeed useful examples of expanding the rhythm and meanings of dialogue and image relations, but they are noticeably less radical than Pudovkin's thoughts on noise, and indeed such devices are now routinely used by dominant cinema. If Pudovkin has already conceded too much ground to the 'talkies', other theorists/filmmakers of his era would largely ignore dialogue altogether in a bid to have no truck with the enemy.

Yet clearly the possibilitites of speech are too important to reject or leave confined to a narrow repertoire of uses and meanings. Before we even think about the ways you might use dialogue formally, it is worth thinking about the range of linguistic variations you can/want to draw into representation. Generally, film and even television have a rather restricted range of dialects and accents which they regard as 'acceptable'. The term 'dialect' refers to vocabulary (word selection) and grammar structure (word combination) common to a group/region, whereas 'accent' refers to the pronunciation of words. In Britain there is a fairly strong correlation between social class and regional dialects and accents. The higher up a speaker is located in the class hierarchy, the less marked the regional accents and dialects become, and the more the speaker is likely to identify with 'standard' English. Of course 'standard' English is itself the dialect and accent of the southern upper middle class, who have merely demonstrated their cultural hegemony rather than their grasp of linguistics by establishing their speech patterns as the norm. Conversely, the closer a speaker is located towards the base of the class structure, the more localised regional dialects and accents become.

There is also the question of language. The domination of English as Britain's national language is historically linked to the political subjugation of Wales, Northern Ireland and Scotland. Thus language use is deeply embedded in questions of resistance/subordination, autonomy/dependence, and different, perhaps conflicting, feelings of belonging and identity. Furthermore, in a world where population movement is increasingly common, there are now more than one hundred languages being spoken in the different ethnic communities in Britain. These include: Punjabi, Bengali, Urdu, Gujarati, Italian, Greek, Spanish and Yiddish. Although there are notable exceptions such as Welsh Channel Four, one could hardly say that such multi-lingual diversity achieves much of a profile in the British media. *Eastenders*, for example, has Asian characters but I cannot recall the series making any use of this potential diversity in order, for example, to explore the interaction of class and ethnic identities.

It is worth pointing out two other dimensions which impact upon language, that of gender and the contexts in which language is used. While less obviously gendered than some languages, for example Japanese, studies have found some gendering patterns to English male and female speech. For example, women are more likely to use emotive adjectives such as 'super' and 'lovely' (something which the Philadelphia soft cheese spread adverts play upon). More seriously, gender patterning has been discerned in cross-sex conversation:

> Women have been found to ask more questions, make more use of positive and encouraging 'noises' (such as mhm) ... men are much more likely to interrupt (more than three times as much, in some studies), to dispute what has been said, to ignore or respond poorly to what has been said, to introduce more new topics into the conversation, and to make more declarations of fact or opinion. [27]

It is easy to see how such speech characteristics are produced by and contribute to the reproduction of patriarchal relations. However, we should be immediately cautious about fastening onto such characteristics in a rigid way. For example, how are masculine and feminine characteristics distributed within same-sex dialogue; how does class cut across gender in terms of power; and how does power in general ebb and flow across different situations and contexts? Indeed, the time and place of verbal communication is a significant determinant on language use in itself. Parties, funerals, interviews, public transport, etc., will all encourage certain types of speech and rule out others as inappropriate A very important component to the meaning of any speech act is the extent to which it recognises, submits to or defies such norms.

Let us now list some of the kinds of language acts which may be drawn upon: a) 'normal' conversation, b) interview, c) reading aloud, d) translation, e) free association, f) interior thoughts, g) voice-over, h) subtitles and titling. These different kinds of language use may be articulated by the various formal strategies already outlined: diegetic synchronic sound, non diegetic, etc. I am less interested here in listing exhaustively examples of such formal strategies in relation to language, than I am in exploring how dialogue can be presented in ways that explore such themes as sociality through language, the articulation of power relations through language and conflicting ideas and values. As Voloshinov reminds us:

> Consciousness takes shape and being in the material of signs created by an organised group in the process of its social intercourse. The individual consciousness is nurtured on signs; it derives its growth from them; it reflects their logic and laws. The logic of consciousness is the logic of ... communication, of the semiotic interaction of a social group ... Consciousness can harbor only in the image, the word, the meaningful gesture, and so forth.[28]

In discussing Godard's use of characters reading aloud from books, magazines, newspapers, etc., Alan Williams suggests that whatever is revealed about specific characters, the general implication of such a strategy is that speech is caught up in the networks of communicaton and the processes of social intercourse which Voloshinov insists on. As Williams puts it, in Godard's films

> language is thus shown to be separable from the people who speak it. It does not merely 'express' them but also works through them. 'One's own' voice is shown to be simply a particular variety of language use.[29]

Thus Godard's films remind us that we do not generate language ourselves: it is never our own private property, or a unique expression of self. For film and videomakers there is also the possibility of exploring the continuities and breaks between writing and/or speech and the world of images by setting the latter (from magazines, newspapers, etc.) in some kind of juxtaposition with the soundtrack. Such asynchronicity would open up the possibility of exploring the contemporary media(ted) world and people's negotiations through it. Or perhaps the continuities and breaks between past and present can be explored by reading aloud from an old text on the soundtrack with visuals from the present on the image track, or alternately, a verbal/written text from the present juxtaposed with images from the past.

Godard also appropriates the documentary strategy of the interview in his dramatic fictions. In *Tout va bien* (J.L.Godard/J.P.Gorin, 1972) all the principal protagonists get at least one direct to camera address where they step outside the narrative and speak to the audience about what has been happening in the film. In this way a range of conflicting perspectives on the action are articulated. At the same time, stepping out of the specific and concrete world of the narrative affords the opportunity to move from the particular to the general/historical/institutional as the interview allows dialogue to shift into reflection, information, philosophy, etc. As far as fictional texts go, it is unusual to use the voice in a non diegetic interview, although

Yellow does just that very successfully, and it is a strategy that could be explored further. As we have seen, *Hour of the Furnaces*, a documentary, uses a collage of non diegetic interviews. Whether diegetic synchronous, asynchronous or non diegetic, the interview provides a space in the text, be it narrative or categorical or some other mode of organisation, for direct exposition of one sort or another.

Fiction also has the possibility of capturing interior dialogue to articulate the continuities and differences between external appearences and/or externalised dialogue and internal thoughts. For Voloshinov, 'the psyche is pre-eminently the word – inner speech ... constitutes the foundation, the skeleton of inner life. Were it to be deprived of the word, the psyche would shrink to an extreme degree'.[30] A common use for inner speech as a device is to articulate the thoughts of one character about a situation and/or other character(s), which cannot, for one reason or another, be exteriorised. Inner speech also exists as a kind of internal dialogue which provides the opportunity to develop a line of thinking in the absence of people with whom such a conversation would be appropriate. Such examples of inner speech are characterised by their relative coherence, by the fact that it is inner speech which closely resembles the logic and grammar of exteriorised dialogue. But there are other forms of inner speech which work in less coherent, linear, metonymic ways. Here representation of inner speech can articulate the psyche's lateral, fragmentary, associational modes of logic.

I have already indicated the multi-lingual possibilities of language use that lie outside the dominant 'national' language. Such possibilities imply the need for translation, achieved conventionally either by a voice-over or by graphic translation in the form of subtitles. In a documentary the original voice is usually retained on the soundtrack at a low volume while an overlaid voice-over translates what is being said. Typically, the voice of the interpreter does not come from the same culture as the speaker, but rather from the presumed culture of the audience. We can tell this by the clash of intonation (pitch and melody), and different accentuation of words and tempo that the disembodied voice has to that of the on screen speaker.[31] Yet despite these clear differences, the voice-over rarely admits to the work of translation (e.g. saying 'S/he thinks that it is unlikely that…') but instead pretends to 'be' the voice of the speaker. It is as if the voice-over is so confident of its status as 'truth' for the assumed audience (compared with the 'unintelligible' signifiers of the speaker) that it can occupy this rather incongruous and peculiar position between translating and being the speaker's voice. It would be interesting to try and expand this repertoire of conventions to foreground the act of translation as interpretation. The repertoire of uses for subtitling could also be greatly expanded. We have already seen how in *Reframe* subtitles are playfully used to foreground various gaps, blockages and interpretations involved in communication. Another example of the comic and political possibilities of subtitling is given by Shohat and Stam:

> In the late 1960s and 1970s, French leftists reportedly 'kidnapped' kung fu films, giving them revolutionary titles … and incendiary subtitles. A sequence of devastating karate blows would be subtitled: 'Down with the bourgeoisie!' thus providing a left political anchorage for what are essentially exploitation films.[32]

Indeed, there are further possibilities: instead of translating, subtitles could also comment on 'native' speech, describing moods, intentions, asking questions of the audience, providing non-narrative, contextual information etc.

The question of subtitling leads on to the wider possibilities of graphic expression. Conventionally, the title and closing credits of a film or programme are presented graphically rather than vocally. The transformation of language into a two-dimensional form presents all sorts of possibilities that are not present in speech. Capitalisation, punctuation, colour, spelling (e.g. variations on normal spelling), abbreviations, and spatial organisation (including size of letters, distance between letters or words, direction, angle, thickness of strokes) are just some of the variables that can be used to give titles an expressive as well as informative role.[33] Fig. 7.3 is a simple title from a documentary on mods.[34] The sudden appearance of the words, in the lower half of the image (underlined by the exclamation mark) gives it a 'titles with attitude' feel and expresses, along with the bold, neat regular graphics, some of the distinctive qualities of the mod style. Use of titles can also be extended throughout a text. *240* for example flashes up the passing seconds at various moments (120, 60), while a student video documentary, *The Most Dangerous Man*[35] (a reference to John Major after his notorious attack on street beggars), conveys information about homelessness through the use of graphic titles rather than a voice-over. *The Box*, on the other hand, uses its red and blue titles as part of the video's coding of the struggle between life and death. With the possibility of

Fig. 7.3

manipulating the graphic materiality of titles, with their direct address and with the impact gained from simply shifting into a new set of stimuli, titles can function as 'attractions' in the Eisensteinian sense. It is very much in this sense of assaulting the spectator's sensory apparatus, that the titles in the opening sequence of *Hour of the Furnaces* shoot out of the darkness, leaping and multiplying, attempting to seize the spectator in their 'hour' of social crisis.

Music

Music can be used diegetically or non diegetically. It can function as a marker in terms of historical period and/or it can express relevant themes, particularly through lyrics. Of course, using pre-recorded music requires you to negotiate the law of copyright. As I have indicated already, the expanding possibilities of mechanical reproduction are in fundamental conflict with the question of ownership and royalties. 'It may seem obvious that a song belongs to the creators and the company that produced it,' argues Colin MacCabe, but, he asks,

> doesn't it also belong to all listeners for whom it is a crucial personal memory? Shouldn't there be some attempt to limit copyright by money as well as time? When the Rolling Stones have made millions of pounds out of 'Satisfaction', shouldn't it by that very fact be in the public domain?[36]

Unfortunately such cultural arguments are unlikely to impress the music recording conglomerates. Copyright law is here stay as long as the profit motive dominates. Thus it may be less time consuming and cheaper simply to produce your own musical accompaniment. *240* uses a simple, electronic based, self-created, non diegetic soundtrack. A basic rhythm comprising bass and drums was laid down using a 6/8 time to approximate the feel of the character's heartbeat. This was then layered with simple riffs from the guitar and organ. Then a collage of sound effects were mixed in from an effects tape, including sirens, crowd chants, babies crying, glass breaking and explosions. All of this then increases in tempo as the video progresses. *Halt*, by contrast, uses a rather more sparse musical accompaniment to equally good effect by employing a single instrument: the bodhran. An interesting example of recording and reinterpreting an old song in the public domain, is achieved by *The Most Dangerous Man*. In this video 'Land of Hope and Glory' is rendered on an old, somewhat out of tune piano and performed in a slow, listless fashion ironically undercutting the song's usual connotations of energy and pride. Here we have an audio example of the debate concerning the ratio between emotion and critical reevaluation which I discussed around intellectual and emotional montage. In its reworked form and new context, the song stirs the emotions in a way that drives home the gap between myth and reality rather than seeking to close that gap in a moment of critical capitulation.

Conclusion

In this chapter I have tried to give some indication of the historical debates around sound and how past theorists and practitioners have engaged with it. As ever, for both them and you, any such engagement takes place in the shadow of the dominant models for sound theory and practice. The principles underpinning these models need to be clear to you (organic aesthetics, verisimilitude, transparency, classical narration, etc.) in order for you to understand how it is that generally, sound use operates within a very narrow range of possibilities. Hopefully, the concepts I have discussed in this chapter will help you to map sound, define its uses, and give it a tangible quality so that you can begin to break down its relationship to the image and explore less commonly used strategies. The question then is why you should want to do this. As with other chapters, I have suggested that there are pragmatic and political issues at stake.

Practical Exercises

The following exercises could be done in camera with a microphone, or with a tape recorder, VCR and television monitor, although access to an editing suite will allow more complex experiments.

- Try playing different musical accompaniments across found images. How, if at all, do the different musical soundtracks alter the possible meanings of the image?

- Play one sound effect across a blank screen. What images does the sound effect conjure up? Play the same sound effect in conjunction with a sequence of images. Now mix in anoth-er very different sound effect. How has this altered the possible meanings of the image track? Mix in a third sound effect, again try to make it as different from the previous two as possible. What is happening to the meaning of the images?

- Wim Wenders' film, *Wings of Desire* (W. Ger./Fr., 1987) makes extensive use of internal dialogue to access the thoughts of characters. Shoot some video footage of people, a scene, etc., and lay down a dialogue track to represent inner speech. What different characteristics and qualities can you give inner speech? What effects does it have on our reading of the image?

Notes

1 R. Altman, 'The Evolution of Sound Technology' in *Film Sound: Theory and Practice*, Weis and Belton (eds), Columbia University Press, New York 1985, p.52.
2 R. Clair, 'The Art of Sound' in *Film Sound, ibid*, p.92.
3 Eisenstein, et al, 'A Statement' in *Film Sound, ibid*, p.84.
4 Pudovkin, 'Asynchronism as a Principle of Sound Film' in *Film Sound, ibid*, p. 86.
5 Clair, *op. cit.*, p.93.
6 Altman, *op. cit.*, p.51.
7 M. A. Doane, 'Ideology and the Practice of Sound Editing and Mixing' in *Film Sound, ibid*, p. 56-57.
8 Doane, *ibid*, p.55.
9 Doane, *ibid*, p.56.
10 M.A. Doane, 'The Voice in Cinema: The Articulation of Body and Space' in *Film Sound, ibid*, p.162.
11 Doane, 'Ideology and the Practice of Sound Editing and Mixing', *op.cit.*, p.58.

12 D. Bordwell and K. Thompson, 'Fundamental Aesthetics of Sound in the Cinema' in *Film Sound, ibid*, pp.191-192.
13 S. Handzo, 'A Narrative Glossary of Film Sound Technology' in *Film Sound, ibid*, p.395.
14 Handzo, ibid.
15 Doane, 'Ideology and the Practice of Sound Editing and Mixing', *op.cit.*, p. 59.
16 Bordwell and Thompson, *op cit.*, p.198.
17 Bordwell and Thompson, *ibid*, p.192.
18 Bordwell and Thompson, *ibid*, p.191.
19 Pudovkin, *op. cit.*, p.87.
20 J. Epstein, 'Slow Motion Sound' in *Film Sound, ibid*, p.144.
21 R. Stam, 'The Hour of the Furnaces and the Two Avant-Gardes' in *Reviewing Histories*, Hallwalls, New York 1987.
22 F. Fanon, *The Wretched of the Earth*, Penguin, 1967.
23 See T. Eagleton, *Ideology: an introduction*, Verso, London 1991.
24 See N. Abercrombie, *et al*, *The Dominant Ideology Thesis*, Allen and Unwin, 1980.
25 A. Cavalcanti, 'Sound in Films' in *Film Sound, ibid*, p.108.
26 Pudovkin, *op. cit.*, p.88.
27 D. Crystal, *The Cambridge Encyclopedia of Language*, Cambridge University Press, 1987, p.21.
28 V. N. Voloshinov, *Marxism and the Philosophy of Language*, Seminar Press, London 1973, p. 13.
29 A. Williams, 'Godard's Use of Sound' in *Film Sound , op.ci*t., p.333.
30 Crystal, *op.cit.*, p.169.
31 Crystal, *op.cit.*, p.169.
32 E. Shohat and R. Stam, 'The Cinema after Babel: Language, Difference, Power' in *Screen* vol. 26, no. 3-4 1985, p.48.
33 Crystal, *op.cit.*, p.179.
34 *Mods,* by Richard Jones (Brunel University, 1994).
35 Made by Cory Peters, Lynne Rennison, Barbel Neumann, Leslie Faiza, Ulrika Rogalla (University of North London, 1993).
36 I. Julien and C. MacCabe, *Diary of a Young Soul Rebel*, BFI, London 1991, p.103.

Chapter Eight

Documentary

In previous chapters I have discussed particular levels or components of the audiovisual text. I now want to discuss a tradition of low-budget audiovisual production which I discussed historically in chapter three: the documentary. Here I want to focus on its audiovisual components in more detail and the philosophies and politics which animate these textual components. The marginal place of documentary in both the culture industries and in academia, means that people often have little sense of the diversity of audiovisual practices which characterises documentary. At the same time, this marginality is often combined with a prestigiousness and authority which can be exclusive and intimidating. Thus many of the possibilities of the documentary and its relevance to low-budget production may be missed.

Documentary and the Enlightenment

The documentary form owes its high status to its roots in the period of the Enlightenment. One can be critical of these roots without necessarily rejecting the Enlightenment ideals which infuse the documentary tradition. The term Enlightenment refers to the climate of rationalism and individualism which developed in eighteenth century Europe. This new intellectual community, inspired by advances in science, were opposed to the divine right of kings (the philosophy of feudalism) and the unquestioning rule of the church in intellectual and philosophical matters. The new intellectuals, very much part of a new rising class in society (the bourgeoisie), believed that science and its methods could understand the natural and social world and therefore contribute to the emancipation of humanity from urgent wants, despotism and other afflictions. The new print media, books and journals carried the message of the Enlightenment through out Europe. This belief in the link between knowledge and progress connects John Grierson, one of the 'fathers' of the documentary movement, to the Enlightenment some two centuries after it first emerged. Grierson saw in the new mass media of film, the prospect of combatting some of the 'pessimism that had settled on Liberal theory' after the first world war.

> We noted the conclusion of such men as Walter Lippman, that because the citizen, under modern conditions, could not know everything about everything all the time, democratic citizenship was therefore impossible. We set to thinking how a dramatic apprehension of the modern scene might solve the problem, and we turned to the new wide-ranging instruments of radio and cinema as necessary instruments in both the practice of government and the enjoyment of citizenship.[1]

Thus progress, ushered in by modernity but then apparently threatened by 'modern conditions' could be set on the right tracks again by the documentary. In this way the documentary likes to locate itself within what Bill Nichols calls, 'the discourses of sobriety'.[2] Seriousness, accuracy, knowledge and social purpose: these are the qualities which underpin such discourses of sobriety as economics, politics, education and the sciences. (It is precisely the documentary's sobriety which is undercut in the spoof documentary. Here, the formal strategies which resonate 'sobriety' – e.g. neutral narration in voice-over – are combined with subjects which are manifestly comic or absurd). A number of Enlightenment themes are evident in the documentary project conceived by Grierson, which remains in many ways, the paradigm today. These themes are: a) that rational knowledge of society is possible; b) that such knowledge is 'objective' which is to say it is true irrespective of who articulates it and to whom that knowledge is said to apply; c) that sociological understanding of society is better than ignorance, superstition, dogma and ideology (i.e. false beliefs); d) and that such knowledge, once acted upon, will (or at least could) lead to progress (for Grierson, by citizens exercising choices at the ballot box).[3] It is b), the assumption of objectivity, which has been particularly vulnerable to criticism. It has been pointed out that the Enlightenment's historic roots in the white, male, Eurocentric, bourgeois subject, inevitably compromised its project. The British documentary's own history reproduces this problem. The first state-supported production base for the realisation of Grierson's ideals was the Empire Marketing Board. As Grierson notes, this existed to 'bring the Empire alive in contemporary terms, as a commonwealth of nations and as an international combine of industrial, commercial, and scientific forces'.[4] As Philip Rosen observes, the contradiction between Grierson's notion of the 'democratic citizen-subject' and support for Britain's colonial structures makes not the smallest of self-conscious ripples across Grierson's discourse.[5] This does illustrate that the Enlightenment belief in the 'objectivity' of knowledge, regardless of who is speaking to whom and about what (in this case colonialist speaking to colonised about the virtues of the Empire) is, to say the least, complacent and problematic. The production of knowledge about a subject/issue must inevitably say something about where you are coming from. There is nothing wrong with being explicit about your starting points, your values, and as we shall see, these can be articulated through the various components of the documentary's audiovisual language. You should not be afraid to use the documentary to express yourself, nor feel that an audience will reject such expressions. Audiences are perfectly capable of assessing the impact your values and beliefs have upon the material you are dealing with, particularly when the text finds ways of being honest and upfront about its position(s).

The Enlightenment project defines not only the emergence of documentary in relation to film, but its contemporary primacy as a component of broadcast television. There was always something of a tension within Grierson's famous definition of documentary as the 'creative interpretation of reality'. The question was whether the 'creative interpretation' part of the definition would be held to be equally as important as the real world the documentary was to reveal. This tension has subsequently been resolved in favour of 'reality' in the dominant model for documentary and no more so than in its televisual manifestation. What this means in practice is that the dominant, most prestigious model of documentary practice is one which distils its signifying strategies (the process of 'creative interpretation') into apparent transparency, thereby conferring on it the promise to its audiences that it speaks from some disinterested position of 'objectivity' and that the sense it makes of the world 'out here' is entirely unproblematic. One would be hard pressed to find a cultural theorist today who would accept with equanimity, the notion that there can be such a thing as disinterested cultural production. Yet the gap between theory and practice, the division of labour between academia and the business world, is sufficiently large that it comes as no surprise to find that this notion remains dominant and unchallenged within the television industry and within political discourses (television news has a statutory duty – like civil servants and judges – to be 'impartial').

Documentary and television

News and current affairs programmes are forged in a set of institutional arrangements, working practices, constraints and opportunities which are quite different from the circumstances of the independent videomaker. The contexts in which television news and current affairs programmes are produced, generate values concerning what is 'news' and what constitutes 'quality' rendering of that news. One can ask two intertwined questions about those values: the pragmatic question is to what extent values generated from one context can be grafted onto all other circumstances and relationships that might obtain between the documentary maker, their subject matter and their audiences; but the issue of how 'objective' these documentary procedures really are, opens very quickly into a critique of the assumptions, coherence and politics of the values which dominate news and current affairs programming.

Typically, the interlocking and overlapping values which govern the documentation of news on television, are: balance, impartiality, and consensus. Balance is the value by which television presents itself as an arena for different and conflicting perspectives. Television's pluralism, however, is rather limited. As Stuart Hall points out, the conflicting perspectives are drawn from within 'the legitimate mass parties in the parliamentary system'.[6] There is a further narrowing of acceptable perspectives insofar as, typically, it is the 'mainstream' representatives within the parliamentary parties whose views are most routinely aired. The 'mass parties of the parliamentary system' function then as the 'norm' against which other political discourses and political practices are to be judged. For example, when a fascist from the BNP was briefly elected as a borough councillor in the east end of London, protesters gathered outside the town hall to air their vociferous objection when he arrived for his first council meeting. The easiest, laziest assumption which news reporters made that evening, and in many other reports on the rise of the fascist right in the East End, was that groups like the Anti-Nazi League were just as bad, just as 'extreme' and stood in a mirror image to the racists and fascists when compared to the norm of parliamentary political discourse and practice. When news does give legitimacy to people other than politicians, the representatives for a plurality of views tend to be drawn from the most 'respectable' or official sources (the police, business representatives, trade union officials) and can be clearly located within the political agenda set by the mainstream parties. Balance, then, is the value which an independent film or videomaker would most want to expand and rework: expand in the sense of greatly extending representation into those parts of the community and those voices who go largely unheard; rework in the sense that balance does not have to interlock with the other values of impartiality and consensus, values which, for reasons I give below, are open to criticism.[7] In other words, a text can map out broadly its position or relationship to its subject while including voices which manifestly disagree with that position.

Impartiality refers to the broadcast programme makers' relationship to the conflicting perspectives which they give air time to. This is achieved by giving roughly equal time, equal space, equal praise or criticism, to the very selectively invited viewpoints on television. At face value this seems entirely fair and uncontroversial, but as Hall points out, the 'symmetry' achieved between opposing viewpoints is a 'formal balance: it has little or no relevance to the quite unequal relative weights of the case for each side in the real world'.[8] News shapes its representations of the world according to the liberal criteria of equality, yet this attempt at impartiality is itself a highly partial decision to ignore the fact that power relations and representation in the world are profoundly unequal. Assuming equality in the 'relative weights of the case', news necessarily ends up aligning itself with the status quo and those already in dominant positions, quite irrespective of truth or the pressing needs for social justice in particular cases. As Hall points out: 'If the workman asserts that he is being poisoned by the effluence from a noxious plant, the chairman must be wheeled in to say that all possible precautions are now being taken'.[9] Thus the notion of impartiality rules out openly committed audiovisual journalism, while at the same time concealing the extent to which all journalism is committed to some values and perspectives and hostile to others.

Television news in particular plays a central role in the formation of a social consensus. Stuart Hall draws on Antonio Gramsci's notion of hegemony to describe the process whereby the intellectual and moral lead of society's rulers can never be assumed but always has to be worked for and shaped if their dominance at the level of ideas and values is to win general consent. As Hall writes:

> The elites are in a powerful position to win assent (a) because they play a dominant role in crystallising issues, (b) because they provide the material and information which support their preferred interpretations, and (c) because they can rely on the disorganised state of public knowledge and feeling to provide, by inertia, a sort of tacit agreement to let existing state of affairs continue. We are thus in the highly paradoxical situation whereby the elites of power constantly invoke, as a legitimation for their actions, a consensus which they themselves have powerfully prestructured.[10]

This suggests that you need to think about your audience and have some sense of the common ideas, values, and responses which they may bring to your subject matter. Which of these ideas and values do you want to challenge, clarify or develop? Remember that your audience are not programmed robots. The concept of hegemony describes a complicated process whereby a consensus on any particular issue or subject is likely to be shot through with tensions and contradictions. The notion of hegemony is not one that many mainstream documentary makers would recognise as relevant to their work. As Bill Nichols suggests,

> the assumption that transformation comes from persuasive intervention in the values and beliefs of individual subjects (not debates about the ideology of the subject as such) [is a] ... cornerstone ... of the documentary tradition.[11]

The belief in the individual as an autonomous, free floating and self-producing entity, is itself an important underpinning of bourgeois hegemony. The concept of hegemony suggests a rather different kind of intervention for the documentary. While asking the viewer to develop their thinking on this or that particular issue/subject, a documentary utilising the concept of hegemony might also attempt to unpack the social consensus on any particular issue; and it might suggest to the viewer how they come to this or that subject/issue as subjects themselves, i.e. subjected to the hegemonic pattern of ideas and beliefs predominating in society over time. As we shall see later, interrogating media images of the documentary's subject (i.e. topic) is one way of exposing the ideological construction of the individual subject watching the documentary, by, among other things, such media images.

Consensus in Britain, in the 1990s, is a complex and contradictory field of opinions and dissent. Indeed, since the 1960s, consensus across a range of political, social, cultural, moral and sexual issues has become increasingly fraught, polarised and mutable. This is not to say that consensus on any and every issue has disappeared. Far from it. There is a growing consensus for example that the environment needs to be protected from the destructive activities of unaccountable private corporations. Yet, in a contradictory movement, a new consensus also emerged during the Thatcher years – at least within the political classes and much of the media – that privileges 'free markets'.[12] The contradictions between these two consensus formations and the internal crisis of others (say on the family or on sexuality) are indications of a conflictual field which has had its impact on television.

In the late 1970s Lord Annan's report into broadcasting found widespread dissatisfaction with the BBC and ITV amongst would-be independent programme makers, the general public and politicians. The Annan report found that as political consensus began to fray,

> people of all political persuasions began to object that many programmes were biased or obnoxious. But some, with equal fervour, maintained that broadcasters were not challenging enough and were cowed by the Government and vested interests to produce programmes which bolstered up the status quo and concealed how a better society could evolve.[13]

In 1982, Channel Four emerged as an initiative attempting to reinvigorate broadcasting. Its role as a commissioner and publisher of programmes rather than a producer in its own right, led to the mushrooming of the 'independent' sector. This provided the industrial base by which Channel Four could meet its statutory duty to bring new voices and encourage new styles in an otherwise moribund broadcasting culture. Documentary programming was often at the cutting edge of this project.[14] However, the 1990 Broadcasting Act altered the channel's funding arrangements. Whereas previously it had received a guaranteed income from ITV, which had in return been allowed to sell Channel Four's airtime to advertisers, the channel now had to raise its own advertising revenue in competition with ITV (now Channel 3) and other commercial broadcasters (Channel 5, BSkyB, cable television, etc.).

That competition will be intense in the context of continuing consumer indebtedness, which in turn depresses advertising expenditure.[15] Critics of the new arrangements have suggested that the knock-on effect is likely to be an increasingly 'safer' Channel Four schedule. Alan Fountain former senior commissioning editor for the Independent Film and Video Department, has indeed suggested that the channel has become 'normalised'.[16] It is interesting that from the start, Channel Four's daily news (as opposed to one off documentaries, series and documentary strands) was supplied by ITV's news supplier, ITN. This arrangement hardly helped open up television to a plurality of new voices in the areas where, arguably, it matters most: daily information, dissemination and opinion formation.

Activists not victims

One news organisation whose sounds and images will rarely feature on television news, is that of Small World.[17] This non-profit-making organisation specialises in covering environmental and social issues. They distribute their material on video in a news magazine called *Undercurrents*. The second video of the series included reports of: protesters trying to stop road-building schemes; squatters transforming a derelict town hall into a shelter for the homeless; the struggle to fight McDonalds' use of libel laws to silence critics; rave parties and police attempts to prevent them from taking place; the role of the IMF and World Bank in perpetuating 'third' world poverty and dependence; ethical shoplifting, where mahogany products being sold by companies are taken from the store and handed in to the local police station as property stolen from the forests of 'third' world countries; a campaign to prevent a Japanese multinational from turning a large tract of common land in Hampshire, into an eighteen hole golf course.

Undercurrents specialises in documenting people in action, people as 'doers', not passive victims. This is important to stress because the victim motif has been very central to documentary cinema. Brian Winston has traced it back in Britain to the documentary movement of the 1930s. It is a tradition continued by television in the 1950s. One difficulty with the victim motif is that it dissipates the critical force of the documentary by encouraging empathy (isn't it sad? isn't tragic? aren't they funny?) rather than analysis. In Brian Winston's words, 'it privileges effect over cause'.[18] The victim motif also suggests that the people who are the subject of the documentary must rely on the enlightened elites of society (like the filmmaker, for instance) for some improvement in their condition, since, as passive victims, they can do nothing to help themselves. According to Winston, as camera equipment became smaller, easier to handle and less obtrusive, and as it became possible to record sound and image simultaneously on location, the possibilities for victim-orientated documentary expanded further. As he puts it '[n]o door, especially the door behind which the disadvantaged were to be found, need or could be closed to the filmmakers'.[19] The American documentary filmmaker, Fred Wiseman, recorded a scene for *Law and Order* (1969) which literally dramatises Winston's point. Wiseman's camera is right behind the police as they kick down a front door and subject a prostitute to violent arrest.

While technological developments have impacted upon the form and content of what has been accessible to audiovisual documentation, the key question is not what kind of equipment one is working with, but where one stands, both physically and ideologically, in relation to the subject matter. *Undercurrents* displays an interest in resistance and understanding how that is organised. Wiseman's films 'stand', physically and ideologically, in a rather different position. He focuses on the interface between individuals and institutional forces and the subsequent moulding of the former by the latter. What remains invisible to Wiseman's camera in, for example, *High School* (USA, 1968), are all those moments when the young might dissent from and subvert the rules of the institution. This is necessarily absent since the camera only ever finds them in the shadow of authority (e.g. in class). Wiseman's documentary has, in sociological terms, a functionalist bent, which overemphasises the integrative and incorporating success of authority. This absence is ironic indeed given that the film was made in 1968, the same year that student protest on the university campuses, against US involvement in Vietnam, intensified.

No matter how much people are affected and shaped by forces independent of them, the victim motif prevents the film or video-maker and the audience from ferreting out the sites of resistance, the strategies of subversion, the possibilities of protest. In *Undercurrents 2*, however, these are all well to the fore. We are encouraged to learn from the tactics of organisation and resistance. The news item 'Justice In the Court' is structured as a manual in how to take direct action. The subject is the occupation of an abandoned Brighton courthouse by a group of squatters protesting against the Criminal Justice Bill.

The period of occupancy provided an important focus in Brighton for the anti Criminal Justice Bill protest at the end of 1994, while also highlighting the issue of homelessness. The formal strategies deployed in this item are straightforward but no less effective and appropriate for that. The item begins with the intertitles: 'First, Pick Your Building…' while on the soundtrack the lyrics of a song urge the viewer towards activism ('Get up, you got to get up'). The item uses intertitles throughout to organise its visual material into sections: 'Get the word out on the street' followed by shots of the squatters going out and making their presence felt in the community with petitions against the Bill, plans for making the courthouse a community centre, street music, interviews with local residents and so on. Other sections are introduced by such intertitles as 'Throw Parties to Raise Funds' and 'Milk the Media'. Sub-titles are also used to provide additional information in conjunction with the audiovisual images.

Occupying the old Brighton Courthouse, left derelict by property developers for five years, was a clever tactical move by the squatters/protesters to raise the profile of their actions within the town. There is also a symbolic resonance to the images as they reveal the occupiers renovating and repairing the building, reclaiming it for a people's justice and a people's court. Like the fictional image, the documentary image is a dense constellation of signs. The item has a simple chronology. Once fit for habitation, we see the courthouse become a thriving community centre with shots of various activities: workshops, theatre, cinema screenings, public debates (drawing in sympathetic, high-profile public figures – in this case Simon Hughes). Thus the item demonstrates the activists carving out a place for themselves in the cultural and political affairs of the community. Once the bailiffs move in, we see how the protest continues by relocating to the rooftop of the occupied building. Thus, even though ultimately the courthouse was 're-secured', the emphasis of the video item is on a general flowering of creativity, on people engaged in ongoing struggles, learning from and becoming empowered by their experiences. Although my example is drawn from an activist video, the debates which it raises have a more general applicability to other documentary subjects. Bearing in mind the legacy of the 'victim-documentary', the videomaker should always be alive to the real creativity and the strategies and tactics people develop in order to 'survive' or carry out whatever it is that the documentary finds them doing.

Counter-Hegemonic Strategies

To exercise hegemony , Gramsci informs us, is to secure,

> the 'spontaneous' consent given by the great masses of the population to the direction imprinted on social life by the fundamental ruling class, a consent which comes into existence 'historically' from the 'prestige' (and hence from the trust) accruing to the ruling class from its position and its function in the world of production.[20]

A counter-hegemonic strategy is one which would seek to break the circuit of 'spontaneous consent'. The notion of 'spontaneous consent' is actually rather more homogenising than is helpful, including as it would have to, a whole gradation of responses, more or less coherent and reasoned and offered with more or less conviction, passion, cynicism or resignation. A counter-hegemonic strategy would also seek to challenge the 'direction imprinted on social life'. This notion would also need to be understood in a generous and broad manner, encompassing a debate about, say the closure of a local cinema, to the global issues of public policy being hemmed in and shaped by international private finance. In both cases, a counter-hegmonic strategy would offer and amplify alternative directions to social life and contest the 'prestige' which the ruling classes have accrued to their organisations and institutions.

'Washes Whiter' is a counter-hegemonic *Undercurrents* news item about the IMF and World Bank. It begins with footage of the ruined European cities in the wake of the second world war, stirring orchestral music and titles explaining that the origins of the World Bank and the IMF lie in the post-war period of reconstruction. Their aims, according to the soundtrack, were to promote prosperity and peace. But then another set of sound and images are intercut with this, coming from the same period in history: a 1950s advertisement for washing powders. This jarring clash between the discourses of sobriety and the frivolity and superficiality of the advert, requires the viewer to re-evaluate the sounds and images which introduced the World Bank and the IMF. Then there is a cut back to the footage of political and financial institutions, in which a spokesman declares that the World Bank and the IMF will promote 'genuine international cooperation'. This is followed by a series of images of military parades with subtitles identifying the leaders of various infamous regimes: Ceaucescu, Romania; Pinochet, Chile; Marcos, Philippines; Mobutu, Zaire; Somoza, Nicaragua; Suharto, Indonesia. Then we cut again to a 1950s advertisement and a man, direct to camera, announces: 'And here's some really good news': cut to another advert/man with direct to camera address: 'We recommend you to use...'. Cut to a shot of a human skull, lying deformed and burnt in a desert terrain; above the skull, titles declare (following on from the exhortations in the previous shot): 'The World Bank'. Below the skull, more titles: '8 out of 10 Dictators Prefer it.'

It is by now clear how, in this video, montage is appropriating the blandishments of advertising to suggest an analogy between them and the self-promotion of the World Bank by itself and a compliant media. We are clearly being addressed here, not only as individuals who have to make some sort of sense of this reworked material, but also as social subjects, i.e. individuals living in a society in which banks are represented as prestigious and respected institutions (Brecht's maxim that robbing a bank is less of a crime than setting one up, can hardly be hegemonic in any capitalist society). The hegemony is not so monolithic as to make such criticism seem outlandish. As I suggested earlier, a hegemony always has fissures and contradictions which can be worked on. In this case many people harbour a healthy scepticism about banks, even if only drawn from their own immediate experiences. At the same time, neither, it may be noted, is the hegemony so vulnerable that it cannot draw the line and make such forthright criticism (via emotional and intellectual montage) of banks, of the fawning media, and even implicitly of advertising culture (which after all frames the news on commercial television) inadmissible within the present regime governing television's 'impartial' daily news.

Macro structures

By macro structures I am referring to the overarching logic by which the material is organised. A number of different organising strategies can be identified. It is important to recognise that these strategies are not mutually exclusive and can be combined in any number of ways. The two main ones that I will look at are narrative structures and expository structures (the latter will be sub-divided into three sub-categories).

i) Narrative structures

There are two senses in which one can talk about narrative in relation to documentary. Firstly there is the sense in which a documentary may use material clearly marked as drama, as par of its 'content'. Reasons for integrating dramatic material with your documentary material may include:

a) representations of people/events which, either because they are in the past, or because they involve people you cannot access, may require some dramatic materialisation: this may be done in either a highly stylised and oblique manner, or it may be done with varying degrees of detail and verisimilitude. Such material may try and suggest interior states of mind or perhaps through monologue to camera, the philosophy or ideas of particular persons.

b) dramatic reconstruction provides the opportunity to introduce a change of tone into your documentary and perhaps articulate, for example through humour or satire, your own perspective on the documentary material.

c) whereas the integration of documentary material allows one to situate the dramatic material within a wider socio-historical space (e.g. *Yellow*'s use of the voice-over), the integration of drama into the documentary may open up the space for a more personal manifestation of the themes in the documentary.

d) dramatic material may give you the control over your mise-en-scène which will allow you to develop an idea in a way insufficiently crystallised in your documentary material; or alternatively, perhaps you want your dramatic material to challenge an idea crystallised in the documentary material (particularly if you are using found footage).

However, we can also to some extent deconstruct the opposition between documentary and fiction by pointing to the ways in which narrative may be constitutive of the documentary form itself, at least in some of its manifestations. Documentaries often (although not necessarily) make use of narrative structures by deploying plots, characters, enigmas, obstacles, heightened tensions, conflicts and closure.[21] Nature documentaries often utilise strategies to explore the life cycle of their subject, constructing animals as 'characters', with goals to achieve (reproduction of the species, getting food, etc), obstacles to overcome and enemies (such as predators) to avoid. Similarly, historical documentaries may tell the history of individuals or whole communities, as a story , with a beginning, middle and end, with conflict and complications, enigmas to be resolved, and dramatic peaks to be climbed. The main advantage with such narrative strategies is clear enough: firstly they draw on the familiar and dominant conventions of the classical fiction film; they present the documentary material in exciting ways, they draw the viewer into the material very quickly and encourage identification.

The difficulty is that one can deconstruct the distinction between documentary and fictional material only so far. In practice one cannot narrativise documentary material as if that material were just another fiction. This is demonstrated by the ethical debates and questions which are continually raised around any documentary material which features people in some sort of distress, need or danger. The viewer inevitably and rightly asks questions pertaining to the conditions under which audiovisual evidence was obtained. What is the relationship between the film/videomakers and those who are their subjects? What power relations are involved? What were the terms by which the film/videomaker acquired consent to record the subject(s)? Were those terms breached in particular instances? What are the film/videomaker's motives? What has the subject gained from the experience? Not only are these questions not raised in the act of producing and consuming fictional texts, nothing so quickly calls the documentary maker's motives into question than evidence that the social actors are being conceived largely in narrative terms (such as heroes, donors, helpers and villains) for the kinds of dramatic effects more associated with fiction.

The documentary raises such questions because the materials (people, events) it works with and works on, do have the same life and the same existence beyond the camera frame, beyond the set-up which records this or that particular moment. I argued in chapter four that recognising the constructed nature of the imagistic sign need not lead us to conclude that the sign has uncoupled itself from all relationships to the real world. This is doubly so for the documentary sign. As Bill Nichols argues, fiction may well offer 'an explanation or interpretation of great power' in relation to the world external to the text, but 'the avenue back to the world is always by means of …[a] detour through narrative form.'[22] The fictional film is a construction orientated towards the imaginary space of its own story and plot, and this imaginary world does not exist independently of the camera and the intentions of the director, producer, etc. For Nichols there is a distinction between a fictional text, which constructs *a* world, and the documentary text, which is orientated towards *the* world; that is the historically contiguous world which the audience shares with the world (even if located in the past) which the documentary text constructs.[23] The grounds on which recognition of that shared world is achieved (which is not all the same as saying that text and audience share the same values and interpretations of the world), is the argument which the documentary offers. Nichols, wanting to defend against the postmodernist tendency to abolish all boundaries between documentary and fiction, suggests that the documentary is above all defined by its emphasis on constructing arguments, marshalling evidence of one sort or another and sustaining some sort of logic in relation to the historical world beyond the text.

ii) Expository structures

The documentary's basis in argumentation is most clearly manifest in what Nichols calls the expository mode. This mode of documentary organisation can be sub-divided further into three kinds. The dominant and most familiar of this kind of expository documentary, tends to be very much concerned with tangible, empirical realities. This mode is very close to what Bordwell and Thompson call the rhetorical documentary, that is, one which attempts to deliver a very precise and focused argument.[24] In order to do this, the expository/rhetorical/empirical mode will usually rely on some direct address to the viewer using a narrator (on and/or off camera) to provide the overall structure to and bridges between interviewees. In this expository mode we tend to make sense of the images in relation to the voice(s) which advance (either on and/or offscreen) the argument. Characteristically, the narrator's voice conveys 'the impression of objectivity',[25] so important, as we have seen, in its dominant television manifestation. There is no doubt that this appeal to 'objectivity' remains strong not only in practice but in theory as well. In discussing the role of the voice-over narrator, Michael Rabiger writes this:

> The key to unobtrusive, effective narration lies in limiting it to the facts and avoiding all value judgments that are not fully supported by evidence in the footage. A good narration avoids predisposing the viewer in any direction but may justifiably draw attention to those aspects of the evidence – visual or verbal – whose significance might be overlooked if they are presented in a casual way. The goal is always to let the viewer make her own judgments from what evidence you can show.[26]

This paragraph is riddled with tensions and ambivalences. The fetishism of unobtrusive technique, which we have come across already in the normative discourse of the dominant industry, becomes particularly urgent in the case of the documentary where it underwrites the genre's status as an authentic, transparent record of events. A binary opposition familiar from the previous chapter can be discerned: evidence (fact) is understood as existing independently of judgments (value), the latter only making their appearance when supported by the evidence. Thus the 'goal' of narration is to let the viewer come to their own conclusions from the evidence presented. However, there is still a nagging question: to what extent has the evidence been shaped by the narrator? Rabiger does allow some minor shaping of the evidence to be justifiable, although, contradictorily, this shaping should not 'predispose the viewer in any direction'. Yet by definition 'shaping' must do just that, and all the more so if the shaping is disguised by an appeal to neutrality. Despite these rather obvious paradoxes, a documentary perceived not to conform to these values, is regarded as flawed.

A good example of this can be seen in relation to Allan Francovich's documentary investigation into the Lockerbie plane bombing. The thesis of *The Maltese Double Cross* (1995) was that early suspicions of Syrian and Iranian involvement were smothered when it became important to secure their support for the Gulf War. The blame for the bombing, the film argues, was shifted by American and British authorities onto Libya for the sake of political expediency. The editorial in the *Guardian* was not unsympathetic to the questions raised by the film, but suggested that, 'Allan Francovich's film threatens to undermine itself by … heavy sarcasm. It would have been better served by a calm, distancing commentary.'[27] The charge refers specifically to the narrator who, in one voice-over, sarcastically expresses disbelief in the official version of events leading up to the bombing in order to emphasise some of the improbable and contradictory elements of that version. Such indications that the documentary has a view, a position on what is being documented, can only be taken to undermine the documentary's case, if one believes, as this editorial clearly does, that truths can filter through the document unmediated by the documentary. Once we reject this position, it becomes possible to think about expanding the repertoire of ways the voice-over is used, beyond the 'calm, distancing commentary' currently the dominant norm. The voice-over may use a range of styles; it may work in relation to the image in a range of ways; there may be more than one voice-over and it/they may ask the audience questions rather than always providing descriptions/analysis of the images; the voice-over may also work in counterpoint with other voices that may be equal 'disembodied' (interviewees) or in relation to sound effects and music which might provide a range of other tones and meanings to the image not included in the voice-over.

I have already noted the problematic distinction between 'facts' and 'values' which underpins Rabiger's passage on narration. This needs further exploration. As an example of how slippery the notion of 'facts' can be, let us take one 'fact' which underpinned recent news coverage. The 'fact' concerned the number of police officers killed in the line of duty, which provided the underpinning for the recurring debate about whether the police should routinely carry guns. Whatever the short-term outcome of the debate, the statistics are always accepted by the media as something that has to be urgently addressed. The 'facts' appeared to speak for themselves. Television news never questioned the interpretation of the 'fact' that x numbers of police killed increases the 'pressure' to arm the police (if not with guns in the short-term, then with other weapons such as with 'improved' truncheons and gas). This is because the news chose not to put the 'facts' into any wider context. Nineteen police officers have been killed in assaults at work over the last ten years. What is extraordinary about this statistic is how low the figure is compared to other statistics for work-related fatalities. Farm workers and transport workers are, respectively, six and five times more likely to be killed at work than police officers,[28] while *Contract Journal*, a magazine for the construction industry, estimates that a hundred workers die each year in building site accidents.[29] On the other hand, in 1994 eight civilians were killed in London alone as a result of police car chases. As E.H. Carr wrote, 'facts' never speak for themselves. They always have to be selected, framed and interpreted from a particular position.[30] This suggests that the role of the narrator(s) might include finding ways of drawing the audiences' attention to the pliable, malleable nature of reading statistical information.

What are the advantages and disadvantages of the expository mode? The empirical/rhetorical expository mode which I have been discussing, tends to be investigative and informational. It can very economically provide the background to a situation, event or process. It can explain immediately and directly, what has happened, what is happening, and what may happen in the future. The argument tends to be linear and the connections between components of the argument straightforward. Facts, particularly little known ones, can still shock audiences, making them re-evaluate their assessments of situations/events. This expository/rhetorical mode is an apt framework for such material. Its emphasis on the empirical also has the advantage of requiring the documentary maker to go out and research their subject. Other forms of documentary making, while possibly opening up greater formal possibilities, can encourage the videomaker to produce something with limited and rather superficial insight into the subject. A formally interesting documentary runs the danger of lacking substance because the videomaker has spent too much time thinking about sound and image, and too little time thinking about and finding out about the subject to which the sounds and images are to be applied. The expository mode at least has the virtue of encouraging you to get in touch with organisations and individuals who will have something to say on the subject; it will at least encourage you to research the print media in the library to find out about the history of the subject and the ways it has been represented previously. The expository mode will also encourage you to find an 'angle', a particular way into the subject matter that provides the main theme or point of the argument.

On the downside, this documentary mode tends to construct a world which has a particular problem to which there is a corresponding solution. While there is nothing intrinsically wrong with having such ambitions, the path from problem to solution often smooths over the more knotty difficulties, conflicting interests and contradictions involved in the passage from problem to solution. For example, such a linear logic can register differences between interviewees, but may leave these unexplored in the interests of moving onto the next stage of the argument and towards the final conclusion. The expository/empirical documentary does tend to make more use of narrative strategies than other modes and so it is unsurprising that it is vulnerable to criticisms also levelled at the classical narrative. The main one is that it leaves the viewer with little to do once they navigate the problem–solution structure. This raises a wider question. Can, for example, this approach invite the viewer to think how they may be part of the problem and not just a separate spectator to an event/issue? If at a formal level a documentary invites a rather passive engagement with the text, can the text invite the viewer to be an active part of the solution proposed?

Another problem with the expository mode discussed so far is simply its dominance. For those happy to work within this macro-strategy, its very dominance may produce a rather uncritical acceptance of it as the 'best' form for the documentary. The reason is dominant on television, however, has little to do with its streng and weaknesses at an intellectual or aesthetic level. It is dominant because it suits the machinery of television production. This requires a hierarchical relationship between the people who make the documentary and the producers/commissioning editors who release the funds and oversee the project. An expository documentary can be easily set down on paper, and thus can be monitored and re-written at the script stage, which provides the people who hold the purse strings with the evidence that they are going to get the particular kind of product they and their organisation want. In other words the expository mode fits snugly into the production process for audiovisual commodities, the centralised control of budgets, the division of labour between planners and workers, and the scrutiny and surveillance of the latter by the planners. An uncritical relationship to the expository mode merely reflects the practitioner's internalisation of this class machinery as the norm. Of course every force has its opposite reaction and so the very dominance of the expository mode can produce overly harsh assessments of it, such as this one by Louis Marcorelles.

> Thousands of bunglers have made the word [documentary] come to mean a deadly, routine form of filmmaking, the kind an alienated consumer society might appear to deserve – the art of talking a great deal during a film, with a commentary imposed from the outside, in order to say nothing, and to show nothing.[31]

I have tried to indicate some of the strengths as well as weaknesses of this expository mode as well as suggest that we can look again at the convention of an 'objective', single 'commentary imposed from outside' and explore ways a narrator or narrators may reflect on the complexity of the documenting process, examine their own position and invite the audience into a more active engagement with the material.

a) *Oral Exposition* One way in which problems around the role of the narrator have been dealt with is to dispense with the visual and/or aural narrator in favour of letting the interviewees' oral contributions structure the text. Oral history, the recounting of history by participants and witnesses, has had an important impact in legitimising such evidence and recollections as important and valuable in their own right. The recent flowering of its audiovisual manifestation is in no small part due to the cheapness of videotape as a recording medium. The British Video History Trust, for example, has been set up by broadcasters to lend individuals and groups broadcast quality video equipment to record first hand testimony and scenes of everyday life. This material is then catalogued and stored as an archive for future broadcasters, researchers and historians. Another organisation, The Television History Centre, also gives advice on audio and audiovisual recording of oral history, as well as housing the Television History Workshop, an independent company using video to specialise in oral history programmes.

The reason that the relative cheapness of videotape is so important for oral history is that it takes time to explore personal memories and reflections. The nature of the information which the documentary maker is after is diffuse and usually not easily extracted in two or three statements, so it is important that the videotape can be left running without clocking up huge expenses. This is particularly so when one is dealing with memories going back many years. For the first memories which people have are often not the most interesting and indeed may be wreathed in nostalgia. For example, people recalling the second world war often stress, initially, how everyone pulled together. But from my own experience I have seen how as the process of reminiscence develops, the memory begins to stir up evidence of a more contradictory reality when it is also recalled how, despite rationing, some middle-class families always had 'luxuries' purchased on the black market. Suddenly the initial memory of unity is fissured by evidence of deep resentment towards such families. As with all interviews, but particularly with those wanting to uncover past experiences, you will need questions, preferably very specific ones to trigger memories. (Although you should also allow the interviewee to digress and follow up any interesting areas they raise). The compatibility of video with domestic VCRs and monitors also allows you to provoke responses by showing interviewees extracts from other interviews (either earlier ones of themselves or other people) or any other audiovisual material. It may be interesting to record and retain in the finished piece such initial prompting to help evoke a sense of dialogue about history and its interpretation, events and people.

What animates oral history most is the value it places on the words and perspectives of the participants and/or witnesses involved in the situations which the documentary takes as its subject. Thus the documentaries from the Television History Workshop reject the convention of the narrator as another example of that version of history which privileges the 'expert', the voice of authority. Rejectin the explicit narrator is one way of not only bringing 'ordinary' peo to the fore, but also encouraging a more pluralistic, even dialogic version of historiography. Classically, the interviewees exist as evidence for the narrator's monologic interpretation of the subject matter (although as I have indicated above, the voice-over need not operate in this way). Without the voice-over, the voices within the text exist more for their own sake, thus demonstrating that there is always more than one version of the subject, and of history generally, to be written. In one sense with the disappearance of an explicit narrator, the act of telling is dispersed amongst the interviewees themselves. However, the process of constructing the text does not of course disappear but is still implicit in the way the material is organised, the way videography and mise-en-scene are used in the interview situation, and the cutting from one interview to the next. I want to briefly discuss each of these in turn.

Once one dispenses with the narrator who can provide the bridges between scenes and develop the argument(s), then the subjects themselves become all the more important in providing a logic by which the material comes together. Yet they can only function in this way if the documentary maker has a clear framework which will make the interviewees' relationships with one another logical. There are a number of frameworks which may be used and again they are not mutually exclusive. You could establish a narrative framework which would allow various voices to take the viewer through a story or stories about particular events. The story itself would help provide logical breaks and continuities across different interviewees. For example, you could use the temporal dimensions of narrative to structure a day in the life of a local street market or an evening in the life of a club or a bar. In both cases the narrative might begin as the market or club prepares itself for its customers, important characters might be introduced, anticipated complications and problems sketched out, etc. This is oral history as it happens, but the narrative form could equally be applied to recollections of events. It is also quite possible to construct a tightly focused argument along the lines of an expository/rhetorical documentary, by carefully asking questions that you anticipate will produce the responses required to plot the next stage of the argument. Another strategy would be to organise the questions and responses into categories which break the overall subject down into parts.[32] For example, interviewees may each give a response to a particular issue or question. What connects one response with the next is not so much the telling of a story or the development of an argument, but a series of discrete opinions/arguments on a theme (in much the same way as the vox pop interview works).

Despite the absence of a narrator, the relationship of the documentary maker to their material, and the role they have in shaping the meaning of that material, is also evident in the use of the camera, image processing techniques and mise-en-scène. In a thought-provoking discussion, Nichols argues that, just as feminist and psychoanalytic analysis has revealed the intermeshing of looking and desire in the classical narrative, the documentary may also be thought to be driven by a gaze, not so much for erotic desire, but an epistephilia, or a desire to know, or to understand.[33] This desire for, and expectation of, knowledge which the documentary attempts to satisfy, will produce costs and benefits of an ethical and political kind, which both the documentary maker and the viewer will have to weigh up and assess.

> The question posed to the spectator, then, is not what kind of imaginary world the filmmaker has created but how the filmmaker acquitted him or herself in relation to those segments of the historical world that have become the scene of the film. Where does the filmmaker stand? What space does he or she occupy and what politics or ethics attach themselves to it?[34]

These questions become particularly pressing in the interview situation where documentary maker and subject(s) meet and negotiate the terms for satisfying audience epistephilia. Cutting across that meeting and that negotiation are ethical and political questions. For example the Television History Workshop has made a point of interviewing people in studio settings with neutral backgrounds. This is done so that the mise-en-scène of the interviewee's own domestic circumstances does not unfairly impinge on their discourse. For example, an ex-manager is likely to be able to situate themselves in a rather more impressive and wealthy mise-en-scène than an ex-worker. Relocating interviewees to a studio setting inscribes the image with ethical questions (admittedly of a rather minor kind) around what is being asked of them in terms of travel, negotiating an unfamiliar environment, etc., but also inscribes the image with a politics which is aware of class differences and which is trying to construct a more equal context from which the respondents can speak.

In many cases though, you may want to use an aspect of the respondent's real world mise-en-scène to reveal something about that interviewee. How you shape that mise-en-scène will also reveal

Fig. 8.1

Fig. 8.2

something about the preoccupations and values of the documentary maker vis-à-vis the world. Take for example Figs. 8.1 and 8.2, both taken from a student documentary, *Mods*. Fig. 8.1 is an interior shot of a shop specialising in mod clothes. The dress style of the mod and modette is the central theme of this documentary and a slow pan right from Fig. 8.1 reveals something of the place where the clothes are bought and the clothes themselves. The pan ends on Fig. 8.2 with a mod looking back at the camera from behind a clothes rail. The conclusion of this shot has a number of meanings. From the stance of the mod we may guess that this is not a browsing customer but a worker in the shop. Thus a social actor has been introduced, and we may expect, mobilising the hints of narrative in this introduction, for this shot to be followed up by the documentary's method of getting to know the social actor in more detail, i.e. an interview. But this introduction also suggests something of the relationship between the text and its subject. The style of the text allows the social actor to enter the scene resonating attitude, street credibility and cool, which are indispensible to most sub-cultures: the mod style is no exception. If the documentary had adopted that rather homogeneous blanket convention for introducing social actors familiar from television news, then we might have seen the same person doing something in the shop apparently unaware of the camera, e.g. serving a customer, arranging the clothes, etc. The alternative introduction which *Mods* uses, suggests a rather less distanced, less formulaic relationship between documentary maker and subject; it suggests a knowledgeable engagement with the Mod scene and communicates a sense of pleasure in the way it incorporates the Mod performance style into its own form.

This reading of a single pan and introduction suggests that the documentary is as densely layered a signifying practice as any fictional text. It is possible to suggest that in arranging the interview situation, the mise-en-scène and videography will function in distinct ways. The mise-en-scène signs are likely to work primarily in relation to the subject(s), indicating to the viewer who they are, what they do, what their values might be, etc. What you do with the camera and other videographic image effects, will produce signs that are likely to indicate something of your preoccupations and values vis-a-vis the subject(s). This is not a hard and fast distinction, however. The camera that moves away from the interviewee's face to study their hands does so to reveal something about the subject, but in the very process of doing so may imply a sympathetic or critical or sceptical attitude towards the interviewee's discourse at that particular moment. However, this distinction between videography and mise-en-scène may provide a useful starting point for thinking about these questions.

Another important aspect of the interview situation is whether subjects are interviewed on their own or in a group. *Mods* for example interviews male mods on their own and the modettes in a group. Whatever the particular and practical circumstances that might have influenced such decisions, the signifying effect of such choices suggests a significant and gendered modification of the mod style. The individualistic image of the male mod buttressed by attitude, etc., is reworked by the modettes to allow greater scope for group experiences, discussion and reflection. This theme remains more implicit than explicit in the video. One way in which the video might have developed this gender contrast (and perhaps offered a critique of the male mod) might have been to montage the interview scenarios in someway once the male/individual interview and female/group interview set-ups had been established.

The question of editing is, indeed, another level at which the construction of the text becomes all the more vital in the absence of an explicit narrator. In particular there is the possibility of juxtaposing conflicting and discrepant views/values between interviewee's against one another. The Television History Workshop's documentary, *Making Cars*, which focused on the factories at Cowley, is a good example of this idea, with its juxtapositions of interpretations within the workforce, between workers and managers, and in relation to company propaganda films. This approach demonstrates that both the making of history and its interpretation is a site of contestation. However, having rejected the kind of contextualisation which the narrator(s) may offer, some of the large scale, supra-individual historical forces which impact upon individual experiences, might be missed in oral history. There is also the sense in which merely cutting between different views reproduces, even if more pluralistically, similar practices of balance and impartiality which I critiqued earlier. For the text need not decide which views and experiences of its subject it takes to have greater explanatory power. As before, this apparent impartiality leaves the more oppositional and critical viewpoints at a disadvantage. For the dominant conceptions of history and the particular subject of the documentary, are likely to have had the 'ears and eyes' of the audience from many media and educational sources in a way that the oppositional viewpoints have not. We have come back here to the question of hegemony.

The question of whether an editing style simply contrasts conflicting statements from a position of 'impartiality' or whether it actually aligns itself with a particular viewpoint, may be a very nuanced matter of timing and rhythm. For an example of this, I want to return to the *Undercurrents* item called 'Washes Whiter', which offered a critique of first world/'third' world economic and political relations. From one interviewee, D.C. Rao, a director of the World Bank, we hear that: 'The main focus of the bank is poverty alleviation'. Immediately the text cuts to Douglas Hellinger, a former World Bank consultant: 'That has never been the case. The Bank is … promoting the interests of western countries and an elite sector in the "third" world'. Here we have balance, but it is not interlocked with impartiality. The juxtaposition exists not as a transparent presentation of conflicting views from two individuals, but as part of the text's construction of an argument. The weighting of the cut, the way Rao's discourse is abruptly interrupted by an instant rebuttal from Hellinger, suggests that the text is aligning itself with Hellinger. This does not of course compel the viewer to agree with Hellinger (and the text), but they are compelled to engage with an argument which makes it clear that 'Washes Whiter' is coming from a position strongly critical of the Bank.

A programme committed to the values of impartiality would avoid such an obviously interventionist editing style, opting instead to give the impression (using continuity editing) of observing the integrity of each interviewee's discourse (i.e. giving the appearance of not chopping into their speech). However, there are ethical problems in simply transferring a more interventionist technique to the discourse of 'ordinary' people. The discourse of expert figures, officials like Rao and Hellinger, exists in the public realm to be disputed and debated. A documentary maker and audiences may well feel that this is an inappropriate method to be applied to 'ordinary' people who have consented to appear before the camera. But then this ethical question of how to treat subjects raises questions about the difficulty of articulating political analysis on 'ordinary' discourses. Perhaps then what would be needed are methods of analysis/critique which make it clear that it is the values rather than the individual, which are being questioned. Perhaps more subtle methods of criticism can also be used. One strategy which documentary makers might use is asynchronic sound–image relations, where the image(s) in some way contradicts or qualifies the words of the respondent or suggests a particular 'blind spot' or partiality in the interviewee's beliefs and value systems.

b) *Poetic Exposition* This mode of documentary strategy is called 'poetic' because it deploys some of the non-linear, associational strategies found in poetry. In less literary terms, such strategies are usually underpinned by montage. Bordwell and Thompson discuss something close to the poetic exposition under the title of associational forms, although, (mistakenly, I believe), they downplay the extent to which the associational mode offers some kind of argument.[35] Certainly, in the poetic/associational mode the advancement of an argument that can be easily summarised and addressed directly to the viewer recedes. Nevertheless, some kind of logical argumentation is very often at work, it is just that it invites the spectator to work out the argument from the associations sparked in the clash of sound and image. However, there are gradations within the poetic exposition in terms of how much work the spectator has to do and how much is already offered to the spectator as anchored meaning.

We have seen in the *Undercurrents* item 'Washes Whiter' that what is primarily being juxtaposed are the verbal statements from adverts, spokespeople and interviewees. In such an example the soundtrack is still concerned to carry concrete and specific information, although in the unusual combinations of different types of material (documentary/propaganda material and advertising material) there is that use of counterpoint and irony characteristic of the poetic expository mode. In chapter two I discussed how one of the choices that one has to make in a production situation vis-a-vis modernist aesthetics, is how determinate or indeterminate your text's meanings are going to be. The modernist strategies *Undercurrents* deploys in news items generally mark out a set of meaning possibilities in fairly circumscribed ways. There is nothing wrong with this and it fulfils the purposes of those items very successfully. Other examples within the poetic expository mode may relax the determination of meaning a little more. For example, a narrator may reappear not as a provider of empirical information, but rather in the form of a poem or song. The poetic expository mode can also depart from the 'diachronic march of cause/effect, premise/conclusion, problem/solution,'[36] which characterises the rhetorical/expository mode. Poetic exposition can move back and forth in time and construct intellectual relationships and connections between disparate subject material that a linear piece – committed to empirical reality – would find difficult or inadmissible.

A short Cuban documentary made in the mid-1980s, *Prayer* (Marisol Trujillo) is a good example of the poetic documentary's ability to construct non-empirical relationships. Using a poem by Ernesto Cardenal, the narrator offers a prayer to Marilyn Monroe. The words and in particular the images, made up of photographic stills and news footage, construct connections between Marilyn Monroe and her struggles and aspirations within Hollywood and the struggles and aspirations of her near contemporaries, American anti-Vietnam War demonstrators, as well as the struggles and aspirations of the peoples of Latin America in conflict with their oppressors within Latin America and North American imperialism. The imagery ranges back and forth from the 1960s, 1970s and 1980s. While the expository/empirical mode would find it difficult to construct a relationship between Monroe and Latin America (given that there are no factual links) *Prayer* achieves this because it is working at the level of metaphor and at the level of conceptual thought promoted by intellectual montage. I have tabulated the final sequence of *Prayer* in Fig. 8.3. Notice that in this final sequence the recurring image(s) which mediate the proposed links between Monroe and Latin American revolutionaries, are those of babies or young children. These links are reinforced by graphic matches, that is there is a focus on faces (and towards the end, on the fist raised in defiance and solidarity). It is not easy to pin down a precise, unambiguous meaning to this synthesis of disparate material, not least because the image of Monroe as a signifier has accumulated a number of different signifieds (innocence, childlike wisdom, unself-conscious sexuality, victim, etc.).[37] The broad parameters of meaning(s) are fairly evident in the poem itself, even though it is the images which make the associations and connections between Monroe and Latin America not explicitly evident in the words.

What are some of the practical difficulties and problems to be drawn from this brief discussion of the poetic mode? The primary difficulty is that the discursive, speculative possibilities of the poetic documentary can also be a weakness unless the documentary maker is wary and disciplined. It may encourage you to think that you need not do any research into your subject and that essentially all that is required is an eye and ear for stitching disparate material together. However, a superficial grasp of the subject will only reflect in a superficial and insubstantial finished piece. The more you learn

Narration	Images (m = moving footage; s = still image)	Music and Sound Effects.
The film ended	Protesters being arrested (s).	
without the final kiss.	Apartment Monroe died in (m).	
They found her dead in her bed; her hand on the telephone. But the detectives did not know who it was she was trying to call.	Monroe's covered body being taken away on a stretcher (m).	
	Latin America: two people carry a child's coffin (m).	
It was	A baby's face in close up (m).	'O Jerusalem' very faintly (music only).
like someone who dials the number of a last friendly voice only to hear a prerecorded tape and a voice say 'wrong number, wrong number, wrong number'.	Monroe's face in close up (m).	
	Baby's face (m).	'O Jerusalem' volume builds.
Or like someone wounded by gangsters, who reaches out towards a disconnected telephone.	Protesters vs police in America (m). Protesters demonstrating for peace (s).	'O Jerusalem' now mixed with crowds shouting, sounds of conflict (e.g sirens).
O lord Whoever she	A child holding a balloon with 'Give peace a chance' written on it (s). Street battles between police and protesters (m and s)	
may have been trying to call but did not call and perhaps it was no-one at all, or someone whose name was not in the Los Angelos telephone book,	Placard of Che Guevara (s). Latin American revolutionaries pointing their rifles skyward (s).	
Lord, please answer that phone.	Child with fist raised (s).	
	Crowds with fists raised (s).	'O Jerusalem' now the only sound (full volume).
	Latin American guerilla/women holding a child (s).	
	Child with arms out: smiling into the camera (s).	

PRAYER

Fig. 8.3

about a subject the more convincing will be the audiovisual connections that you make. Moreover, poetic exposition would often be strengthened by the inclusion of empirical material, whether articulated through titles, interviews or some other sort of explicit discussion of the issues involved.

The poetic mode also presents a difficulty with regard to anchoring the meanings of the images to some authorial intention. If your intention is to provide contradictory and/or multiple meanings, and/or provide a lot of space for the spectator to construct their own meanings, this ambition still, paradoxically, has to be combined with your own authorial purpose. There is, usually, a perceptible difference between ambiguities and contradictions which are fruitful and meaningful, rewarding the work the audience has to put into the piece, and ambiguity and contradictions which are simply the product of confused intentions. It is very important, then, to remember that each and every image is potentially polysemic, bubbling with different meanings and possibilities.[38] Thus you should not assume that any one image which you select will function in the way you intend it to. One way of giving some patterning to your images is through the soundtrack, as we have seen with *Prayer*. Alternatively, or in combination with the soundtrack, you may group the sound–image juxtapositions by dividing a general subject up into various categories. In this way, by producing variations on a specific theme, the spectator is offered a number of chances to make sense of the associations proffered by the text.

Another way in which links between images can be made might be to find contrasts and similarities in the graphic and rhythmic qualities of the image(s). Bordwell and Thompson identify this strategy as one which makes links at the abstract level of the shape, size, density, colour, angle, movement, light, etc., of the things depicted. In *Prayer* a certain abstract logic is at work in the graphic matches achieved between the faces and then later, the fists. However, such abstract links play a supportive role only in the linkage between images, remaining very much subordinate to the structure of poetic exposition. Some texts, however, are concerned to explore this abstract logic in and for itself. Such texts operate at a considerable distance from Nichols' definition that argumentation 'forms the organisational backbone of documentary.'[39] Comparing this mode with categorical forms, Bordwell and Thompson remark that a 'ball and a balloon might be put side by side, not because they are both toys but because they are both round or both of an orange

of the images with the original version. How, if at all, do they differ? Think about whether and why your commentary would be accepted by the news organisation if you worked for them?

- Taking your cue from *Prayer*, select a star and jot down some of the films they have been in, some of the gossip and 'knowledge' about the star which is in general circulation. Try and identify the meanings that are associated with the star (see Dyer's work on stars) and then montage the star into the context of other documentary footage (found or shot by you). What effects have you achieved? Are you subverting the star image or celebrating it? What does it add to the documentary material?

Notes

1 J. Grierson, *Grierson on Documentary*, Faber and Faber, 1966, p.78.
2 B. Nichols, *Representing Reality*, Indiana University Press, Indianapolis, 1991, p.3.
3 G. McLennan, 'The Enlightenment Project Revisited' in *Modernity and its Futures*, Polity Press/Open University, 1993, p.330.
4 Grierson, *op.cit.*
5 P. Rosen, 'Document and Documentary: On the Persistence of Historical Concepts' in *Theorising Documentary*, Routledge, London 1993, p.78.
6 S. Hall, 'Media Power' in *New Challenges for Documentary*, University of California Press, London 1988, p.359.
7 S. Harvey, '"Those Other Voices": An Interview with Platform Films' in *Screen*, vol. 25, no. 6, 1984.
8 Hall, *ibid.*
9 Hall, ibid, p.360.
10 Hall, *ibid*, p.363.
11 Nichols, *op.cit.*, p.63.
12 W. Hutton, *The State We're In*, Jonathan Cape, London 1995.
13 P. Scannell, 'Public Service Broadcasting: The History of a Concept', in *Understanding Television*, Routledge, London 1990, p.19.
14 S. Harvey, 'Channel Four Television: From Annan To Grade' in *Behind The Screens*, Lawrence and Wishart, London 1990.
15 W. Hutton, 'Forebodings in a Cold Climate' in *Media Guardian*, November 2nd, 1992, pp.15 and 17.
16 P. Keighron, 'Channel Four's Fuzzy Focus' in *Red Pepper*, January 1995, p.35.
17 Small World can be contacted at 1a Waterlow Road, London N19. Tel. 0171-272 5255.
18 B. Winston, 'The Tradition of the Victim in Griersonian Documentary' in *New Challenges for Documentary, op. cit.*, p.24.
19 Winston, *ibid*, p.275.
20 A. Gramsci, 'The Formation of Intellectuals' in *The Modern Prince and Other Writings*, Lawrence and Wishart, London 1957.

21 Nichols, *ibid*, p.107 and M. Rabiger, *Directing the Documentary*, Focal Press, 1992.
22 Nichols, *ibid*, pp.112-115.
23 Nichols, *ibid*, pp.112-115.
24 D. Bordwell and K. Thompson, *Film Art*, McGraw-Hill, 1990, pp.99-105.
25 Nichols, *op. cit.*, p.35.
26 Rabiger, *op. cit.*, p.236.
27 The *Guardian*, May 13th, 1995, p.22.
28 *Socialist Worker*, 20th May, 1995, p.2.
29 The *Guardian*, 3rd August, 1995, p.5.
30 E. H. Carr, *What is History?*, Penguin Books, Harmondsworth, 1964, pp.10-20.
31 Quoted by Trinh T. Min-Ha, *op. cit.*, p.95.
32 Bordwell and Thompson, *op. cit.*, pp.91-99.
33 Nichols, *op. cit.*, p.76.
34 Nichols, *ibid*, p.79.
35 Bordwell and Thompson, *op. cit.*, pp.113-122.
36 Nichols, *ibid*, p.36.
37 See R. Dyer's *Stars*, BFI, London 1979, and *Heavenly Bodies*, Macmillan, 1986,pp.19-66 on Marilyn Monroe.
38 R. Barthes, *Image, Music, Text,* Fontana, London 1977, pp.38-41.
39 Nichols, *op. cit.*, p.125.
40 Bordwell and Thompson, *op. cit.*, p.105.
41 Grierson, *op. cit.*, pp.150-151

Conclusion

In making an argument for theorising your own cultural practice, I would not seek to claim that theory is a prerequisite for producing interesting cultural work, simply that it need not, as is often assumed, cast a stultifying shadow over creativity. I have advocated theorising practice because I think the videomaker has more to gain than lose from such efforts. There are, I have argued, two reasons for this. One is pragmatic: theory can help generate aesthetic strategies from your own conditions of production rather than from the conditions and aesthetics which obtain in the mainstream audiovisual industries. These industries are of course the reference points for many instruction manuals in which 'theory' constitutes a prescriptive code of practice. The other strand to my argument has been that it not only makes sense to develop alternative strategies for pragmatic reasons, but that there is also a debate to be had around the politics of cultural representation which you, as a videomaker, engage in as soon as you make certain choices and decisions in the construction of the audiovisual text. Theory can help ground the cultural worker in those debates.

In part the choices and decisions which you make are framed by the other video and audiovisual practices which precede and surround your own. Video as playback technology, as art, as familial or community representation, as a component of the dominant entertainment industries, as a cheaper, more accessible substitute for 'film' – these are some of the manifestations of video use that have cropped up in this book. I have also tried to explore the politics of cultural representation through the various layers of textual language itself. I hope to have drawn the reader's attention to the construction and political resonance of the image, its various modes of combination with other images via editing, the patterning of sequences into larger macro structures whether of a narrative or non narrative kind, the question of sound and its relationship to the image and finally documentary as a distinct form, weaving in and out of various video practices as well as interacting with or being co-opted by fictional or dramatic representations. However, I want to end with some thoughts on the future prospects and possibilities that exist for greater access to the means of distribution and to audiences.

I suggested in the introduction to this book that there is no reason why video production could not become as popular an independent cultural activity as musical production. However, there is one very obvious block. When people produce their own music, they have a reasonably good chance of finding a site of exhibition where their work can find public recognition and receive public feedback. Live performances can be supported by small-scale distribution of audiotape. By contrast, people can produce videos but, outside a small circle of friends, will anyone else see the fruits of their labour? Will it be able to achieve any amplification through consumption, thereby giving it some kind of cultural impact? The most obvious medium for distribution is television, where video has already made considerable inroads. As we have seen, one area low-budget video has had an impact is around questions of access and the prospect of opening up broadcasting to voices outside the established institutions and their routine contacts.

It is very important that questions of access have achieved new prominence and critical favour on the national terrestial channels, not only for what might be further achieved on those channels in terms of broadening the meaning and possibilities of broadcast programming, but also for the example it holds out for access programming in a multi-channel future. What might that future hold? The spread of cable distribution could democratise television considerably, opening it up to local and community audiences to produce, at least in part, their own television. On the other hand, the terminus of cable television might be another example of the subordination of the local into the global economy, with cable networks recycling already dominant symbolic goods (overwhelmingly originating in North America).

We know that technology determines nothing in itself, but rather that its uses and applications are shaped by its social and economic context, which, of course, has a certain structure, hierarchy of power and dominant logics. But this insight can quickly develop into pessimism if that context is viewed as exerting an iron law determinsim over all aspects of technology. In other words, some left thinkers see a social context dominated by capital as completely dominating the deployment and benefits of technology. Yet what often underpins this left position is a political desire to point out the limitations of reformist gains achieved within the system, rather than a sociological understanding of the (limited) room for manoeuvre within the social structure.

Now there are two observations to make about the relationship between social context and technology in the case of cable. Capital has invested in cable largely for the telecommunications services, which it is hoped that the new optical fibre cables will carry. But, in addition to banking and shopping services, cable will also carry various forms of cultural/symbolic goods. These may include ordering up your own television/video programmes or linking up live to locally produced video from around the world. The point is that the future of cable television is relatively unknown and still open, in the sense that the huge capacity which fibre-optic cable has to carry information means that new, as yet barely conceived cultural forms will have to be developed.

The development of cable could offer limited, constrained, but nevertheless real, opportunities for the independent videomaker. If cable operators could get away with using the network as an extension of their global media industry, no doubt this would be their preferred option, since it would probably be the most profitable one. But whether this is acceptable, politically and culturally, is really another question. And to simply accept their terms as somehow inevitable is to forget the point about human agency. The latter complicates the temptation to see the social context determining technology in too predictable a manner. The surest way for a new echnology to end up serving the interests of capital in an ntrammelled way, is to see the fight as unwinnable in the first place. iis is to return to Gramsci's notion of hegemony. If the multi-annel television of the future is to develop along more democratic l progressive lines, we need to contest and intervene in that elopment now; we, as audiences and practitioners, need to make the arguments against the dominant logics of capitalism, that is to extract concessions from it.

There are two key groups to lobby and make demands on in pursuit of this aim. Firstly there are the cable operators themselves. In this early phase of operation they are desperate for material to fill air time. This is a chance to set precedents, to demonstrate that cable television need not look like The Big Breakfast twenty-four hours a day. The rhetoric which has surrounded cable television has been to sell it in terms of local and community programming. The need now is to challenge cable operators to turn that rhetoric into a reality. But crucially, if cable is to expand access to audiovisual communication, rather than merely expand the power of international media capital, then the political sphere has to be won over.

Again, to paraphrase Gramsci, looked at intellectually, the omens are not particularly encouraging, but one should not, because of this, abandon optimism of the will. If we take the case of British cinema, the legislation that the two main political parties have been responsible for during the twentieth century suggests that culture does not rate very highly on the political agenda and that when it is addressed, the conception of what a British film culture might look like, who it might address and why it might be important, is very narrow and conservative, while the legislation is always framed with the aim of causing least offence to the powerful American film companies that dominate the British market. This period of flawed intervention into the crisis of the British film industry covers the period when it became increasingly acceptable, politically, for the state to intervene in the economy. Given that, since the early 1980s, the political consensus has been shifting away from Keynesian political economy and towards a deregulated market system, it is likely that the political will to force private capital to have any substantial public service obligations may well be drying up. However, political parties, like the social structure itself, are contradictory. During its period in opposition, the Labour Party has shifted over to a more or less wholesale embracement of the 'free' market. On the other hand, its discourses of decentralising power, of local accountability, and of 'communitarianism', may provide some crack, some fissure, in its relation to market forces, that may be worked on. Certainly, without political will and without a legislative framework that compels cable companies to give a genuine commitment to access programming, then the potential of cable will be constrained inexorably by profit margins. However, we have also seen that video can itself be a mode of distribution. From the example set by Small World in the genre of magazine news, to the possibilities of extending video culture via festivals and audiovisual clubs, alternative avenues for video communication still remain to be explored and expanded upon.

In the introduction and first three chapters of this book, I stressed the importance of context as a defining and shaping force on the video practitioner. But that context is not fixed or static. It is always in flux, and there are contradictions to be worked on. In the last five chapters I have sought to introduce some of the key debates and theories associated with the various components of audiovisual language. Theoretically, there is certainly more to be done. One can envisage more specialised interrogations of video practices, perhaps in relation to digital media, in relation to community video, in relation to media pedagogy, etc. But hopefully, for now, this book will have amplified some of the textual strategies of the work I have been discussing, made the theory I have discussed relevant to practice, and made some small contribution to enlarging the use, creativity and diversity of video's productive potential.

Selective Bibliography

Ades, D., Photomontage, Thames and Hudson, 1986.
Alvarado, M., Video World Wide, UNESCO, 1988.
Armes, R., Third World Filmmaking and the West, University of California Press, 1987.
Armes, R., On Video Routledge, London 1988.
Arnheim, R., Film As Art, University of California Press, Berkeley, 1971.
Anderson, P., 'Modernity and Revolution' in Marxism and the Interpretation of Culture, Nelson, C. and Grossberg, L. (eds), Houndmills, 1988.
Andrew, D., Concepts in Film Theory, Oxford University Press, Oxford, 1984.
Aspinal, S., 'The Space for Innovation and Experimentation' in Screen vol.25, no. 6, 1984.
Aston, E. and Savona, G., Theatre as Sign System: A Semiotics of Text and Performance, Routledge, London 1991.
Bakhtin, M. M., The Dialogic Imagination, University of Texas Press, Austin, 1992.
Balazs, B., Theory of the Film: Character and Growth of a New Art, Dover Publication, New York 1970.
Barker, M. (ed), The Video Nasties: Freedom and Censorship in the Media, Pluto, London 1984.
Barthes, R., Mythologies, Paladin, London 1986.
Barthes, R., Image , Music, Text, Fontana, London 1977.
Bazin, A., What Is Cinema? vol 1, U.C.P, London 1967.
Benjamin, W., 'The Work of Art in the Age of Mechanical Reproduction' in Curran, J., Gurevitch, M., and Woollacott, J., (eds), Mass Communication and Society, Edward Arnold/Open University Press, London 1977.
Berger, J., Ways of Seeing, British Broadcasting Corporation and Penguin Books, London 1972.
Berman, M., All That is Solid Melts Into Air, 1983.
Bordwell, D., 'The Art Cinema as a Mode of Film Practice' in Film Criticism, vol 4, no. 1, 1979.
Bordwell, D., Staiger, J., Thompson, K., The Classical Hollywood Cinema, Routledge, London 1988.
Bordwell, D., The Cinema of Eisenstein, Harvard University Press, London 1993.
Bordwell, D., Thompson, K., Film Art: An Introduction, McGraw-Hill Inc., London 1993.
Bourdieu, P., Distinction: A Social Critique of the Judgement of Taste, (trans. Richard Nice), Routledge, 1984.

Bourdieu, P,. Photography: A Middlebrow Art, Stanford University Press, Stanford, 1990.
Brecht, B., 'Against Georg Lukacs' in Aesthetics and Politics, Taylor, R. (ed), Verso, London 1988.
Burger, P., Theory of the Avant-Garde, Manchester University Press, 1984.
Callinicos, A., Against Postmodernism : A Marxist Critique, Polity Press, Cambridge, 1992.
Carey, J., The Intellectuals and the Masses, Faber and Faber, London 1992.
Carr, E. H., What is History?, Penguin Books, Harmondsworth 1964.
Caughie, J., 'Progressive television and documentary drama' in Screen, vol. 21, no. 3, 1980.
Chanan, M. (ed), Twenty Five Years of New Latin American Cinema, BFI/Channel Four, 1983.
Cook, P., The Cinema Book, BFI, 1985.
Crystal, D., The Cambridge Encyclopedia of Language, Cambridge University Press, 1987.
Cubitt, S., Timeshift. On Video Culture, Routledge, 1991.
Cubitt, S., Videography: Video Media as Art and Culture, Macmillan, London 1993.
Debord, G., The Society of the Spectacle, Detroit, 1970.
Doane, M. A., 'The Voice in the Cinema: The Articulation of Body and Space' in Cinema/Sound, Yale French Studies, no.60, 1980.
Doane, M. A., 'Ideology and the Practice of Sound Editing and Mixing', in The Cinematic Apparatus, de Lauretis, T. and Heath, S. (eds), St Martin's Press, 1980.
Dovey, J., 'Copyright as Censorship: Notes on *Death Valley Days*', in Screen, vol.27, no.2, 1986.
Drakakis, J. (ed), Alternative Shakespeares, Methuen, London 1985.
Eagleton, T., Criticism and Ideology, Verso, 1976.
Eagleton, T., The Ideology of The Aesthetic, Basil Blackwell, Oxford 1990.
Eagleton, T., Ideology: an introduction, Verso, London 1991.
Eisenstein, S., Essays In Film Form, Harcourt Brace Jovanovich, London 1977.
Elam, K., The Semiotics of Theatre and Drama, Methuen, London 1980.
Espinosa, J. G., 'For an Imperfect Cinema' in Twenty Five Years of New Latin American Cinema, Chanan, M. (ed), BFI/Channel Four, 1983.
Evans, D. and Gohl, S., Photomontage: a political weapon, Gordon Fraser, London 1986.
Fanon, F., The Wretched of The Earth, Penguin, 1967.
Fowler, B., 'The Hegemonic Work of Art in the Age of Electronic Reproduction: An Assessment of Pierre Bourdieu' in Theory, Culture and Society, vol, 11., no. 1, Feb 1994.
Frith, S., Music For Pleasure : Essays in the Sociology of Pop, Polity Press, 1988.
Faludi, S., Backlash: The Undeclared War Against Women, Chatto and Windus, 1992.
Garnham, N., 'Public Service versus the Market' in Screen, vol 24, no.1, 1983.
Garnham, N., 'The Myths of Video: A Disciplinary Reminder' in Capitalism and Communication: Global Culture and the Economics of Information, Sage, London 1990.
Geohegan, V., Marxism and Utopianism, Methuen, London 1987.
Gidal, P., Materialist Film, Routledge, London 1989.
Glasgow University Media Group, More Bad News, GUMG/Routledge Kegan Paul, London 1980.
Gombrich, E. H., Art and Illusion, Phaidon Press, London 1962.

Goodwin, A. and Whannel G.(eds), Understanding Television, Routledge, London 1990.
Goodwin, A., 'The Structure of Music Video: Rethinking Narrative Analysis' in Dancing In The Distraction Factory: Music, Television and Popular Culture, Routledge, London 1993.
Gramsci, A, The Modern Prince and Other Essays, Lawrence and Wishart, London 1967.
Grierson, J., Grierson on Documentary, Faber and Faber, London 1966.
Gunning, T., 'The Cinema of Attractions, Early Film, Its Spectator and the Avant Garde'; Gunning, T., 'Primitive Cinema: A Frame-Up? Or The Trick's On Us', both in Early Cinema: Space, Frame, Narrative, Elsaesser, T. and Barker, A. (eds), BFI, 1990.
Hall, S., 'Media Power' in New Challenges for Documentary, Rosenthal, A. (ed), University of California Press, London 1988.
Hartley, J., Understanding News, Methuen, 1982.
Harvey, D., The Condition of Postmodernity, Basil Blackwell, Oxford, 1989.
Harvey, S., '"Those Other Voices": An Interview with Platform Films' in Screen, vol.25, no. 6, 1984.
Harvey, S., 'Channel Four Television: From Annan To Grade' in Behind The Screens: The Structure of British Television in the Nineties, Hood, S. (ed), Lawrence and Wishart, 1994.
Haug, W. F., Critique of Commodity Aesthetics: Appearance, Sexuality and Advertising in Capitalist Society, Polity Press, Cambridge, 1986.
Hawkes, T,. Structuralism and Semiotics, Methuen, 1977.
Henderson, B., 'Two Types of Film Theory' in Movies and Methods, vol. 1, Nichols, B. (ed), University of California Press, London 1976.
Hogenkamp, B., Deadly Parallels: Film and the Left in Britain 1929-1939, Lawrence and Wishart, London 1986.
Holland, P., Spence, J., Watney, S., Photography/Politics: Two, Comedia, 1986.
Hood, S., On Television, Pluto, London 1987.
Hood, S. (ed), Behind The Screens: The Structure of British Television in the Nineties,Lawrence and Wishart, London 1994.
Hutton, W., The State We're In, Jonathan Cape, London 1995.
Jameson, F,. 'Reflections in Conclusion' in Aesthetics and Politics, Taylor, R. (ed), Verso, London 1988.
Jameson, F., 'Video: Surrealism Without the Unconscious' in Postmodernism, or, The Cultural Logic of Late Capitalism Verso, London 1993.
Julien, I., MacCabe, C., Diary of a Young Soul Rebel, BFI, London 1991.
Kaplan, E. A., Women In Film Noir, BFI, London 1978.
Keighron, P., 'Condition Critical' in Screen, vol.32, no.2, summer 1991.
Keighron. P., 'Video Diaries: What's Up Doc?' in Sight and Sound, vol. 3, issue 10, Oct 1993.
Kellner, D., Media Culture, Routledge, London 1995.
Kirkham, P., Thumin, J., You Tarzan:Masculinity, Movies and Men, Lawrence and Wishart, London 1993.
Kuleshov, L., Kuleshov On Film, University of California Press, London 1974.
Lefebvre, H., Rabinovitch, S., Everyday Life In The Modern World,Allen Lane, 1971.
Lesage, J., '*S/Z* and *The Rules of The Game*' in Movies and Methods, vol. 2, Nichols, B. (ed), University of California Press, 1985.
Lewis, R., The Video Maker's Handbook, Pan/Marshall Editions, 1987.
London Video Arts, London Video Arts: 1984 Catalogue.
London Video Arts, Video Tape Catalogue 1987.

Lovell, T., Pictures of Reality: Aesthetics, Politics and Pleasure, BFI, London 1983.
Lucas, M., Wallner, M., 'Resistance by Satellite' in Channels Of Resistance, Dowmunt, T. (ed), BFI/Channel Four, 1993.
Lukacs, G., History and Class Consciousness, Merlin Press, London 1971.
Lunn, E., Marxism and Modernism, Verso, London 1985.
MacCabe, C. 'Realism and the Cinema' in Screen, vol. 15, no.2, 1974.
Marshall, S., 'Video: from art to independence' in Screen, no.26, 1985.
Marshall, S., 'Artist's Tapes' in ICA Video Library Guide, ICA, 1986.
Marx, K., Engels, F., The Communist Manifesto, Penguin Books, Harmondsworth 1967.
Moretti, F., Signs Taken For Wonders, Verso, London 1988.
Masterman, L., Teaching The Media, Comedia, London 1986.
Millerson, G., Effective Television Production, Focal Press, London 1993.
Minh-Ha, T. T.. 'The Totalising Quest For Meaning' in When The Moon Waxes Red: Representation, Gender and Cultural Politics, Routledge, 1991.
Mitchel, G., 'The Consolidation of the American Film Industry 1915-1920' in Cine -Tracts, no. 6, 1979.
Molyneux, J., 'The "Politically Correct" Controversy' in International Socialism, no. 61, winter 1993.
Mulvey, L., 'Visual Pleasure and Narrative Cinema' in Screen, vol.16, no.3, autumn 1975.
Murdock, G. 'Authorship and Organisation' in Screen Education, no.35, summer 1980.
Musburger, R. B., Single Camera Video Production, Focal Press, London 1993.
Neale, S., 'Masculinity as Spectacle: reflections on men and mainstream cinema' in Screening The Male, Cohan, S., and Hark, I. R. (eds), Routledge, 1993.
Nichols, B., Ideology and the Image, Indiana University Press, Bloomington, 1981.
Nichols, B., Representing Reality, Indiana University Press, Indianapolis, 1991.
Paget, D., True Stories? Documentary drama on radio, screen and stage, Manchester University Press, Manchester, 1990.
Pasolini, P. P., 'The Cinema of Poetry' in Movies and Methods, vol 1, Nichols, B. (ed), University of California Press, London 1976.
Place, J. A., Peterson, L.S., 'Some Visual Motifs of Film Noir' in Movies and Methods, vol 1, Nichols, B. (ed), University of California Press, London 1976.
Penley, C., 'Feminism, Psychoanalysis, and the Study of Popular Culture' in Cultural Studies, Grossberg, L., Nelson, C., Treichler, P. (eds), Routledge, London 1992.
Potter, C., Image, Sound and Story: the Art of Telling in Film, Secker and Warburg, London 1990.
Pudovkin, P., Film Technique and Film Acting, (trans. I. Montague), Vision Press Ltd, London 1958.
Rabiger, M., Directing The Documentary, Focal Press, 1992.
Reisz, K., Millar, G., The Technique of Film Editing, Focal Press, 1968.
Renov, M., Theorising Documentary, Routledge, London 1993.
Rosenthal, A., New Challenges for Documentary, University of California Press, London 1988.
Ryan, T. 'The New Road To Progress: The Use and Production of Films by the Labour Movement, 1929-39' in British Cinema History, Curran, J., Porter, V., Barnes (eds), Noble Books, 1983.
Sanjines, J. 'Problems of form and content in revolutionary cinema' in Twenty Five Years of New Latin American Cinema, Chanan, M. (ed), BFI/Channel Four, 1983.

Scannell, P., 'Public Service Broadcasting: the history of a concept' in Understanding Television, Routledge, London 1990.
Shatz, T., New Hollywood/Old Hollywood: ritual, art and industry, UMI Research Press, 1983.
Shohat, E., Stam, R., 'The Cinema after Babel: Language, Difference, Power' in Screen, vol. 26, nos. 3-4, 1985.
Sorlin, P., European Cinemas/European Societies: 1939-1990, Routledge, London 1991.
Stam, R. '*The Hour of The Furnaces* and the Two Avant-Gardes' in Reviewing Histories: Selections from New Latin American Cinema, Fusco, C. (ed), Hallwalls, New York 1987.
Stangos, N. (ed), Concepts of Modern Art, Thames and Hudson Ltd, London 1994.
Sturrock, J., Structuralism and Since: From Levi-Strauss to Derrida, OUP, London 1979.
Thompson, E.,P., The Poverty of Theory and Other Essays, Merlin, London 1978.
Tulloch, J. Television Drama, Routledge, London 1990.
Vertov, D., Kino-Eye: The Writings of Dziga Vertov, Michelson, A. (ed) (trans K. O'Brien), Pluto Press, London 1984.
Volosinov, V.N., Marxism and the Philosophy of Language, Seminar Press, New York & London 1973.
Wayne, M. 'Television, Audiences, Politics' in Behind The Screens: The Structure of British Television in the Nineties, Hood, S. (ed), Lawrence and Wishart, London 1994.
Weis, E., Belton, J. (eds), Film Sound:Theory and Practice, Columbia University Press, New York 1985.
Widdicombe, R. 'Discovering Legends in his Own Lifetime' in the Sunday Times Supplement 4th September, 1994.
Williams, A., 'Godard's Use of Sound' in Camera Obscura, nos. 8-9-10, Fall, 1982.
Williams, R., The Long Revolution, Pelican, Harmondsworth 1961.
Williams, R., Television: Technology and Cultural Form, Fontana, London 1974.
Williams, R., Keywords, Fontana, London 1983.
Williamson, J., Consuming Passions: The Dynamics of Popular Culture, Marion Boyars, London 1986.
Wolff, J., The Social Production of Art, Macmillan, London 1981.

Index

Index